The McGraw-Hill
36-Hour Course

Entrepreneurship

Other Books in The McGraw-Hill 36-Hour Course Series

Arredondo
THE MCGRAW-HILL 36-HOUR COURSE: BUSINESS PRESENTATIONS

Bittel
THE MCGRAW-HILL 36-HOUR MANAGEMENT COURSE

Cooke
THE MCGRAW-HILL 36-HOUR COURSE IN FINANCE FOR
NONFINANCIAL MANAGERS

Cummings
THE MCGRAW-HILL 36-HOUR REAL ESTATE INVESTING COURSE

Dixon and Arnett
THE MCGRAW-HILL 36-HOUR ACCOUNTING COURSE

Rosenfeld
THE MCGRAW-HILL 36-HOUR BUSINESS STATISTICS COURSE

Sartoris and Hill
THE MCGRAW-HILL 36-HOUR CASH MANAGEMENT COURSE

Seglin
THE MCGRAW-HILL 36-HOUR MARKETING COURSE

Schoenfield and Schoenfield
THE MCGRAW-HILL 36-HOUR NEGOTIATING COURSE

The McGraw-Hill
36-Hour Course

Entrepreneurship

James W. Halloran
Entrepreneur in Residence
Muhlenberg College

McGraw-Hill, Inc.

New York   San Francisco   Washington, D.C.   Auckland   Bogotá
Caracas   Lisbon   London   Madrid   Mexico City   Milan
Montreal   New Delhi   San Juan   Singapore
Sydney   Tokyo   Toronto

Library of Congress Cataloging-in-Publication Data

Halloran, James W.
    The McGraw-Hill 36-hour course : entrepreneurship / James W.
    Halloran
        p.   cm.
    Includes index.
    ISBN 0-07-025876-7 (cloth : alk. paper)
    ISBN 0-07-025877-5 (pbk. : alk. paper)
    1. New business enterprises.   2. Small business—Management.
    I. Title.   II. Title: McGraw-Hill thirty-six hour course.
    HD62.5.H352   1994
    658.4'21—dc20   94-1904
                                                                            CIP

1 2 3 4 5 6 7 8 9 0   DOC/DOC   9 0 9 8 7 6 5 4

ISBN 0-07-025876-7 (HC)
ISBN 0-07-025877-5 (PBK)

*The sponsoring editor for this book was David Conti, the editing
supervisor was Fred Dahl, and the production supervisor was Pamela
Pelton. It was set in Baskerville by Inkwell Publishing Services.*

Printed and bound by R. R. Donnelley & Sons Company.

This book is printed on recycled, acid-free paper containing a
minimum of 50 percent recycled de-inked fiber.

This publication is designed to provide accurate and authoritative information in regard to the subject matter covered. It is sold with the understanding that the publisher is not engaged in rendering legal, accounting,
or other professional service. If legal advice or other expert assistance is
required, the services of a competent professional person should be sought.
    *—From the declaration of principles jointly adopted by a committee of the
    American Bar Association and a committee of publishers*

Contents

Preface

The high rate of small business failures is well publicized. It does not have to be this way if entrepreneurs would take the time to plan and research their business ideas. By taking this course, you will be building such a plan, and the probability of success for your venture will certainly be on the positive side.

The McGraw-Hill 36-Hour Course in Entrepreneurship has proven to be successful in the classroom and in the marketplace. The author is an experienced entrepreneur who has helped thousands of aspiring entrepreneurs reach their goals. At times, it is a demanding course; however, if you follow through as directed, you will create a business plan that will serve as the tool needed to launch an exciting enterprise and reap the rewards of entrepreneurship.

Being an entrepreneur is a way of life. It is demanding but challenging. It requires creativity, confidence, and determination. This course will show you how to apply these personal characteristics. The only prerequisite required to take the course is that you be a goal-oriented individual—a person who is willing to do what it takes to get what he or she wants. There is no quick and easy way to build a successful business—it takes planning, research, a good idea, and the support of those around you. Starting a business is the hardest, most challenging, and exciting career change you will ever make. Once accomplished, I assure you that as you go to work each day, you will feel more satisfied and fulfilled than at any other time in your career. You will be working for your own goals and not the goals of others.

Acknowledgments

Creating this course required the help of many—particularly those un-named sources who have shared experiences. In addition to these entre-preneurs, I owe an expression of gratitude to my son Tim for his editing and indexing skills; Gary Salman, a senior Entrepreneurial Studies student at Muhlenberg College who wrote the business plan in Chap. 24; and David Conti, my editor at McGraw-Hill, for making the course a reality. Also, thank you to the faculty and staff in the Business and Accounting Depart-ment at Muhlenberg College for their support and for putting up with me while putting the book together.

And last, but not least, I dedicate this book to my wife Diane, the one constant in the ever-changing lifestyle of an entrepreneur.

James W. Halloran

About the Course

The course is comprised of 24 chapters and demands approximately 90 minutes to be spent on each lesson. The majority of those 90 minutes will not be spent reading, but completing the Next Step exercises at the end of each lesson. The chapter readings will prepare you to take the necessary action called for to write the next step of the business plan.

- The first of six parts is entitled "Opportunity Knocks." This part of the text gives you the chance to evaluate yourself and the business opportunities available to you.

- Part 2, entitled "Marketing," will start you in the research process of determining whether there is a market for your idea and how to capture and retain your share of it.

- Part 3, entitled "Financing a Small Business," takes on the always difficult problem of securing the needed capital and the best way to put it to work.

- "Managing Your Small Business" is the title of Part 4, which will prepare you for how to control and build your enterprise.

- Part 5 on "Legal Considerations" will alert you to the legal responsibilities you must adhere to, and will give you instruction on deciding the proper form of ownership for your business and how it should be formulated.

- The last part is called "Looking Ahead." It will supply you with some tips for the future and show you an example of a completed business plan.

Each part is followed with a case study of an actual experience of an entrepreneur from whose experience you can learn. The cases emphasize the lessons learned in the part just completed.

The key is to do the Next Step exercises. Often they will ask you to pick up a telephone, write for information, or visit a valuable resource. Find the time to complete these steps and at the end of the course you will have a business plan that you can take to the bank or show to investors.

The course concludes with an optional Final Examination. You may take the examination and send it to the McGraw-Hill certification examiner for grading. A score of 70 percent or better (70 correct answers) entitles you to a handsome certificate of accomplishment presented by McGraw-Hill, Inc. Details are provided with the "Final Examination" at the end of the book.

PART 1

Opportunity Knocks

Risks

- To place your ideas, your dreams before a crowd is to risk their loss.
- To hope is to risk despair.
- To try is to risk failure.
- But risks must be taken, because the greatest hazard in life is to risk nothing.
- The person who risks nothing, does nothing, has nothing, and is nothing.

SOURCE UNKNOWN

1
Assessing Your Entrepreneurial Aptitude

Objectives

1. To understand the characteristics of successful entrepreneurs.
2. To learn how to evaluate your personal aptitude for being a successful entrepreneur.
3. To learn the importance of choosing the right environment in which to apply your ambitions.
4. To understand why so many business start-ups fail.
5. To determine why and when you should consider opening a business.

Key Terms

Entrepreneur	Full Function Wholesaler
Retailer	Limited Function Wholesaler
Service Marketer	

Bob Dylan's song in the 1960s, "The Times They Are A-changin," is appropriate for the 1990s as a description of current corporate and occupational lifestyles. The massive corporate downsizing going on around us has forced many to re-evaluate their careers and what is important to them. Since the corporate career no longer offers security, the question being asked is, "If I am going to be at risk anyway, why not do it myself?" The decision to embark on an entrepreneurial career has never been so appealing as it is today.

What Is an Entrepreneur?

Let's begin the course with a look at the word *entrepreneur*. Entrepreneur is of French origin; *entreprende* meaning "to undertake." A standard definition is "one who assumes the risk of gaining profits or incurring losses in the undertaking of commercial transactions." This broad description could include anyone from the casino gambler to the corner drug dealer. Therefore, for the purpose of this study, we will confine our meaning to the description of a successful entrepreneur. *Successful entrepreneurs* assume only calculated risks of gaining profits or incurring losses in the undertaking of commercial transactions within a market in which they have developed a sense for its needs. By inserting the word "calculated" before risks and demanding that the individuals research the needs of the market, we have eliminated the "flim flam" connotation of the term entrepreneur and have significantly improved the individual's chances for achieving success in reaching their intended goals.

Desired Entrepreneurial Characteristics

The first and most important question is: Do you have what it takes to be a successful entrepreneur? Think through this section very honestly and then discuss it with those close to you, because if you are not ready to assume entrepreneurial risks at this point in your career, put this book aside until the proper time.

You Must Be Goal Oriented

The late Sam Walton, founder of Wal-Mart, put it very simply, "knowing where you want to go and being willing to do what it takes to get there."[*] So much of what we accomplish is through sheer determination of achieving important goals and *then* once they are achieved, setting even loftier goals

---

[*]*Sam Walton: Made in America*, Sam Walton with John Huey, Doubleday, 1992.

to pursue. When you look at those who have reached great heights as entrepreneurs you will quickly notice that profits became a secondary objective. The real objective was reaching new goals for personal satisfaction. Sam Walton became the country's wealthiest person, yet he continued getting up early and working at an ever-increasing pace when he could have been fishing in the South Pacific. His motivation came from reaching goals, not strictly making money, and that is what will make the difference in the type of entrepreneur you will become.

If your entrepreneurial ambition is strictly to make a quick buck, you need to rethink your ambitions. However, if you have goals in mind that are not strictly financial, but include considerations such as a desired lifestyle and accomplishments you wish to achieve, a long-term entrepreneurial career is a path you might wish to consider.

Do You Have Creative Energy?

Most successful entrepreneurs are people who come up with a better way to serve an existing market. It does not require reinventing the wheel, but it does require that you are able or willing to find those ways of doing things better. In many instances, this means a more efficient method to serve a customer or a more creative way of telling the market that you exist and that you have a product to sell. The successful entrepreneurs have a certain flair to the way they approach the things that they do—always curious, always wondering if a particular idea will work. Do you carry this flair in the way you think?

Do You Have an Abundance of Self-Confidence?

As an entrepreneur you will be the decision maker in your enterprise. Making decisions requires confidence. Confidence not only in making the right decision, but also in not being afraid of making the wrong decision. Often the difference in determining success is in how you react to making a poor decision. Not all decisions are going to be right. Therefore you must be able to learn from the decisions that are wrong. Self-confidence is evident in those who are able to honestly believe that although the decision made today was wrong, the decision that you will make tomorrow will be the right one.

Successful Entrepreneurs Have Tremendous Determination

Most of us get knocked down numerous times in pursuing goals, but not all are willing to keep getting up and trying again. After 99 rejections, are you willing to try for the 100th time? A successful entrepreneur's answer is not only yes, it is "yes, but with a different method." If determination is coupled with creativity you will be successful on try number 100. The world is filled with would-have been successful entrepreneurs, if they had been willing to keep creatively trying long after they gave up the fight.

Determining Your Entrepreneurial Aptitude

The best way to look at your future is to look at your past. Take the time to examine your past career pursuits before deciding on whether the entrepreneurial track is for you. Describe your working career to present. Look for what brought you the greatest satisfaction and the greatest dissatisfaction. What type of changes in your job responsibilities have you enjoyed the most? When have you felt the most fulfillment from your work? When has it been most important for you to achieve recognition from your efforts? What has caused you to feel the most frustration?

These questions are designed to ascertain whether you have been doing what you should be doing. Many of us have been placed in careers through circumstance and not through choice. You might work in accounting, although your greatest satisfaction has come when you have been placed in a position to work with solutions to interpersonal problems in your organization. It is quite possible that you have developed a mindset as to what you are suppose to do, as opposed to what you want to do and what you are best at doing. Look at your past. If the satisfaction you seek is not there due to lack of freedom to pursue what is important to you, you are a candidate for an entrepreneurial career. Entrepreneurs work for their own goals, employees of large organizations work for the goals of the organization. Many cannot be satisfied working for someone else's goals.

Successful entrepreneurs cling to a strong value system of honesty, authenticity, and achievement. Self-reliance carries them through the difficult times. They learn to understand that being an entrepreneur is more than making business decisions, it is a way of life.

The Right Environment

If this is you, it is time to look for an environment that will allow you to work to your potential. Your background review should allow you to describe that area, at least in general terms. If you like working with specific skills, consider a trade or profession that allows you the environment to develop your expertise. This might be a photographer, an auto mechanic, a computer specialist, or any specialty that requires skill enhancement and development.

If you like working with and through people, consider an environment that will allow you to manage people and responsibility. Although in the initial start-up phase of a business, capital limitations will limit the number of people you hire and the range of responsibilities you handle, choose an area that can grow to one that you will be able to use your abilities as a manager. This might be as an owner of a number of retail outlets, a multiple product and market manufacturer, or a many faceted service provider.

If you feel stymied by not being able to put your creative instincts to work, choose an environment that is idea driven. Promotional businesses (i.e., advertising, designing, merchandising, or direct one-on-one marketing experiences) might appeal to you. Or if you absolutely cannot stand for anyone telling you what to do, or how to do it, and do not enjoy working with others, consider an environment of complete autonomy such as inventing, writing, art, or mail-order selling.

One word of caution as you review your past: If you find that you have built a dependency on the regular paychecks and benefits of an employer and the thought of uncertainty causes extreme anxiety, consider part-time business opportunities that will allow you to continue your employment until your confidence level grows.

Industry Choices

Entrepreneurs are found in every field of commercial activity. Using a yardstick of businesses that employ fewer than 100 employees, Fig. 1.1 illustrates the strength of the small enterprises in our country's industrial output.

Small enterprises dominate in most industries in not only sales but also as employers. Over half of the country's workforce are employed by small businesses. The small enterprises also are responsible for more product development than the larger companies. The businesses with 100 or fewer employees are managed and have been developed for the most part by the actions of one individual who set out to achieve a goal. Some of these businesses will grow to take the place of the large downsizing corporations of today. Contrary to many opinions you hear, there are many opportunities for the right individual to achieve success in today's marketplace.

For the purpose of this course, the broad industry classifications for the entrepreneur will be retail, service provider, and the small manufac-

Small Businesses by Different Categories

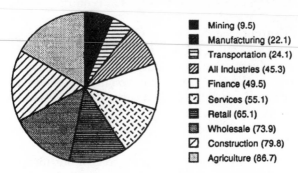

Legend:
- Mining (9.5)
- Manufacturing (22.1)
- Transportation (24.1)
- All Industries (45.3)
- Finance (49.5)
- Services (55.1)
- Retail (65.1)
- Wholesale (73.9)
- Construction (79.8)
- Agriculture (86.7)

Figure 1.1. Revenue share of small businesses to industry totals.

turer/wholesaler. You should begin your search for the right environment with an understanding of what is involved in these three industries.

The Retailer

Retailing is the selling of products to the intended final consumer. They may be retail store merchandisers, vending machine distributors, or mail order and catalog merchants. In many cases, particularly the store owner, it is an occupation which requires extraordinary hours of time. However if you like retailing, you will not mind the hours because the rewards can be many. Retailing allows a lot of creative expression in buying and merchandising, it can be very profitable once established. It is an occupation that gives the owners much pride as they will feel very much an integral part of their community. Successful retailers are very people oriented as they understand that one of their roles is to entertain and please. Initial investment will vary greatly depending upon the choice of the retail path but it will normally take five years to recoup the investment.

The Service Provider

Service businesses have blossomed during the past decade and should be expected to continue their rapid rate of growth. The lure of being a service provider is that talent is required more than investment potential. Service businesses normally succeed or fail depending on the originator's commitment and talent. In providing a service, you are assisting someone or some organization for a fee. Either that service becomes very valued if performed well, or it becomes something the client can do without if not satisfied. Our ever-changing lifestyles seem to constantly demand more services as many do not have the time available to do the responsibilities they once assumed.

One of the greatest changes that has given momentum to the service industry has been the tremendous number of women electing to enter the work place. The dual working couples and the single parent have created great opportunities for service providers in such areas as child care centers and fast food restaurants. Industry downsizing has given greater opportunities for industrial service providers since corporations and government are now "outsourcing" work previously performed by employees. Consulting services, commercial cleaning, and other business services are in demand as they are a method of controlling the employee payroll benefit expense of large organizations.

Successful service providers are perfectionist and have an innate understanding of what pleases people. They must gain a reputation for thoughtfulness, therefore, they are most diplomatic and tactful. Doing the extra is what will distinguish one service provider from another. Their profit potential is determined by the amount of time they are able to give the business and the size of their market.

The Wholesaler and Small Manufacturer

Wholesalers act as middlemen between manufacturer and retailers, or they may assemble, store, and distribute products to industrial users. In some instances, they assume title to the goods and act as full function wholesalers. Others act in a limited function and market products without assuming title. The wholesale industry is dominated by small enterprises.

Small manufacturers do not dominate their industry due to capital limitations, labor unions, and large business competition. However there are many strong and profitable smaller manufacturers particularly in the areas of clothing design, machine shops, and packaging firms. Many of the more successful operations are family owned and have been passed down from previous generations. Construction businesses are sometimes grouped as manufacturers but are mostly small enterprises.

To be successful as a small manufacturer or wholesaler, the entrepreneur must be a very efficient time manager. They must insist on high standards of quality as this will, in the long run, determine their fate. They must work whatever hours are necessary to complete a project on time and must possess good negotiating skills. It is difficult in that they are very dependent on the efforts of many suppliers and they must keep abreast of all technology developments within their industry. If the manufacturer performs all of the wholesale marketing efforts of his or her product, there is the added reward of being in control of all steps and the added incentive of additional profits.

It is extremely important that you as an aspiring entrepreneur look closely at all areas of opportunity. You must decide the very important question of what industry classification is the best environment for your ambitions and talents.

Why and When

Why Are You Taking This Course?

For many, it is the elusive chase for the American dream—wealth, independence, and the right to control your own destiny. It is possible to acquire all of these desirable benefits through business ownership, however you must be aware of the risks. Before jumping off the deep end, take a close and realistic look at what is in store for you. Most new businesses fail—that is a fact. Over 60 percent of businesses started this year will not be in existence five years from now (see Fig. 1.2).

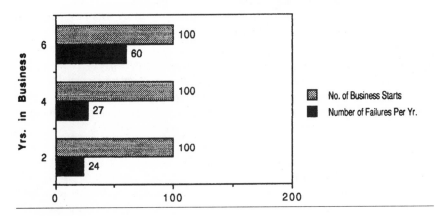

Small Business Start-Ups and Failures

Figure 1.2. Business failure graph.

Not all of these businesses fail, some will close voluntarily, others will be sold to larger businesses—but the fact remains the odds are against the start-up business. So why will close to one million entrepreneurs attempt to start a business this year?

It has something to do with the entrepreneurial spirit within us. The challenge of overcoming the odds and the confidence we can succeed. The good news is that by taking this course, you have appreciatively improved your chances for success. Many of the business failures are coming from the great percentage of individuals who open a business with little or no training, education, or planning in regards to what they expect to accomplish.

Completing a course such as this and following through with proper planning and specific training in the type of business you wish to operate will put you into the plus side of the businesses that do succeed. Too many, who have received proper education and training in their current fields of endeavor, do not take the time, or make the effort, to properly prepare themselves for their new careers. There are no guarantees, however those who point only to the business failure statistics are not seeing the complete picture of the hundreds of thousands of entrepreneurs who properly prepare for a business opening and go on to a successful career as an entrepreneur.

Business conditions are cyclical. Inflationary times, recessions, growth periods have always fluctuated throughout our economic history. Although opening a business in recessionary times poses a more difficult challenge, good ideas will weather the storm and will come out stronger during the following growth periods. The recession of the early 1900s took its toll, but those businesses who have survived are stronger as their weaker competition was eliminated. Your decision as to when to enter a market should take into consideration the economic indicators for the particular industry, however, keep in mind that if you wait until all indicators are perfect you may never have the opportunity you seek.

A word of caution must also be presented as to what is considered success. This course is not about the few who, through a twist of fate, and a lot of luck, turn a business idea into millions of dollars of profit overnight. The theme here is that if you do your homework and research your idea, you will build a business over a period of time that will support your lifestyle, give you the freedom you desire, and instill within you pride of ownership. If you can build that, you will have achieved success and along with it you will have also developed the potential to make much more money than you presently do. The big profits come last, but the freedom to do it your way comes first and in the end that is the most important asset you will have acquired.

When to start a business becomes a personal question. It is not necessary to rush a business idea. If an idea is good and the plan is right, it will succeed at any time if the market need exists. Many rush into a business start-up within a few weeks of a pink slip or an inheritance. Take the time to learn, study, and research before proceeding. Often it is best to start on a part-time basis as this gives time for the market to develop. The best possible scenario is for the market to demand that you enter, as opposed to forcing your way into a market. Some great businesses have started in the garage or workshop on Saturday mornings and in the evenings after work.

Also you must consider the timing as it effects those around you. Getting a business off the ground while trying to pay for a child's college education or when other financial obligations must be settled first, is a barrier that can be difficult to overcome. Opportunities will strike more than once and if need be your entrepreneurial ambitions can be put on hold until all indications are positive.

Chapter Summary

Your journey into an entrepreneurial career begins with evaluating your personal characteristics and potential in regards to achieving success in reaching your goals. To be successful it is imperative that you review your past, set your goals, and choose an environment that will allow you to reach your full potential. Be aware of the risks that you are undertaking, but build the confidence needed to be successful as an entrepreneur.

The First Step

The first step is to make a written commitment to what you wish to achieve. Written because writing gives clarity and commitment. This is the time to discuss ideas with those close to you to receive support. It is extremely important for you to have the support of your family. The path you are about to follow is filled with excitement and hazards. Those close to you must have an appreciation for what you are about to commence because it will become very much a part of you. Starting and operating a business becomes an appendage to your person. It will absorb you in many ways and those around you must understand this. Therefore don't hide your dreams and your goals, you want your support staff to feel your excitement and to get caught up in it themselves.

Write a very clear description of your goals and why they are important to you. Share this statement with your family and receive their input. At this point, these goals might be general but they will be the glue that holds the upcoming plan together because this part of your plan will not change. The goals stated should include the personal satisfaction you expect to receive and the minimum financial rewards you must receive to go ahead with the idea. In one paragraph, state the type of enterprise you wish to consider, why, and how much profits must be received in the first year to meet your immediate financial obligations. A second short paragraph should address the timing of the start of the project and the profit goals three to five years down the road. You have now started your journey into an entrepreneurial career. *Good luck !*

Review Questions

1. *What is the difference in definition of an entrepreneur as opposed to a successful entrepreneur?*
2. *Describe the primary personal characteristics of successful entrepreneurs.*
3. *Why is it important that you look at your past career achievements before deciding on your future goals?*
4. *Why is the choice of environment an important determinant to your future success?*
5. *Describe the industry choices available for your consideration.*
6. *What is a prime reason that so many businesses fail?*
7. *Why should you consider an entrepreneurial career?*
8. *When is the best time to start a business?*
9. *Why is family support considered an essential ingredient for success?*
10. *What is the first step in starting a plan to become an entrepreneur?*

2
Finding the
Right Idea

Objectives

1. Describe the approach for discovering the right business for you to pursue.
2. Receive an overlook of current trends in small business start ups.
3. Learn the questions to ask yourself in deciding on a business venture.
4. Learn where to go for help in achieving your objective.
5. Understand the purpose and importance of developing a business plan.

Key Terms

Small Business Development Centers   Business Plan
Service Corp. of Retired Executives

Many inspirational messages have come from Henry David Thoreau's philosophies. One in particular, "The mass of men lead lives of quiet desperation. What is called resignation is confirmed desperation," has a profound meaning to entrepreneurship. Ross Perot for one states that this expression changed his life.

Successful entrepreneurs do not know the meaning of resignation. Their lives are comprised of constantly reaching for what others think is not possible.

Where to Look for Ideas

The best small business opportunities are found in niches throughout any marketplace. There is no particular industry or any particular type of business that is an immediate gold mine. It depends on what is not being adequately supplied or serviced in a particular market area. Your goal is to identify a particular segment where you can fulfill an unsatisfied need.

The greatest area of growth through the 1980s and into the 1990s has been the service market. *INC.* magazine annually ranks the 500 fastest growing small businesses in America.* Service businesses have dominated this list (55 percent in 1991) during the past decade. The greatest industry growth in the 1991 ranking has been in computers. Growth by industry includes:

Computers	23.0%
Consumer goods and products	14.4%
Business products and services	12.4%
Health care	8.6%
Real estate and construction	6.4%
Environmental products and services	6.4%
Industrial equipment	4.4%
Telecommunications	2.8%
Media	1.8%
Transportation	1.8%
Other	18.0%

Entrepreneur magazine projected the 17 hottest small businesses for 1993 as:

Medical claims processing	Baseball card stores
Computer training for children	Coffeehouses
Translating services	Pasta restaurants
Exports	Temporary services
Upscale billiard halls	Auditing services
Food delivery	Mail order
Women's formalwear rental	Environmental services
Computer and printer maintenance	Audio bookstores
Home health care	

*The Inc. 500, October 1992, p. 74.

These projections fit the trend of the small business market towards the services. *Entrepreneur* backs up these projections by citing national trends towards the aging of America, the rise of child consumers, privatization (the shift away from government services to the private sector), health food consciousness, and the need for more career enhancement. If you need ideas to stimulate your exploration, Figs. 2.1 and 2.2 are just a partial list of full-time and part-time occupations that are open to entrepreneurs.

Many communities have researched their market areas to determine what industries are undersupplied. Check with your community resources to see if such a list exists.

Retailing	Services
Clothing store	Preschool/day care
Fashion boutique	Print shop
Bicycle shop	Landscaping
Bookstore ·	Rental service
Antique shop	Interior decorating
Camera shop	Warehousing and storage
Art gallery	Home/commercial maintenance
Drugstore	Auto repair franchise
Stereo shop	Accounting and tax service
Gift shop	Business services franchise
Liquor store	Car wash
Florist	Employment agency
Plant shop	Travel agency
Pet shop	Real estate agency
Auto dealership	
	Industrial
Food and Recreation	Manufacturing
Fast-food franchise	Machine shop
Restaurant	Distributorship
Convenience-store franchise	Wholesaling
Bar/cocktail lounge	Manufacturer's representative
Boat marina	Cartage/delivery
Riding stable	
Campground franchise	**Other**
Motel	Mail order
	Auctioneer
	Farming
	Artist
	Contractor
	Restaurant designer
	Dog kennel

Figure 2.1. List of small business opportunities.

1. Mail Order	14. Firewood Service
2. Catalog Sales	15. House Sitting
3. Mailing Service	16. Sell Home Safety & Energy Devices
4. Freelance Writing	17. Novelty Button Making
5. Desktop Publishing	18. Handicrafts
6. Garage Sale Service	19. Repair Service
7. Flea Market Sales	20. Parking Lot Striping
8. Recycling	21. Janitorial Service
9. Pet Sitting	22. Cake Decorating/Birthday Services
10. Child Care	23. Lawn Maintenance
11. Tutoring Service	24. Balloon Delivery
12. Pamphlet Distributing	25. Pet Grooming
13. Paint House Numbers	

Figure 2.2. List of 25 part-time business opportunities.

Making Personal Choices

Very simply, just as in making the decision to pursue an entrepreneurial career, look to yourself in deciding exactly what will be the greatest opportunity. After all the reason you are doing this is to work for your goals and not someone else's. Therefore, what do you really want to do with your career?

Any idea must fit the description of what is right for you. You will most likely spend the majority of your waking time at this endeavor so make sure that it is right or else you will regret the day owning your own business ever entered your mind. Write out the answer to these questions:

1. What is important to you in terms of personal satisfaction? Do you seek challenge, family fulfillment, community service, fame, status or possibly a combination of many factors to assure a feeling of self-worth and self-actualization?

2. What is the minimum income level you need to meet your current obligations and what income level do you hope to reach in the future? Your personal financial obligations will continue as you start your business. They must be met regardless. You will need to establish a personal cash flow budget to illustrate what minimum amount of money must be generated for you to consider any idea. You cannot consider any idea that does not assure you of reaching the minimum profit figure that permits you to meet your basic financial obligations. After you ascertain this figure, then you can look further down the road to determine, in a realistic manner, the profits you would be satisfied with after the business is established.

3. What type of work really turns you on? Do you enjoy sales, technology development, administrative tasks, working outdoors, arts and crafts? Whatever, this is a starting place. Ideally you would like to do for a living, the things you do for enjoyment.

In considering the type of work, make sure you address how you feel about working with people. Different occupations have different degrees of personal interaction with employees, suppliers, and customers. Be aware of how effective you are and how much you enjoy working with and through others.

Also check your stamina for work. Different types of work have various degrees of physical and psychological requirements. Are you a 12-hour-per-day person, a nine-to-fiver, or a part-timer? Do you thrive under anxiety and time pressures or do you require a quiet and less tense environment?

4. What lifestyle considerations are important to you? Do you enjoy travel? Are you a night person or an early morning dynamo? Do you enjoy community involvement—chamber of commerce meetings, civic clubs, etc.? In many businesses, these activities are essential for networking customers and building goodwill.

5. What are your personal capabilities? Are there areas of expertise that you have accumulated through past experiences that you wish to carry into the future? Or, are there areas that you seek training that might require going back to school to develop? Certainly you should use the abilities that you have acquired, even if applied differently.

6. What are your financial capabilities? We will spend considerable time discussing how to build financial options later, however you need to address your basic financial situation at this point. For now, figure what you have immediately available to invest times two for a ball park estimate.

7. What type of risk factor is acceptable to you? There is a definite correlation between risk and immediate profit potential. The higher the risk the greater the potential for greater profits or losses. How does your psyche hold up when considering risk? Are you more comfortable with a slower growth, lower risk situation or are you the high stakes gambler who is more willing to roll the dice?

Writing out the answers to these seven questions, honestly, will eliminate many options available for you to pursue. You should be able to write a short description of the type of opportunities that appeal to you based on these answers. Keep the answers to these personal choice questions handy because they serve as your tool for considering whether or not a particular idea is worth considering. Many factors must be weighed in choosing the right opportunity, however the answers to these questions should remain quite stable and can guide you in this decision-making process.

Where to Go to Develop
Your Idea

With a general description in mind from answering the personal choice questions, you can start a basic research on some specific endeavors. Take your ideas to the following sources of assistance:

1. *Friends.* Ask them what they think of your ideas. Listen to the feedback, it will stimulate more questions. Insist on honest feedback.

2. *Industry sources.* The people with the greatest knowledge are those who are already in the field. Contact manufacturers, wholesalers, or retailers currently or recently employed in the industry. Making these contacts are invaluable, you will use them throughout your career. Many of them will be quite helpful, particularly if you represent a future customer. If you don't know anyone, contact corporate offices by phone and ask them for the name and number of the closest company representative.

3. *Local business community members.* Visit your chamber of commerce, local bankers, accountants, lawyers, or realtors. These are the people for a feel for the local market and its potential. Even if you have to pay an initial fee for a professional interview, the cost might save you thousands down the road.

4. *Small Business Development Centers.* The Small Business Administration and your state government have teamed together in developing a resource of help for the small business owner and developer, the SBDC. SBDC offices are often located at many college campuses or chambers of commerce. They are manned by individuals with training in assisting you with writing and researching business plans. They can also be helpful to you in determining whether you qualify for SBA loans or other government assistance programs. There is no cost for their services, therefore you have nothing to lose by arranging a visit to one of their offices. Small Business Development Centers also offer a series of low-cost seminars on various aspects of opening and managing a small business which can be very helpful.

5. *The Service Corp. of Retired Executives (SCORE).* This is another SBA sponsored program which puts you in touch with retired executives, who will act as your consultant, once again at no charge. Call your nearest SBA office for information.

6. *The local library and bookstores.* You will find an abundance of published information on many types of businesses and markets.

7. *Business and economic professors at area colleges and universities.* An increasing number of colleges are offering courses in entrepreneurship

and are staffed with knowledgeable sources who are usually glad to visit with you to discuss your ideas and give direction.

8. *Small Business Consulting Firms.* In many instances, these companies offer for a fee what you can receive free through the SBA. However, if you are seeking information and help in a highly specialized area they might offer more depth and more direct involvement.

The idea is to learn to ask questions and not be afraid of rejection or negative feedback. The boldness to ask for help is a requirement for your ultimate success. Start now. Once you have done this initial screening on your ideas, you are ready to start your business plan.

Creating a Business Plan

Among the options you can consider is creating your business from scratch, buying an existing business, or possibly becoming a franchisee. Regardless of what path you decide to follow you will need to write a business plan. In many cases, if your description at this point lends itself to a number of business opportunities, you should write a business plan for each. It is quite possible that you may end up with three, four, or five different plans. All will be somewhat related since they come from the same fundamental reasoning, and once written you should be able to compare them to make a final selection.

The reason you write a business plan is to give you a map to follow to reach your objectives. Without it you will wander and miss obvious important information. A good plan illustrates the "what-if" situations that might arise from good fortune or bad. It is imperative that you take the ideas that you are carrying around in your head and write them down in a clear and orderly fashion. Initially, the business plan is for you. However, in its final format it can be shown to bankers or potential investors to raise capital.

The Ingredients of a Business Plan

Upon completion of this course you will feel comfortable writing a business plan. We will discuss in detail how to research and write the following parts of your plan.

1. *The Executive Summary.* The first part of the plan is the last part that you will write. It is the capstone that clearly tells the reader the objectives that will be reached by the entrepreneur if the business plan is followed.

2. *The Business Description.* A business description should state the type of business to be opened, what market it will serve, who will be responsible for it, and why it is needed.

3. *The Market Analysis.* A description of the target market. How large and how comprised? Its growth trend and future projection. If a consumer market, it should include a description of the lifestyles of the market members (psychographics), per capita income information, education level, gender and race ratios and all other pertinent demographic information. If the business is to sell industrial products or services, it should include all pertinent information as it relates to the particular industry. As stated the successful entrepreneur is able to sense the needs of the market, but not without first validating those senses. The market analysis must also include a geographical market analysis in regards to where the business will be located.

Also an analysis of all competitive factors in the direct and indirect marketplace. Who will the entrepreneur compete directly against? What are their strengths and weaknesses? What indirect competitors are capable of influencing the market? What is the anticipated market share of the new business? What is the anticipated response from the competition when the new business opens?

4. *The Marketing Strategy.* How will the entrepreneur attract and retain customers? This will include a description of all marketing activities including advertising and promotional plans. The marketing strategy also addresses pricing strategies and reasoning. What influence does the choice of location have in regards to influencing customer appeal?

The market analysis and strategy sections of a business plan are the most important ingredient. Small businesses exist because they know their market better than large businesses. This should be evident even in the initial business plan.

5. *Management and Operations Plan.* What organization structure is planned and why? A proprietorship, partnership, or corporation? How will the operation be managed and by who? How will personnel be recruited? This section should include a description of suppliers, terms, and inventory control systems. What type of accounting system will be used? What legal restrictions, regulations, and licensing requirements need to be addressed? What types of insurance will be carried?

6. *Financial Data.* Normally three years of projected (pro forma) financial statements should be included. This would include income

statements and balance sheets. You will have to defend your reasoning for your sales forecast and for the amount budgeted for the capital assets and inventory purchases needed to operate. In addition you will need to include at least a 12-month cash flow analysis that shows how cash comes in and goes out of the business operation on a monthly basis.

7. *Supporting Documents.* The final section of the plan consists of any reinforcements you may wish to include to defend your proposal. They might include letters from potential customers, references of past successes, sample marketing pieces, and personal resumes of owners and managers.

It sounds like a lot, however once you get involved in the research it is surprising how it will all come together. Follow along the course and you will be assured of a well written business plan. A sample business plan is illustrated in Chapter 24.

Chapter Summary

In choosing to become an entrepreneur you have made a conscious decision to do what you want to do for a career. Make sure you closely examine what is important to you. Those who enter businesses who are uncertain of their aptitude become quickly disenchanted and often have unrealistic expectations as to what can be achieved. When you have an idea in mind, start to research by asking questions of resources that can be helpful to you. Once an idea has passed the initial screening it is time to write out your course of action in a business plan. A business plan is essential for success and must be thoroughly researched to be complete.

The Next Step

Write out answers to personal choice questions. This should allow you to better formulate your idea and will give you an initial business description(s). Take your idea to the assistance sources discussed and start the first step of the business plan, a clear and concise description for your intended business.

Review Questions

1. *What are considered the "hot spots" for business start-ups?*
2. *Why is it necessary for you to write out descriptions of your personal choices in choosing a business opportunity?*

3. *List five sources in your community that you consider good information resources.*

4. *What is a Small Business Development Center?*

5. *Why are industry sources so important to you?*

6. *What is the purpose of writing a business plan?*

7. *What are the ingredients of a business plan?*

8. *What should be included in a market analysis?*

9. *What is a cash flow analysis?*

10. *What might you include as supporting documents to a business plan?*

3

Investigating Buying an Existing Business

Objectives

1. Understand the advantages and disadvantages of buying an existing business.
2. Learn the different methods of evaluating a business for sale opportunity.
3. Learn how you can find business for sale opportunities.
4. Understand the procedures to use when buying and negotiating a business purchase.

Key Terms

Business Broker	Earnings Approach
Goodwill	Replacement Value
Market Value	Liquidation Value

Many individuals find the best way to enter the world of self-employment is through the purchase of an existing business. Before deciding to start a business it is wise to investigate the business for sale market for three reasons.

1. Discussing a business for sale with the seller is a very good way to learn the conditions of the marketplace. It enables you to see, first hand, the sales revenues from a member of the industry and possibly a future competitor.
2. It educates you to the potential market value of a particular type of business after it has been established.
3. It might lead to an opportunity to enter the market at a lower cost than originally intended.

Even if your original intention is to create a business on your own, it is always wise for the potential small business owner to investigate businesses for sale. You might find an existing business very similar to the one you envision—one that you can adapt easily to fit your own personality.

Why Buy an Existing Business?

There are many advantages to buying an existing business, particularly for the inexperienced. It is an ideal way to learn the ropes because, in most cases, the previous owner will stay on for a period of time to train the new owner. Procedures are in place, suppliers are lined up, and a customer base is intact.

There is less anxiety since the existing business has a track record. This gives the new owner an idea as to what he or she can expect in regards to revenues, expenses, and profits. If the purchase of a business is approached properly, there will be less risk.

Purchasing an established business might be financially advantageous. In some instances, sellers will assist by financing the purchase either partially or, in some cases, totally. This is likely to happen if the seller needs to get out quickly or the business has been on the market for an extended period of time. The buyer should negotiate for the seller to accept a minimum downpayment with the remainder in the form of a note spread out over a period of time. This arrangement might eliminate the need for bank financing and is often negotiated at a more attractive interest rate. If the note is secured solely by the business, the seller incurs a risk that the new owner will be able to make the payments, or else he or she will have to take the business back. Presuming he or she does not wish this to happen, the previous owner will want to help the new owner in any way possible.

Businesses are sometimes purchased because it is the only way to successfully enter the market. If a particular business dominates the market due to superior location and reputation, buying it might be the only method of assuring success.

Other advantages to buying the existing business might include:

The business suppliers will already have been established, saving the time necessary to find them.

The necessary equipment will be on hand.

The hard work of physically setting up the business will have been done.

Experienced employees will already be on hand and will not require training.

There will be less planning required.

Why to Not Buy an Existing Business

Many businesses are for sale due to problems. You are better off starting with a clean slate than inheriting someone else's problems. If a business has a poor reputation with customers, has trouble with suppliers, or is poorly located, it is not wise to assume that because there is new ownership, customers will automatically change their opinion about a struggling concern. Too many business buyers have learned the hard way that it takes a long time to restore confidence in a business and have regretted not starting anew.

Buying a profitable business will cost more initially. The seller has built an established business and will expect to be rewarded with a high selling price. Capital limitations might prevent the purchase of such a business and it might be more economically feasible to take the risk of creating a new business with less investment.

Also you can consider purchasing part of, or investing in, an established business. The risk is that there might be little compatibility between the parties that have been more or less forced together for economic reasons. A bad partnership arrangement prevents a business from building the teamwork that is so essential for its success.

The employees currently working in the business may have to be replaced due to poor training and habits of the former owner. In this case, you are better off starting anew than to try to change old habits.

It may be necessary to invest money to modernize the operation. You do not want to buy equipment or machinery that will not perform to your expectations for future business activity.

Reasons That
Businesses Are Sold

In considering the purchase of a business you, as the potential buyer, need to determine the real reason the business is for sale. Determining the reason a business is for sale will help the buyer in negotiating the final price. If the seller is under great pressure to sell, he or she will be more flexible in the negotiation stage. The following is a list of the many reasons businesses are sold.

Insufficient profits

Death or illness of a working partner

Disinterested heirs of a business

Partner or shareholder dispute

Management burnout

Geographic relocation

Forced liquidation or sale

Fear of new competition

Fear of current or predicted economic conditions

Lack of desire or capital to do necessary remodeling

Desire for a change of career direction

To take advantage of an opportunity requiring the liquidation of business assets

Often the real reason a business is for sale is not stated. It is the buyer's responsibility to uncover any missing information through proper research of the opportunity.

Evaluating a Business for Sale
Opportunities

Normally an investigation of businesses for sale opportunities will produce a range of opportunities from the good to the bad to the promising.

Bad Opportunities.   The first sign of a bad opportunity is poor bookkeeping. If a business has been derelict in maintaining its financial records, it has more than likely been under poor management. Often failure to present adequate validation of sales revenues and expenditures is a sign that the seller is attempting to hide information. This type of situation should be avoided.

Good Opportunities. Good businesses keep good records and maintain a good customer image. Buying a business that has been properly managed is much better because time and money will not have to be spent convincing customers that they will be treated better under the new management. However, if the business has been profitable and managed well, it will cost more to buy. In cases of successful businesses for sale, it is customary to add a dollar amount for goodwill. *Goodwill* is the amount the seller believes he or she should be paid for the efforts of building a successful business and a good reputation with customers and the community.

Promising Opportunities. Many opportunities are not as easy to distinguish. Recordkeeping is adequate, but not totally complete, a solid, but unspectacular, customer base has been built, and relationship with suppliers is generally satisfactory. Many times, these are the best opportunities because their greatest need is for better management. Proper management might generate greater sales and better customer reception. Since previous management has not been able to reach all of its objectives, the selling price of the business should not include goodwill, therefore, it might be a bargain for the right person(s).

An example might be a business that has leveled off in sales at a certain point and can't seem to get above that level even though the surrounding market is good. Management is evidently not doing some things right or else does not have the capital available to aggressively pursue the market. If a new owner can make some changes like a remodeling, adding new inventory, and increase advertising expenditures, it is quite possible to change the profit picture and receive a healthy return on investment for the new owner. In looking for opportunities, the potential buyer should keep an open eye for this type of opportunity.

Opportunities for buying a business must be evaluated in terms of profit earnings and return on investment. Using the earnings approach, the buyer needs to determine the likelihood that the business will be able to pay him or her a salary for the time invested in working and also return the amount of money invested over a period of time. Usually that period of time is five years, or 20 percent per year. Too often businesses are bought with the assumption that as soon as the new management takes over, business will improve dramatically. Just as in a new business, it takes time to change customer buying habits, therefore, opportunities must be evaluated considering the long-term potential.

If a business is bought without proper evaluation of the return on investment, the buyer runs the risk of buying a job and not receiving a return on the money that was used to purchase the business. Suppose a business is for sale for $100,000 with the following simplified income statement:

Sales	$200,000
Cost of Goods	−110,000
Gross Profit	90,000
Operating Expenses	60,000
Net Profit	$ 30,000

The seller might try to present the $30,000 profit as a 30 percent return on investment (30,000/100,000). However, if the business is a proprietorship, profits are declared before any distribution to the owner. If the buyer is planning on managing this business and being paid, the needed salary must be deducted from the net profit before determining the true return on the $100,000 investment. If the needed salary is $25,000, that allows only $5000 to be paid back on the original investment or five percent.

The potential buyer must also research the market value of the business for sale. This requires discovering the selling prices of similar businesses and comparing to the proposition being investigated. The replacement value of assets to be purchased must be determined as well. Since a balance sheet listing of asset valuation is based on the original purchase price of assets including equipment and inventory, the buyer should determine the current replacement value of the assets listed. A final measure of valuation should be the liquidation value of the business's assets. Using a worst case scenario, you should determine the immediate cash value of all assets in the event a problem arises that causes an emergency exit from the business.

A final step in the evaluation process is for the prospective owner to review the current income statement of a business for sale and project adjustments to that financial statement due to the new ownership. This should be done in a realistic manner without assuming that new ownership will automatically cause an immediate drastic increase of revenues. Figure 3.1 is an example of such a list of adjustments.

When considering the purchase of a business, you must form a strategy for what you would do with the business to improve its position. Each situation must be looked upon differently.

Suppose two businesses, making roughly the same profit, are for sale at the same price—$250,000. One is old and rather worn looking and is selling for its cost inventory value. The other is very up to date, obviously under good management, and has $150,000 of inventory. Certainly, first impressions would

Projected Income Statement for the Year Ending December 31, 19XY

	19XX actual year-end results	% of sales	19XY adjusted results	% of sales
Sales	$200,000	100.0	$220,000	100.0
Cost of goods sold	114,000	57.0	121,000	55.0
Gross margin	86,000	43.0	99,000	45.0
Operating expenses				
Payroll	31,000	15.5	32,000	14.5
Rent	20,000	10.0	22,000	10.0
Operating supplies	4,200	2.1	4,620	2.1
Utilities	3,800	1.9	4,400	2.0
Other	14,000	7.0	15,400	7.0
Total cash operating expenses	73,000	36.5	78,420	35.6
Depreciation	5,000	2.5	5,000	2.3
Interest	6,000	3.0	5,000	2.3
Total operating expenses	84,000	42.0	88,420	40.2
Pre-tax profit	$ 2,000	1.0%	$ 10,580	4.8%

Figure 3.1. Adjusted income statement.

favor the up-to-date operation. However, a more in depth investigation might reveal that the only way to improve the profit picture of the up-to-date business would be to increase the inventory selection by $50,000 thereby increasing the investment and the risk to $300,000. On the other hand, the older operation might be carrying too much out-of-date inventory. The strategy here would be to sell off $50,000 of old inventory at cost, use some of the proceeds to buy some newer inventory, and the remainder to update and remodel the operation. The investment remains at $250,000, however, the new look might make it a very promising opportunity with less risk than the first option that you considered. You must look at opportunities from all angles before making the final decision.

Steps in Buying and Negotiating a Business Purchase

Buying a business is an intricate process which requires the same thoroughness as creating a business plan for starting a business. A buyer should follow these steps:

1. Just as in the start of a business plan, personal and financial objectives must be clearly written out. Whatever the business for sale, it must match these statements to be considered.

2. Locate business opportunities with the potential to grow and offer an attractive return on investment. By reading classified advertisements, discussing opportunities with business brokers, and checking industry sources, a list of potential opportunities can be made.

3. Visit with the business sellers or brokers for an initial introduction to the opportunity(ies). The initial material available should include a brief financial report, history, price, and reason for sale.

4. If after reviewing the material presented it fits the stated buyers objectives, a second meeting should be requested to probe for more information.

5. Review the facility closely to determine how well it has been managed and maintained. Prepare a checklist of information needed. The checklist should include:
   a. A complete financial accounting of operations for at least the past three years or from the beginning of operations if not established that long. This should include all income tax returns and state sales tax forms.
   b. A list of all assets to be transferred to the new owner. This should include an item breakdown of all inventory as of the last accounting period.
   c. A statement as to any legal action past or pending against the present operation.
   d. A copy of the business lease or mortgage.
   e. A list of all major suppliers to the business to include names and addresses of those to contact who are familiar with the operation.

6. Upon a satisfactory personal examination of all information received the potential buyer should then visit:
   a. An accountant for further interpretation of financial information.
   b. The landlord or mortgage holder to inquire about the transfer of the premise to a new owner. In the case of a lease, the expiration date should be discussed and if possible renegotiated to the intentions of the new owner. An on-site review of the facility should be conducted to assure it is in satisfactory condition.
   c. The chamber of commerce and other local assistance centers to discuss the future of the market and the location.
   d. Industry representatives presently selling to the business to validate the sales reported and an opinion as to the likelihood of future growth of the business.

7. Arrange a convenient time with the seller to spend time at the operation observing and surveying customer satisfaction.

8. Determine a fair price to offer for the business. Determine what financing arrangements can be made available through a lending institution or the seller. Present the offer in writing to the seller. Normally, at this point, there will be negotiation. Successful negotiating comes from confidence in your position. The more information that you have collected and analyzed, the more confident you will be in presenting your case. Without full confidence you can be persuaded away from your best interests. As the buyer, you will have to use your best persuasion techniques to point out the validity of the offer and the advantages to the seller of accepting the offer. Be prepared to walk away if a major obstacle prevents you from obtaining important objectives. Some buyers, not confident of their persuasive skills use a third party, or agent, to explain the offer to the seller. If you do your homework this is not necessary and shows a weakness to the seller.

9. If an agreement is reached contact an attorney to draw up a suitable sales contract and research state records for any liens against the property for failure to pay a debt. The contract should be contingent upon examinations of all assets to validate what is represented is true.

10. Before signing a sales contract, the buyer should be present when a final inventory count of assets, including inventory, is taken.

Finding the Opportunities

Business owners wishing to sell their businesses will let their intentions be known through classified newspaper advertising, by listing their businesses through business brokers, or by getting the word out through industry and community sources.

Classified Advertising

Potential buyers should check first in the business opportunities section of the classified section of local newspapers. There they will find numerous advertisements similar to the one shown in Fig. 3.2.

The initial information will be very sketchy, however, a quick phone call, or mail inquiry, should bring the basic information as whether it is worth investigating. If the idea shows promise, a time should be prearranged to visit the seller to become acquainted and make initial direct inquiries. Buying a business requires very intensive research. The first meeting is

Figure 3.2. Business for sale advertisement.

normally a general discussion of why the business is for sale and how the seller foresees the future potential of the business. If the buyer is still interested after this meeting a schedule to investigate the opportunity should be arranged with the seller including meeting and observation times.

Business Brokers

Business brokers act as selling agents for business sellers, just as real estate brokers sell homes. They assist the seller by bringing the potential buyer and seller together. In order to complete a sale they advise the seller as to the information that will be needed to answer questions. They also handle advertising the business for sale. Many sellers use brokers in order to keep the selling intention confidential. A broker will advertise without giving the name of the business and will give their phone number and address as the contact. When they feel a prospect is qualified to buy the business they will put the buyer in contact with the seller. They will also assist in drawing up the sales contract and possible financial arrangements. Brokers are paid for their services by the seller a stipulated percentage of the selling price. The percentage is normally 10 to 15 percent.

Industry Sources

Many businesses are sold by getting the word to the industry that a business is for sale. This works through either direct referral from sales people or by advertising in industry publications. It is an effective means of selling since potential new business owners will make inquiries as to opportunities to companies of the products that they will be selling. Many companies have referral systems in place to put those making inquiries in touch with those who wish to sell. They will normally not get directly involved with the selling process except as a referral.

Other sources for leads in finding a for sale business include:

Landlords

Attorneys

Bankers

SBA and Small Business Development Centers

Management consultants

Shopping center management offices

Venture capitalists

Chambers of commerce

Acquaintances

Bankruptcy announcements

Often the best business opportunities will come from businesses not for sale. If there is an existing business that meets all of the requirements, the potential business buyer is looking for, an offer can be made to the owner. The owner may refuse, however, if the offer is attractive enough, he or she might consider the opportunity to sell.

Chapter Summary

Many entrepreneurs choose to buy an existing business rather than create a business. The advantages to buying a business as opposed to starting one from scratch include owning a business with a history which reduces the risk factor by knowing what to expect. Also the new business owner will inherit an immediate customer and supplier base, and may receive preferable financial arrangements through seller financing. However, many businesses for sale do not have these advantages. They have poor customer relations, an image that takes a long time for a new owner to overcome.

Buying an existing business requires extensive research and planning. The buyer must make sure that all documents presented are true and the final price is fair. If the opportunity does not represent a good investment it should be avoided. The buyer should realistically project how the change of ownership will impact the growth of the business and should not expect an overnight turn around of profits and growth.

To find business-for-sale opportunities, research the classified sections of the newspaper, inquire to business brokers, discuss your interest with industry representatives, and inquire throughout the marketplace.

The Next Step

Review the classified section of the newspaper to find a for-sale opportunity for a business similar to the one you are researching. If applicable, visit the seller. Also contact a business broker to inquire if he or she has any current listings of a similar business. Inquire to an industry representative or trade association as to their knowledge of any businesses for sale. Follow the procedures mentioned for investigating opportunities.

Review Questions

1. *Why is it a good idea to investigate business for-sale opportunities before deciding to start a business?*

2. *What are the advantages to buying an existing business?*

3. *What are the disadvantages to buying an existing business?*

4. *Why is it important to determine why a business is for sale?*

5. *What information is necessary to collect before a business opportunity can be properly evaluated?*

6. *What is a sign of a bad business for sale opportunity?*

7. *What is determined by using an earnings approach to evaluating a business for sale?*

8. *What is determined when calculating liquidation value?*

9. *Why is it wise to make an adjusted income statement before purchasing a business?*

10. *Describe a promising business opportunity.*

11. *Explain the advantage of using seller financing as opposed to conventional financing.*

12. *Describe the steps taken in investigating a business for-sale opportunity.*

13. *How would you find business for sale opportunities?*

14. *A business is advertised for sale for $150,000. The stated profit is $40,000 after all salaries including the owner. Is it worth investigating? Why?*

15. *Why does replacement value differ from the asset value listed on a balance sheet?*

4

Investigating Franchise Opportunities

Objectives

1. Understand the franchisee-franchisor relationship.
2. Understand the advantages of owning a franchise.
3. Understand the disadvantages of franchise ownership.
4. Describe the current franchise market.
5. Learn how to find franchise opportunities.
6. Learn what you should expect from a franchisor.

Key Terms

Franchise	Uniform Franchise Offering Circular
Franchisee	Franchise Agreement
Franchisor	

Franchising is booming and will continue to do so into the 21st century. The reason is very simple, the success rate is much greater than for the independently created business. However, keep in mind what was said about the correlation between profit and risk—the lower the risk the lower the profit potential. Therefore although the failure percentage is lower, often the profit potential is lower when measured against the return on investment.

What Is a Franchise?

A franchise agreement is when one party, the franchisor, grants to another party, the franchisee, the rights to market/distribute a trademarked product or service in exchange for payment or royalties. Or in some cases the franchisee is granted the right to offer, sell, or distribute goods or services under a marketing format designed by the franchisor.

Why Consider a Franchise?

The U.S. Department of Commerce reports that less than 5 percent of franchised businesses have been discontinued in any particular year since 1974. Compared to the independent small business first-year failure rate estimated to be as high as 30 percent, it is easy to see the attractiveness of franchising. Even during the recent recessionary times, franchise sales have continued to grow at a rate of approximately 6 percent per year and now total over $246 billion.

Franchising has a particular appeal to the victims of downsized corporations who wish to use their severance and benefit packages to invest in proven concepts. It is an opportunity for small business ownership for those with little or no small business experience. It can be a way of becoming an entrepreneur with a built-in market and proven product. It is easier.

As an independent entrepreneur you have to do all the advertising, merchandising, buying, and researching plus run the business operation. Purchasing a proven franchise will give you instant customers. As a franchisee you will receive the necessary training to operate a business, instead of learning through mistakes. Your support system is in place from day one. It is indeed a more comfortable avenue for many, however....

Why to Not Consider a Franchise

Franchise owners will often feel that they have just changed jobs. The restrictions and regulations of many franchisors will take away from the feeling of independence and the satisfaction of self-determination that comes from starting your own business. In addition the revenue-sharing agreement with the franchisor that seemed so fair at the start may not be so agreeable a few years down the road when the franchisee knows the business better than the parent organization.

Also the initial cost is going to be higher. The security, identity, and training that you are going to acquire is going to cost more. The average franchisee is 40-years old and has a net worth of over $300,000 before investing. Approximately 90 percent of all franchisees are college educated and more than one third are corporate refugees.* This general description does not fit many would be entrepreneurs.

Franchise Opportunities

Franchise industry growth reflects the same trends as the small business market in general. Services head the list as they account for the majority of franchise start-ups and over 35 percent of total franchise revenues.

Entrepreneur magazine rated the following as the top 10 franchises for 1993 based on a formula accounting for history, number of franchises, growth, and financial stability.**

1. Subway—submarine sandwiches

2. Dunkin Donuts—donuts

3. Little Caesar's Pizza—pizza

4. McDonald's—hamburgers

5. Mail Boxes Etc.—packaging/miscellaneous business services

6. Burger King—hamburgers

7. Chem-Dry—carpet, upholstery & drapery services

8. Jani-King—commercial cleaning

9. Dairy Queen—ice cream

10. Coverall North America Inc.—commercial cleaning

In the same study *Entrepreneur* rated the fastest growing franchises, the top low investment franchises, and the top new franchises. The 10 fastest growing franchisees (based on number of units added over past year) are:

*Generic terminology.

**Entrepreneur*, January 1993.

1. Subway—1082 units, submarine sandwiches
2. 7-Eleven—878 units, convenience stores
3. Jani-King—786 units, commercial cleaning
4. Burger King—776 units, hamburgers
5. Dunkin Donuts—600 units, donuts
6. McDonald's—521 units, hamburgers
7. Coverall North America Inc.—478 units, commercial cleaning
8. Clean Net—346 units, commercial cleaning
9. Little Caesar's Pizza—344 units, pizza
10. Mail Boxes Etc.—285 units, packaging/business services

The top 10 low-investment franchises (franchises with a minimum total investment of less than $10,000) are:

1. Jani-King—commercial cleaning
2. Coverall North America Inc.—commercial cleaning
3. H&R Block—income tax services
4. Jazzercise—fitness centers
5. Duraclean—carpet, upholstery & drapery services
6. O.P.E.N. Cleaning System—commercial cleaning
7. Sport It—sports equipment and apparel
8. Fax-9—miscellaneous business services
9. Triple Check Income Tax Service—income tax services
10. National Maintenance Contractors—commercial cleaning

The top 10 new franchises (companies that began franchising since 1988) are:

1. Merle Norman Cosmetics—cosmetic aids
2. CleanNet—commercial cleaning
3. GNC Franchising Inc.—health food/vitamins
4. Mrs. Fields Cookies—cookies
5. Ramada Franchise Systems Inc,—hotels & motels
6. Fax-9—miscellaneous business services
7. Color Tile Inc.—miscellaneous decorative products and services
8. Play It Again Sports—sports equipment and apparel

9. Futurekids Inc.—computer learning centers
10. Valvoline Instant Oil Change Franchising Inc.—oil change and lubrication services

How to Find Opportunities

Finding available franchise opportunities is as simple as buying an issue of *INC.*, *Entrepreneur*, or *Franchise Opportunities* magazine at your local bookstore. There are many magazines that advertise opportunities which will tell you how to make contact. Another avenue is to attend a local franchise opportunity trade show. These shows occur quite frequently in most metropolitan areas and are an excellent way to preview multiple opportunities in person.

A word of caution to keep in mind: There are thousands of franchise offerings, many of which are not good opportunities. Too many franchise agents will use hard-sell tactics to persuade you to join their operation.

As is true of many business decisions, timing and ability to calculate risks, play a major role in selecting a franchise. The list of top franchises is mainly comprised of well-established names that carry little risk, yet considerable investment. The McDonald's, Burger Kings, and Pizza Huts which at one time were considerably less, now require an investment of several hundreds of thousands of dollars to those who can qualify. Many of these giant organizations that require such steep investments are like buying a good stock that will give you a good, but unspectacular, dividend if you work hard. The original franchisees who took some of the initial risks have done extremely well. You would like to find the next super franchise and buy in now. Not long ago, Subway was one of these. In 1987, you could have purchased a Subway franchise for less than $10,000, now it is closer to $75,000.

Look for franchises that are solidly managed, well financed, and are positioned in a growth industry. Be aware of current marketing trends within industries that indicate potential weaknesses such as price wars. Also how will changes in our society, such as the aging population, affect industry growth? Environmental services, children's products, recreation, and unique food offerings markets are projected to be strong in the nineties. Investigate any regional franchises that are doing well but have not yet gone national in their distribution.

What You Need to Know

If you decide to enter a *franchise agreement* you will be the *franchisee*. You will enter into a contract that obligates you to the *franchisor* for certain payments and methods of conducting your business. Prior to entering this agreement the franchisor must disclose certain specified information to you in a disclosure document called the Uniform Franchise Offering Circular (UFOC).

The Disclosure Document

The Federal Trade Commission requires all franchisors to supply prospective franchisees with a UFOC at least 10 days before entering a purchase contract. This document must contain:

1. The legal name of the franchisor and a concise history of the business for the preceding 15 years or since its inception.
2. The names, titles, and business experience of the franchisor's directors, executive officers, and franchise brokers.
3. An account of all administrative, criminal, or material civil litigation currently pending or completed against the franchisor involving any alleged violation of franchise law, misrepresentation, or fraud.
4. A disclosure of any bankruptcy filings made by the any officers, general partners, or previous officers of the franchisor.
5. Disclosure of the full initial franchise fees and other initial payments.
6. Disclosure of all additional and recurring fees—includes royalty fees, training fees, lease payments, assistance fees, and insurance fees.
7. Any obligations to purchase from designated or approved sources— including the franchisor, and under what circumstances.
8. Any financing arrangements—including payments, terms and conditions.
9. An explanation of all assistance, supervision, and services offered by the franchisor. This includes a description of all training programs and the experience of the trainers. Also the process used in selecting and approving the location of the business.
10. Description of the territory served and the rights to the territory.
11. Explanation of the rights to use a commercial symbol such as a trademark, service mark, or logo.
12. Any copyrights and patents involved in the agreement.
13. Explanation of the obligation of the franchisee to manage the operation.
14. Description of the terms of the agreement to include renewal rights, termination, cancellation, repurchase, and assignment.

15. Disclosure of all franchisees currently and formerly operating, including addresses and telephone numbers.

16. Explanation of any earnings clause. If the franchisor makes an earnings claim it must be clearly represented and documented.

17. Audited financial information concerning the franchisor.

18. All franchise contractual documents.

19. Public figure involvement in the franchise system. If a famous person's name is used in conjunction with the franchise, that person's true involvement and investment with the franchise must be disclosed.

20. A statement of the acknowledgement of receipt of the disclosure information. It must be signed and dated.

The Franchise Agreement

The contractual agreement between the franchisor and franchisee is the legal document that spells out the relationship. It will show how the information in the UFOC applies to the franchisee and also outline all procedures to be followed in regards to:

Site preparation specifics.

Reporting responsibilities of the franchisee.

Specific lease arrangements and responsibilities.

Regulations and requirements for promotion and advertising.

Dates, location, nature and cost of training programs.

Franchisor's rights of inspection.

Confidential information related to trade secrets.

Covenants not to compete.

Specific information as to suppliers.

Legal information as to licensing and registering for business operation.

Specific operating guidelines and standards.

Miscellaneous provisions.

The franchise agreement is a lengthy and sometimes complex legal document and should be reviewed by your attorney before making a commitment.

Questions to Ask

Although the franchisor is required to provide the preceding information, do not assume that is all you need to know or that the information is solid fact. The Federal Trade Commission is lax in the enforcement of franchise law, so it is advised that you confirm and challenge the information provided to you.

Often the best information will come from visiting current franchise owners to ask some penetrating questions. The owners you visit should not come from a list of recommended, satisfied franchise owners given to you by the franchisor. The questions should include:

How pleased are they with their decision?

Is the franchisor responsive to their needs?

Would they open a second unit if one becomes available?

How good was the training?

What surprises have they encountered?

How good is their business? Have they met projections?

How does their family feel about their occupation?

Have they had any problems with territorial rights?

Also make sure you have a good feel for the franchisor's financial condition. Have your accountant review the audited financial statements presented to look for problems. You do not want to be a franchisee whose franchisor has declared bankruptcy or has been unable to uphold their end of the agreement due to financial pressures. Franchisors sometimes sell out to other companies which can present management and relationship problems with the franchisees, you and your accountant should investigate to discover if a sale might be eminent.

As you can see, buying a franchise carries risk as does any entrepreneurial venture. The more information you collect, the less risk you will be exposed to.

Chapter Summary

Franchising plays a growing and important part in our national economy accounting for sales of approximately $250 billion annually. Whether it is for you depends to a great extent on your investment and risk capabilities. For the most part, franchises offer a safer road at a greater investment.

Many do not like to work under the restrictions and guidelines of a franchisor. They often feel they have just traded jobs.

Finding franchise opportunities is quite easy through magazine advertisements or attending franchise opportunity trade shows. Buying a franchise is complex and must be approached with caution. The potential franchisee must review carefully the disclosure document, The Uniform Franchise Offering Circular, and the franchise agreement to make sure they are in compliance with the law and the franchisee's expectations. In addition, important questions should be asked of the franchisor and franchisees currently and previously in business.

The Next Step

Visit a franchise opportunity trade show or contact a franchise agent to learn of opportunities. Such as in investigating business for sale opportunities this is an educational experience whether you have a franchise interest or not. Follow up any interest with a visit to a local franchise owner.

Review Questions

1. *Describe what is a franchise.*
2. *Why does franchising appeal to so many?*
3. *Describe current trends in franchising. What industries are doing the best in the current market?*
4. *What are the advantages to owning a franchise?*
5. *What are the disadvantages to owning a franchise?*
6. *How would you learn about franchise opportunities?*
7. *What is the Uniform Franchise Offering Circular?*
8. *What is contained in the UFOC?*
9. *What is contained in a franchise agreement?*
10. *What additional questions are in order to the franchisor and franchisee system members before entering an agreement?*

Part 1 Case Study—
To Create or to Franchise?

Barry Ross pondered over his choice. His retail background and interest had led him to investigate the possibility of opening a gift shop in the community mall. During his research he found a new franchise opportunity, The Gift Managerie, which had started franchising its name and operation just two years ago on the West Coast. They had opened 16 units during that time and were evidently experiencing some success. Barry would be the first in his state if he bought into the franchise now.

He was tempted, however, he also felt that he could create a business of his own for considerably less investment. He studied his business plan, which he had named The Gift Tree, and compared it to the franchisor's offering.

Original investment	Gift Tree	Gift Managerie
Inventory	$45,000	$ 55,000
Fixtures	15,000	30,000
Equipment	5,000	12,000
Leasehold improvements	7,500	16,000
Franchise fee	-0-	25,000
Miscellaneous	5,000	8,000
Total	$77,500	$146,000

The franchise agent had made a good presentation. The Gift Managerie would certainly be more up to date with the latest in fixtures and state of the art equipment, including a sophisticated cash registering system and a central computer terminal. Their plans for the leasehold improvements to outfit the store required more expensive carpeting, wallpaper, and lighting systems than were in Barry's original plans. They were willing to finance up to 50 percent of the initial outlay, therefore, the cash required was approximately equal.

Operations would be simpler. The franchisor was plugged into a national buying network which would allow Barry to order all of his merchandise needs through one computer terminal that would save him 5 percent in his cost of goods. They had also developed attractive advertising copy which he could use for all of his promotional events and were exploring doing some regional magazine advertising which could benefit him greatly.

Of course there was a price for all of this assistance. In addition to the initial franchise fee, Barry would pay the franchisor 4 percent of all revenues for help in operations and 1 percent as an advertising assessment. The agent was quick to point out that in view of the anticipated savings on his cost of goods, the franchise fees were really quite moderate. He also noted by being one of the first of an anticipated 200 franchisees, Barry was coming in at the right time. He projected that the cost of the franchise package would probably increase by 25 percent within the next year. Since the other franchises were still in their infancy, their sales figures were not consistent and, in some cases, not available. Some were doing more than Barry's original sales forecast for his store, while others were below.

Barry had received the disclosure document (UFOC) and a sample contract to review. They were well presented and the company appeared very solid on initial review. The company had very detailed plans on how the store should be merchandised, what inventory control systems should be used, a sophisticated reporting system was designed for bookkeeping purposes, and personnel policies were in place including an employee handbook. It was truly a turn key operation that Barry could walk into all set up and in operation.

Barry was tempted. Although he had worked in retail stores (as a matter of fact, he was a manager for five years in a large apparel store), he had little experience in gift merchandising. On the other hand, he was concerned about having to work under the predetermined guidelines of a franchisor. The monthly inspections and weekly reports could become bothersome. It was a tough decision.

Questions

1. What suggestions do you have for Barry to help make his decision?
2. What would you do?

Case Suggestions

Barry is in a very familiar situation for an aspiring entrepreneur. There is some research he should do. Most importantly is to visit other franchises and talk to the owners. Even though in this case he might have to travel to a neighboring state or even farther, he should not hesitate to get in his car. He can not make a good decision without experiencing first hand the operation of a Gift Managerie. He should visit several and those he cannot, he should contact by phone and ask the questions suggested in the chapter.

The other part of his decision-making process lies in his personal goals. If working under supervision, no matter how limited, is a problem for Barry he needs to address the future implications of inspections and reports. If he truly seeks independence, he will not struggle with running his business as someone else sees fit. Decisions of what to buy and how to merchandise are the creative part of the job and he may wish to keep these responsibilities as his own.

The profit motive of joining the franchise might be the determining factor. If there is reasonable assurance that profits will soar as a franchisee, it might overcome many of his reservations. Barry must closely look at what he is getting for his fees. Five percent of gross sales will accumulate into a great amount of money over a number of years in business. Is there enough evidence to warrant the expense. Is the name, The Gift Managerie, an asset that will attract customers that he would probably not have? Probably doubtful at this point since it is a relatively new franchise, but what about the future? If the anticipated growth does occur, it might be a very timely decision as the resale value of the business should grow appreciatively. He also must factor in the cost of financing the purchase from the franchisor, including the terms.

Barry will have to find these answers through questioning, research, and self-examination.

PART 2

Marketing

**Creative Thinking—Looking
at the Same Thing as
Everyone Else and Thinking
Something Different**

1. Pay attention to your ideas and then take them further.
2. Don't believe there is only one answer.
3. Don't be afraid to be wrong or be different
4. Read—question—break away from ruts.
5. Brainstorm, but don't judge.
6. Don't be afraid of humor.
7. Give your ideas time—back off and then come back.
8. Stick to your guns.
9. Don't allow the environment to inhibit ideas.
10. Look for what is right, not wrong, with ideas.

5

Identifying a Market

Objectives

1. Describe how to conduct a demographic market research.
2. Learn how to use demographic information in forming an initial sales forecast.
3. Understand the importance of correctly identifying a target market.
4. Learn why the entrepreneur must understand the behavioral aspects of the target market.

Key Terms

Demographics	Needs
Market Research	Perceptions
Target Market	Motivations
Customer Profile	Attitudes

Many businesses are born with a product but die without a market. It is not enough to have a good product, you must identify a need that is unsatisfied, and then bring the product to the attention of the potential customer with the unsatisfied need. Success comes when you offer a good product to a market with sufficient customers to earn a profit. It is not hard to sell candy, but it might be hard to sell enough candy to make a profit. Therefore it is imperative to make sure that there is a large enough market for your product or service before starting a business.

A good marketing program comes from using your creative flair with a whole lot of common sense. The real question is: How can you serve a market better than it is presently being served? Once you are able to clearly define the advantage that you are bringing into the marketplace, you will be able to identify that niche in the marketplace where you belong. It is not necessary to reinvent the wheel, however, you must create a differential advantage, whether it is better service, faster delivery, lower prices, or any other distinct competitive advantage and then determine those in the marketplace who are demanding the advantage you offer. This group is your target market—finding it is essential.

Who Are Your Customers?

Customers are individuals or organizations who have unsatisfied needs and have the means to satisfy those needs. It is important to emphasize that they must have the means to be able to satisfy their needs, as this determines the size of your market. If you market a high-priced specialty good that appeals to many, such as a 48-inch television screen, you must eliminate those who cannot afford such a luxury item from your potential market as they do not qualify as customers.

Where Are Your Customers?

Defining your market starts with research. Research should follow six steps:

1. Ask the question: Is there a large enough market to support my business?
2. Determine the information needed to answer that question.
3. Collect the data. Determine where you should go for information and the best method to obtain it.
4. Analyze the data. Once you have the information, what should you do with it?
5. Implement the data. Determine how you should test your suppositions?
6. Evaluate action. How can you validate your results?

The information that you will collect will come in two forms: secondary and primary data. *Secondary data* is previously published information available through scholarly research. *Primary data* is information that you must get firsthand through questioning, surveys, and sampling as it relates to your specific mission. A complete business plan includes both types of data.

In the beginning it is a maze of statistical data that as developed breaks down to a very definable target. Let's review two methods—one for the consumer market, the other for an industrial market.

Researching a Consumer Market

All communities are sources of demographics. *Demographics* are population studies and can be found at your local chamber of commerce, library, government business support agencies, or commercial developers. The research should include:

1. Population Statistics.   Study the population tables for the community and surrounding communities where you are considering opening a business. Look closely at the past, present, and future of population growth or loss. Compare the 1980 census figures with the 1990 census and the future projected population. The growth trend is very important. A growing population is desired, particularly if you are entering a market with strong competition. More people means more demand for products or services. Get a perspective on the local trend as it compares to the state-wide population growth trends.

If the population is stagnant you will be successful only by persuading customers away from your competition. If this is the case make sure there is a strong indication that your competition is weak and relatively ineffective. A declining population is a danger sign. Consider opening a consumer business in such an economy only if you are the sole entry in your market.

2. Age Breakdown.   A good demographic study will break down the population into age segments. It should show the past, present, and future trends by age group. This is important if your product has an appeal to a particular age group. For instance, do not open a store whose primary market is young adults, age 20 to 24, in an area which is aging quickly. This indicates that the young people are moving away to find jobs.

3. Racial and Gender Ratios.   If your product has an appeal to a particular gender or race, make sure you become familiar with its composition within a marketplace.

4. Education Levels.   Becoming familiar with a communities' educational level will tell you important information regarding the lifestyle of that population. You'll find indications about whether the area has a blue collar or white collar population. This data will reveal your potential customers' lifestyles including leisure activities and outside interest.

5. Per Capita Income/Average Annual Pay/Unemployment Statistics. The higher the per capita income and the lower the unemployment level, the healthier the economy. Communities experiencing economic problems due to plant layoffs or relocation are going to lose population. Compare this information to surrounding areas and state-wide figures to determine if it is a healthy and vital community. If it is not, look for a community that reflects a stronger economic base.

After you have collected the initial information you should start to dig deeper to support your initial assessment opinions. Other information available includes:

The birth count of the communities

The number of marriage licenses issued

Car registration statistics

Number of telephone hookups

Housing market information

New shopping centers and commercial building permits issued

Also check with your state department of revenue for a breakdown, usually by county, of retail sales by product or service classification.

There is a lot of available information if you are willing to make the necessary phone calls and visits. Once you do, you will be able to put together a pretty complete summary of the overall market you are considering. It's possible that as you get familiar with your immediate marketplace, you might learn that an adjoining market area might be a better choice for your business idea. The more information collected, the less risk you will take. Figures 5.1, 5.2, and 5.3 are examples of statistical tables from one marketplace.

How to Use Demographic Information

If you do your research properly, the pieces will come together and you can start to form your business plan. Once you've ascertained that your marketplace has a healthy and growing economy, and is comprised of compatible ratios of race, gender, and education levels for your type of business, you can get a better feel for the needs of your market.

Combining this information with the total revenues of your industry and the per capita spent on your product in your market, you can make a ball park

The Official JPC Population Forecast for Lehigh and Northampton Counties: 1990–2020					
	1990	1995	2000	2010	2020
Lehigh County	291,130	297,486	306,864	318,860	334,537
Northampton County	247,105	253,483	269,265	291,790	320,026
Two County Region	538,235	550,969	576,129	610,650	654,563

SOURCE: U.S. Bureau of the Census for 1990 data; all other data forecasted by the Joint Planning Commission.

Figure 5.1. Population table.

estimate of the revenues you should expect. For example, let's say that you are interested in opening a furniture store. The economic conditions appear favorable and the per capita spent on furniture of $90 per year is in line with the national average quoted from an industry source. The market population is 40,000 which means that roughly $3,600,000 ($90 × 40,000) is spent on furniture per year in your marketplace. There are six direct competitors dividing the market share. Depending on the size and location of your intended business, you can estimate the percent of the market that you wish

Employment by Industry Group—1989 Place of Work Data (in 000s)					
	Lehigh County	Northampton County	ABE Area*	PA	USA
Manufacturing	36.5	26.5	76.9	1,069.4	19,943
Mining	0.5	0.1	0.8	33.4	915
Contract construction	9.4	6.5	20.8	330.0	7,225
Transportation and public utilities	8.9	4.6	15.0	292.4	6,380
Finance, insurance, real estate	10.9	7.1	21.4	419.7	10,304
Retail trade	29.8	17.9	58.9	1,062.9	22,562
Wholesale trade	7.9	3.8	13.3	296.5	6,698
Services	51.9	26.1	93.1	1,789.5	36,764
Agriculture/foreign fishing service	1.0	0.7	2.4	40.6	2,374
Government	14.8	11.5	34.0	762.4	20,737
Farming	1.0	0.9	3.0	82.2	3,168

*ABE area includes Lehigh Co., Northampton Co., Carbon Co., and Warren Co., NJ
SOURCE: U.S. Dept. of Commerce, Bureau of Economic Analysis.

Figure 5.2. Per capita income table.

Per Capita Income and Annual Average Wage			
Per capita income (by place of residence)			
Year	Lehigh County	Northampton County	Pennsylvania
1990	$15,458	$14,562	$14,068
1980	$ 7,873	$ 7,382	$ 7,078
1980*	$13,195	$12,372	$11,862

*1980 adjusted for the increase in consumer prices (1.676 × actual 1980 medial per capita income).
SOURCE: U.S. Bureau of the Census.

Annual average wage (by place of work)			
Year	Lehigh County	Northampton County	Pennsylvania
1989	$22,707	$21,638	$22,312
1988	$21,697	$20,717	$21,488
1987	$20,374	$19,345	$20,408
1986	$19,583	$18,314	$19,358
1985	$19,111	$17,948	$18,611
1984	$18,143	$17,315	$17,896
1983	$17,235	$16,609	$17,161
1982	$16,358	$16,605	$16,451

SOURCE: U.S. Department of Labor, Bureau of Labor Statistics, PA Dept. of Labor, Office of Employment Security.

Figure 5.3. Trade percentage table.

to pursue. If you are going to be the largest and most centrally located, you may wish to aim for 20 percent or $720,000. If you are to be more specialized, with a more limited budget, your goal might be 10 percent or $360,000 of the market.

Population × Average Per Capita Expenditure = Projected Potential Market × Projected Share of Market = Sales Forecast

Researching for an Industrial Market

A slightly different approach is used for an industrial market, but the objective remains the same: Is there an unsatisfied need for your product? Researching an industry starts at the library. Ask the reference librarian for the *Thomas Register of Manufacturers*. This will allow you to determine who, and how many, are selling to your industrial market. Companies are listed by Standard Industry Codes (SIC) with description of size by assets, revenues, and employees. If you are considering making widgets, find out who else makes widgets, where they are located and how big they are. Published industry information can tell you the size of the potential market. Your primary research will tell who in the industry is doing the lion's share of business. Determining your intended share will be dependent on your anticipated production capabilities, your sales force and marketing strategy, and your location. Figure 5.4 is an example of an industrial advertisement from the *Thomas Register*. The primary research can be gathered by visiting industry trade shows and asking questions of company representatives.

Determining Your Target Market

As noted, small businesses exist because they know their markets better than large businesses. In order to know a market well the entrepreneur must address a market small enough so that he or she is able to learn. As an individual entrepreneur you can not possibly learn or serve a general consumer market description such as women who wear cosmetics, or an industrial market of all companies in America that buy linen supplies. Therefore you must narrow your market to one that you can reach and serve. This starts with *market segmentation.*

Segmenting a market means breaking it down into parts. A consumer market can be segmented by age, education level, and income level. An industrial market can be segmented by geography, size, and use. Once segmented into logical parts, the entrepreneur can then begin to target his or her particular market or niche.

The goal is to get as specific as possible. Since you are limited by both time and capital, it is mandatory that your resources are not squandered chasing a market that is too big for you to reach. Targeting your market allows you to describe your best customer very clearly. If you sell ladies' fashions, the market segments can be further targeted into women of certain careers, lifestyles, size, income, family descriptions, type of housing and location.

The industrial linen market, for example, can be targeted by industry specifications such as hospital size (under 400 beds), location (Southeast United States), etc. You must keep working the description until you feel you know your target market quite well. Eventually you should be able to write a customer profile of that customer similar to Fig. 5.5.

The customer profiled is not the only customer your business will serve. There will be a high percentage of customers who will fit only parts of the

Figure 5.4. Thomas Register.

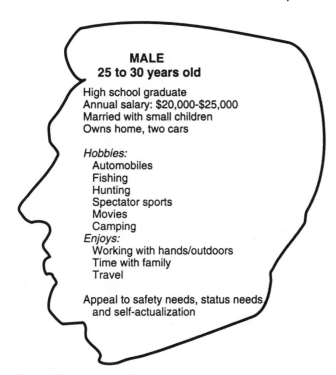

Figure 5.5. Customer profile.

profile—they are your secondary market. As your business matures your target market will widen to include a larger audience. However, start-up businesses must concentrate on pleasing and developing the primary market first before reaching to the secondary market. Figure 5.6 illustrates a target market strategy.

One of the current buzz words heard around entrepreneurs of the 1990s is *niching*. Market niching is another way of putting emphasis on target marketing. When you employ a *niche strategy* you are concentrating very specifically on a well-developed target market. We are witnessing more and more small business specialization as a means to compete particularly in the large metropolitan areas. Businesses such as sunglass stores or gift shops which carry only gifts with cats on them are examples of entrepreneurs who are carving out a very particular target market or market niche.

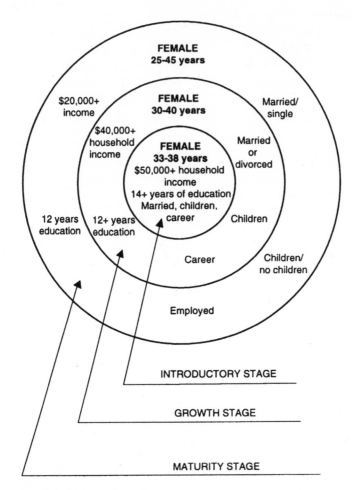

Figure 5.6. Target market strategy.

Understanding Needs, Perceptions, Motivations, and Attitudes

It is not enough to describe your target market statistically; to be effective you must know how they think and live. Learning their needs, perceptions, motivations, and attitudes comes from primary data research.

Needs

We all have different levels of need. Dr. Abraham Maslow was one of the pioneers of the *need satisfaction theory* when he formulated his *Hierarchy of Needs* in the 1920s. He stated that as we fulfilled our lower level needs for physiological and safety requirements, we crave more for the upper echelon needs of love and belonging, self-esteem, and self-actualization. More simply, we have a need to maintain and improve our standard of living. As an entrepreneur, it is your job to identify how your product or service will allow your customers to fulfill their needs to allow them to do exactly that. Once identified you must learn to sell to that need.

For instance, a clothing store might sell to a multitude of needs depending on the customer. Customers looking to buy a more basic outfit suitable for work are satisfying a "belonging" need. They have a need to look properly in order to belong to the work force. However those in the market for a high fashion social event outfit are seeking a self-esteem and self-actualization need fulfillment as they wish to appear attractive in the eyes of others and believe that they deserve such an outfit for achieving a particular level of sophistication. Each need requires a different approach and market strategy tailored to that need level. Through experience, questioning, and testing you must learn the needs that your product is appealing to, if you are to be successful.

Perceptions

Perceptions are how we understand and view things depending on our background and mental framework. They are largely formed by the amount of information and knowledge we carry inside our heads. What are perceived as needs by some, are perceived as unnecessary wants or desires by others. Just because you perceive someone's needs for a fashion item as whimsical, do not assume that the other person's needs are not sincere in their minds. In learning your market, find out about your customers perceptions. As a seller you must learn how to alter those perceptions to fit an unsatisfied need for your product.

Motivations

Motivations are the reasons we take action. To persuade a customer into action, the entrepreneur must give them a reason. Unsatisfied needs create tensions within us which give motivation to act to fulfill the need. If you understand what motivates your target market, you will be able to create reasons for them to act. Knowing your target market well will allow you to devise advertisements, displays, and sales presentations that will expose unsatisfied needs, thus creating tensions that may be relieved by buying your product or service.

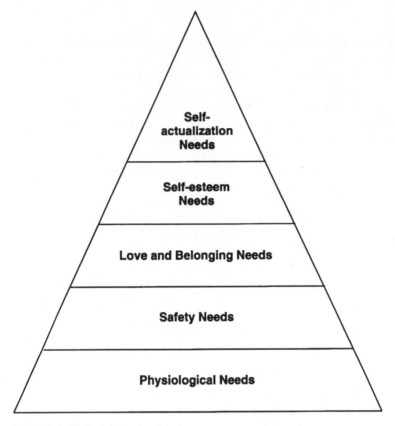

Figure 5.7. Maslow's hierarchy of needs.

Attitudes

Attitudes are how we feel about something. The entrepreneur wants the customer to feel positive about his or her product. Large businesses do this through brand identification, entrepreneurs must do it through personal interaction with the customer that builds confidence. Knowing the attitudes of your target market allows you to create a strategy that appeals to positive influences. The more confidence instilled into the customer, the more sales for the entrepreneur.

Some of your primary data will come from experience. However, in the initial stages of developing a business plan, you should learn as much about how your target market behaves as possible. Talk to prospective customers, learn their likes and dislikes, what excites them, and what are their expectations as to what you are planning.

Chapter Summary

Start your business plan as a research project. Collect the necessary data to determine the size of your potential market. Analyze and compare it with other markets. As a small business it is most important to target your market as specifically as possible, including doing primary research on the behavioral aspects of potential customers. The identification of the target market dictates all marketing decisions of the business owner.

A complete market analysis will enable you to make a sales forecast of the market potential for your business.

The Next Step

Visit available community resources for secondary data on your intended market. After comparing and analyzing the data, attempt to form an initial sales potential projection. Design information collection tools such as surveys and opinion polls to help you collect primary data concerning the lifestyle and behavioral tendencies of your potential customers. Take the information tools to shopping malls, trade shows, or wherever your potential customer may be and ask questions. Write out a complete customer profile of your best customer.

Review Questions

1. *What are the steps of completing a market research project?*
2. *What can be learned from a demographic study?*
3. *Why is it important to compare market demographics?*
4. *What is the formula for making an initial sales forecast from demographic information?*
5. *What is the difference between secondary and primary data?*
6. *What is target marketing?*
7. *What is a customer profile?*
8. *What is the* Thomas Register?
9. *Why must an entrepreneur learn the behavioral aspects of the target market?*
10. *What are needs? Perceptions? Motivations? Attitudes?*

6
Knowing Your Competition

Objectives

1. Learn the difference between direct and indirect competition.
2. Understand the importance of researching the competition.
3. Learn procedures to follow in researching the competition.
4. Learn how to apply the data gathered in constructing your business plan.

Key Terms

Direct competition   Indirect competition

A vital part of the market analysis is the study of the competition and how they will react when there is a new market entry.

Market Entry

You can surely expect the competition to react when you enter a market. There may be no immediate reaction, but in time, you will feel the wrath of your competition at some point. Unless you have developed some form of new technology, you will be taking business away from someone else when you open. If you open a sandwich shop and sell but one sandwich the first day, that sale has more than likely come at the expense of another business. As your competition becomes aware of the impact that you have on their market, they will try to counter you with obstacles. Since they have been in the market longer, they will have more weapons (experience). Therefore you must be alert to what is going on around you. A thorough research of the competition from the outset will better prepare you for the difficulty of market entry.

Types of Competition

There are two types of competition—*direct* and *indirect*. Direct competitors are those whose existence relies primarily on the selling of similar products or services in the same marketplace as you. Although maybe not exact, they share a common target market description and serve the same unsatisfied needs. An example of direct competition would be two bridal stores in the same town.

Indirect competitors are those who sell similar products or services but are not solely dependent on the relative success or failure of selling these products or services. A simple example is Kmart. Kmart is an indirect competitor to many retailers but a direct competitor to just a few other discount stores. Although indirect competitors may not be as dangerous as direct competitors, they are often strong enough to capture enough impulse purchases from your target market to make a serious dent in your profit figure. You cannot ignore their presence in your plans and research. As you research your intended market you must learn as much as possible concerning your direct and indirect competition.

How to Research Competition

To research your competition, simply start with the yellow pages listing for consumer markets and the *Thomas Register* for industrial markets. These two sources will give you a list of your direct competitors.

Consumer Product or Service Competitor Research

For a consumer market survey, mark the location of all direct competition on a local map. Measure the distances between locations in an attempt to find product dispersement. You are interested not only in miles but also travel time between competitors. You might be able to discover a pattern or an area lacking product or service distribution.

With a map, list, and note pad in hand, set out to visit all direct competitors. You should have a pre-arranged checklist of the information you hope to obtain from your visits. This list should include:

1. *Size.* Discreetly walk off the physical interior boundaries of the business to determine its approximate size in square footage.

2. *Location appeal.* Make notes as to why the particular location was chosen. Include a description of the surrounding neighborhood, traffic considerations, and mix of surrounding businesses.

3. *Number of employees.* Record the number of employees working at specific times for comparison to other competition. Also note the number of cash register stations for an idea of store traffic at peak times.

4. *Inventory levels.* A low level of shelf inventory may represent credit and supplier problems. Too much old inventory means poor inventory turnover.

5. *Customer traffic count.* During your visit how many customers enter and how many leave with purchase in hand? Compare your observations with other businesses visited.

6. *Management availability.* Is the manager present? Is the manager the owner? Or is it an absentee management situation? Lack of management availability indicates either simplicity of operation or, in some cases, the owner/manager works another job to keep the business afloat.

7. *Appearance.* Is it neat and up to date, or neglected? Find out the last time it was remodeled. Most consumer oriented businesses should undergo remodeling on a regular basis. If it has been longer than three to five years since the last facelift, management might be postponing things due to financial restrictions.

8. *How long has it been established?* Tactfully inquire as to how long the business has been operating to ascertain their level of stability.

9. *Customer satisfaction level.* Listen to customer comments to get a sense for satisfaction. How are they treated? Are some leaving because they can not find what they wish?

10. *Suppliers.* Record the names of the businesses' vendors. Discreetly pick up merchandise to inspect for the manufacturer's name and city of origin. You can develop a list of those you might wish to order from and can get the phone numbers by calling information of their cities.

11. *Community reputation.* Visit the surrounding stores and businesses and tactfully inquire to employees how they feel about the health and stability of the potential competitor.

During your search, make mental notes and then record your thoughts immediately after leaving the establishment. Depending on the number of competitors, you may wish to start a separate folder on each to use as a reference now and for after you open.

In addition to visiting the competition, you should get to know the supplier representatives to your competition. Sales representatives can be invaluable to you for information if they regard you as a future customer. They are often willing to discuss the weaknesses and strengths of their present customers, particularly if you are able to develop a relationship of confidence with them.

Certainly include the indirect competitors on your list of visits. By evaluating the amount and type of inventory they carry and its prominence in display, you will get a sense of the importance they place on selling your product.

Industrial Competitor Research

Since geographical restrictions may prevent you from a physical inspection of your competition, the best plan is to go to one place where the competition gathers—industrial trade shows.

Practically all industries have regional and national trade shows and conventions to sell their products and exchange information. You will need to wrangle an invitation to attend the next show. Usually this can be done through an acquaintance as a visitor or through the invitation of a supplier who considers you a potential customer. Once there you will have the opportunity to roam the convention center, witness the competition's displays, and discreetly make inquiries to the industry members. Your best bet is to visit with one business to learn about another. Your list of questions to industry members should include:

1. Who do they consider the industry leader and why?
2. Who do they consider their leading competitor and why?
3. Who seems to be losing ground and why?
4. What businesses are strongest in particular geographical areas?
5. What are their selling terms and how fast are they able to ship?

By checking and cross checking through the different industry members you will be able to eventually sort out a picture of the competitive field. Keep an eye out for the companies that are most often mentioned during your interviews. Once the field is narrowed down you will need to research, through secondary data, more specific information on potential competition.

Another way to learn more about the competition and the nature of the market, whether industrial or consumer, is to study the advertising strategies of the various members of the industry. During this planning period you should keep a constant eye on what and how the competitors are advertising. Through this you will learn who is discounting, what companies sell on reputation, who spends the most on advertising, and who are the most creative, aggressive and innovative. Some strategies, such as price wars between members, may indicate the condition of the market. Pay attention to the advertising strategies of the indirect competition as well since you will gain some insight into the importance they place on your product as it relates to their other offerings. Start to keep a folder of these advertisements for future reference.

One of the best sources for information is making contact with ex-employees of your competition. They are often quite open and candid with valuable information. They might also be potential employees of your new business.

Applying Information

The goal in studying the competition is to determine where your business should position itself in the market. Market positioning is deciding on the most advantageous strategy to compete for market share. Through knowledge of the competition you can learn who is doing what well and what areas of the market are not currently being adequately served. Also you seek to determine what is going to happen in the future. Studying competition will expose opportunities, give insight into new developments in the market, and allow you to determine the level of business you can expect.

Part of the success formula is timing. You are looking for the best time to open your business—the best time to launch your assault on the competition. There is normally a window of opportunity that exists that makes market entry easier. It may be when a certain competitor is struggling, or one has undergone a change of ownership, or there has been the development of new services or products that further develop a market. A changing market is more appealing to enter than a stagnant one—keep your eye open for the best time to enter the market.

By learning about your competition you will be able to gauge the impact your entry will have and the reaction that you may expect. You will know who in your marketplace might counter your entry with price reductions, who might expand, or who will add services or products to counteract you. With these thoughts in mind you will be better able to devise plans to compete with their actions.

Ranking the Competition

After you have collected all competition data you should be able to rank the competition as to their various strengths and weaknesses. You might wish to devise a form such as Fig. 6.1 to serve as a reference while you make your plans.

The more knowledge you possess of the competition, the better your initial marketing plan will be. Knowledge of your competition cannot be overemphasized. Copy the strengths and correct the weaknesses. Your goal is to be the very best in the marketplace.

Chapter Summary

Competition comes in two forms, direct and indirect. A good market analysis demands that you thoroughly investigate all who are serving your target market. Through observation and questioning, the entrepreneur can learn the various strengths and weaknesses of each and rank them accordingly. The knowledge gathered will allow the new entrepreneur to plan an effective initial marketing strategy and also be prepared to counter efforts by the competition to obstruct his or her entry into the market.

The Next Step

Follow the suggestions in this chapter to rank and evaluate your competition. Discuss your findings and impressions with your support staff to

Direct and Indirect Competition			
Names of Competitors	Strengths	Weaknesses	Direct/Indirect
1. _____	_____	_____	_____
2. _____	_____	_____	_____
3. _____	_____	_____	_____
4. _____	_____	_____	_____
5. _____	_____	_____	_____
6. _____	_____	_____	_____
7. _____	_____	_____	_____
8. _____	_____	_____	_____
9. _____	_____	_____	_____

Figure 6.1. Competition ranking chart.

see if they concur. Check with county officials, developers, and local bankers to determine if there is any other new competition planning to enter the market.

Review Questions

1. *What is direct competition?*
2. *What is considered indirect competition?*
3. *Why is it important to research competition?*
4. *What is normally the starting place for information for the consumer market? An industrial market?*
5. *List the procedures you can use to investigate a consumer market?*
6. *How would you research an industrial market?*
7. *What are you hoping to discover by researching potential competition?*
8. *What can competitive advertising tell you?*
9. *What might you discover by interviewing a former employee of the competition?*
10. *Why rank the competition?*

7

Choosing a Location

Objectives

1. Understand the importance of convenience in choosing a business location.
2. Learn the various types of consumer and industrial locations.
3. Learn the reasons for home based businesses.
4. Understand the importance of learning leasing terminology.

Key Terms

Neighborhood shopping center
Community shopping center
Regional shopping center

Industrial park
Incubator
Percentage rent clause

In many businesses, particularly in regards to the consumer market, the location decision is the most important decision the entrepreneur will make. Although normally aware of this, time after time, business owners are influenced by expense factors into making the wrong choice. They fail to realize the importance of convenience.

Convenience

Our society is a lazy and spoiled one. Our consumers expect everything to be at their fingertips and, if they are not, they simply change their purchase intentions. Being convenient to your market cannot be overstated. To give practical input to this statement simply consider a few basic facts about consumer psychology.

Convenience breeds greed. The easier it is to make a purchase, the more we purchase and want to purchase. Go back 10 or 15 years when pizza was not served on every corner and pizza delivery trucks were not causing traffic jams—you probably did not buy as much pizza as you do now. Back then it was not as convenient, therefore, a trip to the pizza restaurant was a greater effort and more of a special occasion. Now through convenience, pizza has become a staple item on many families' menus. Convenience has enticed us to buy more, therefore, there are more and more pizza establishments.

Convenience saves time. The consumer has only so many waking hours each day to fulfill his or her responsibilities. In our hectic lifestyles, consumers are often fearful of not spending enough time with family and friends. The more convenient a business, the stronger the perception that shopping that business will save time. Many retail businesses are able to charge greater prices by offering convenience (i.e., your corner convenience store).

Greed and fear are the two strongest purchase motivators in the consumer psyche. By locating your business convenient to your potential customers you will increase their appetite for wanting more and ease their conscience by effectively using their time.

Choosing a Site

In choosing a proper location for a business, locate where your customer wants and expects to find you. To find this location, refer to your demographic study and a map. If you are dealing with a consumer target market of high income, highly educated women you should find where they live, where they currently shop, and where they work. Plot this information on a map and put yourself in a very accessible location. If you are an industrial producer, place your plant accessible to transportation facilities that will allow you the quickest delivery. Put yourself in the customer's position and decide what would be the greatest convenience to you. Look upon location as a customer service.

Finding a Retail Location

The importance of location varies from important to vitally important for various retailers. Retail goods are classified as *convenience, shopping,* or *specialty goods.* If you sell convenience goods you sell mainly on impulse which means the more people who pass by, the more sales you will generate. If you sell shopping goods, the consumer will do some price comparison and research before purchasing, therefore, you must make this as easy as possible by being clustered close to competition. Some specialty goods retailers have an advantage since customers will seek them out. Specialty goods require a more intensive search for the right product and customers are willing to put forth more effort. However, more effort does not mean inconvenience.

For example, selling convenience goods such as food snacks or everyday staple items requires a high drive-by or walk-by traffic location to be successful. Shopping goods such as tires require that you be convenient to your competition in order that your customers can readily see the advantage of doing business with you. A specialty good such as bridal gowns can be set off from the highest shopping traffic areas (malls), but should be in an accessible area to those areas (adjacent to the mall).

Types of Retail Shopping Areas

Downtowns

Many downtown shopping areas are being rejuvenated with the hopes of bringing the customer back downtown to shop as in the old days. However, it is not the old days and, for the most part, these projects are not working. People want to shop where they live and where they can fulfill all of their needs in one place. Most downtowns offer neither, but large shopping centers offer both. In addition, the exodus to the suburbs, high crime rates, limited parking, and unattractive buildings have contributed to the downfall of downtown shopping.

Operating costs of downtown retail areas, in most cases, are significantly lower than shopping centers. You pay for what you get and in downtown areas you do not receive the amount of consumer traffic nor the extra hours for evening shopping that has become a way of life for the dual-income families in this country.

Therefore, unless you have a retail business that can profit from selling to the citizens who work downtown or the businesses that are located in downtown, do not locate in a downtown area to save money. If there are not enough customers, the savings are meaningless.

Stand-Alone Locations

If your business is one that will not be dependent on the attraction of many businesses being clustered together (i.e., motels, fitness centers, certain types of restaurants), you can locate in a self-standing building as long as you are assured of good drive-by traffic and adequate parking facilities. When considering such a location, check with your State Department of Transportation for drive-by traffic statistics for particular locations. Locating independently is less expensive than being in a developed shopping area and has the added advantage of possible site ownership as opposed to leasing.

Shopping Centers

Different types of shopping centers should be considered for different types of retail outlets. *Neighborhood shopping centers* are small, relatively inexpensive and serve the immediate neighborhood in which they are located. These shopping centers are dominated by businesses whose nearby residents require convenience. They often consist of a small supermarket or convenience store, a dry cleaners, a drug store, and other services to serve the everyday needs of the neighborhood.

Community shopping centers are centrally located in the community they serve. Often they are small malls or large strip centers comprised of supermarkets, smaller department stores, specialty apparel stores, gift and floral shops, drug stores and other businesses which are able to attract the attention of the entire community. In smaller towns of 50,000 or less, they are often the dominant shopping area.

Regional shopping areas are dominated by the large enclosed malls. They serve an entire region of many communities. The larger, or super regional malls, have a very strong attraction and serve customers from a radius of 50 miles or more. They have multiple department stores and a collection of smaller stores from every merchandising segment. They are expensive and sometimes difficult to get into, however, if your business is one that requires the most convenient of locations you must consider a regional shopping area. The big malls offer the important ingredient of being able to offer one-stop shopping for all the consumer's needs which fulfills the requirement for time saving and increased buying potential.

Finding an Industrial Location

Industrial producers or service providers must decide on a location based on how can they best and most efficiently serve their customer. Operations must be safe and efficient and able to get goods to the customer quickly. Look for locations close to transportation facilities for shipping and also accessible for travel to the customer as well as for the customer to visit you. The space itself must fit all requirements for fast and efficient production.

Industrial Parks

Most communities have set aside land for use by industrial users. The cost and taxes to the property are often subsidized by the community in order to entice businesses which will bring in jobs. Theses areas are normally well lit with good road access and have suitable shipping and transportation facilities close by for the tenants. Go to city hall or the chamber of commerce to find out where industrial parks exist in a particular community.

Incubators

In recent years, communities, agencies, and private developers have created business incubators. These are industrial facilities shared by a number of small start-up businesses in order to minimize the cost of operation for a new business. Incubator tenants share many services such as receptionist, copy machines, fax machines, etc. The rents are often partially subsidized making incubators very appealing to many small start-ups. Check with your community to see if and where there are any small business incubators.

Commercial Office Space

Many professional office services will require an office suitable to receive clients. The type and location of the office must fit the clientele's expectations. The office must communicate confidence and knowledge. Many realtors, lawyers, accountants, and other professional services pay extremely high rent in order to look successful to their clients. After all, who wants to use the professional services of someone who doesn't appear professional.

There are office arrangements similar to incubators, which allow the tenants to share the common expenses of receptionist, copier, fax machines, etc. Although not subsidized as many industrial incubators, they can save money and are often a good way to get started. In leasing a commercial office you still follow the same commandment of locating where your customers expect to find you.

Working from the Home

The number of home-based businesses is booming for very good reasons. Operating expenses are minimal and it is now possible to set up a very complete office in your home at a very reasonable investment.

If you are starting a business in which you visit the clients as opposed to them visiting you, you should consider an office in your home. Not only is there no rent to pay, there is a tax deduction given for the portion of your home used in conducting a business. You will need to make sure your business qualifies, however. If you use a portion of your home strictly for business purposes you will be allowed to deduct the percentage of your housing expense used as a business deduction and this can be quite a savings. Instead of paying perhaps $500 per month rent plus utilities, you may be able to deduct 15, 20 percent, or more of your housing expenses from your gross profits.

It has become increasingly easy to operate professionally from your home. A personal computer, professional stationary letterhead, and a separate telephone line are the basic necessities. For other equipment needs you can use your most convenient Mail Boxes, Etc. or other business assistance center. Many offer private post office boxes, copier equipment, fax machines, graphic design help, and mailing services. It is quite possible to set up a home-based business which will appear so professional that only your family will know that you are working from a basement or spare bedroom.

Be aware that operating a business from your home requires discipline from all who occupy the residence. When you arrive in your home office it is imperative that you be cutoff from those around you. It should be the same as if you have gone downtown to the office. Close a door behind you and there should be no family interruptions. You cannot babysit, be an answering service, or a car pool driver while you are at work. This is one reason you must install a separate phone line. In addition, it gives you a separate answering service for your business.

Leasing versus Buying

New businesses should, in most cases, lease. There is too much uncertainty in the initial stages to incur the long-term obligation of property owner-ship. This argument also can be made for leasing expensive operating equipment versus buying. Businesses which eventually may wish to own their equipment and property should inquire to the availability of lease/ purchase arrangements. This allows part of the rent payments to be deducted from the eventual purchase price of the land or equipment.

Leasing expenses are tax deductible operating expenses as are interests costs of mortgage payments. If most of the initial mortgage payments are going toward interest expense, the tax considerations of leasing versus buying will be equal.

Take the time to closely scrutinize any facility that you are considering for lease or purchase. Just as you would examine a home purchase, check the commercial facility for structural soundness including plumbing, electrical, and heating and air conditioning equipment. You do not want to experience any additional preventive expenses in the initial start up phase of your business.

Leasing Arrangements

A lease is a legal commitment between the tenant and landlord that guarantees the landlord a stated rent payment for a specified period of time. This commitment does not cease to exist if you terminate your business operation prior to the lease termination date. There are many one time proprietors still paying rent on commercial space, months after business termination. Therefore, it is extremely important that you understand what you are getting into before signing a lease commitment.

Leases are usually very long and detailed and, for the most part, written to protect the interest of the landlord. It is not uncommon for a commercial lease to be 30 pages or longer. If you are new to leasing, it is advisable to review prospective lease arrangements with an attorney to make sure you are getting what you expect from the arrangement. The following discussion covers some of the particulars you should be aware of.

Rent Charges

Commercial rent is charged on a cost per square foot basis. A commercial space of 1200 square feet might be leased at $8 per square foot annually or $9600. The tenant normally will pay in 12 equal monthly installments, in this case $800 per month. The base rent charge is the guaranteed amount to be paid to the landlord, however in many instances, particularly in retail shopping centers there may be additional charges.

HVAC Charges. Enclosed shopping centers and some office complexes will pass on the cost of operating the heating, ventilation, and air conditioning of common areas to the tenants based on their percent of gross leasable space.

CAM Charges. Common area maintenance charges are often charged separately, once again dependent on the amount of square footage rented. These maintenance fees are used by the landlord to keep all common areas clean and operational, including parking facilities.

Real Estate Taxes.   Property taxes for the landlord's property are often divided proportionately among the tenants and are billed either on a monthly or annual pro rata share basis.

Merchant's or Tenant's Association Fees.   Community and regional size shopping complexes often will have an association comprised of the tenants to promote the shopping or service location. These fees are used for advertising special promotions and the advantages of the shopping complex.

A nother clause that has become quite commonplace in larger shopping centers is a percentage of gross sales charge. A charge is assessed if the tenant's gross sales exceed a certain stated level of revenue. It is the landlord's way of benefiting from the success of a tenant. It is written in terms that, if a stated percentage of the tenant's revenues exceed the guaranteed base rent charge, the tenant will pay the higher of the two. For example, a retail tenant must pay $8 per square foot or 6 percent of gross sales, whichever is higher. For a 1200 square foot store this would be $9600 or 6 percent of sales if the tenant's sales exceed $160,000. Too often new business owners are too casual about this charge as it is normally set at a sales level that probably will not be reached until year two or three of the operation. However, once it is reached it will surely be a point of friction between the landlord and the tenant. Therefore, make sure you understand its ramifications before signing the lease. It is often a negotiable figure.

Duration.   Leases can be written to cover any period of time but usually will run from one to three years. The longer you are willing to lease, the lower the initial rent fee should be. You should request inclusion of an option to renew the lease clause at the termination at a stated rent fee. This will assure that the decision to continue operations at a particular location is yours and will protect you from being put out at the landlord's discretion.

Option to Sublease.   Since the lease is a legal commitment, make sure that you have the right to find another suitable tenant for your space if you decide to call it quits. This clause should state that if another tenant is found for your space your obligation will dissolve. Of course the landlord has the right to approve any tenant.

The body of the lease will include all obligations of tenant and landlord. Included will be the type and amount of insurance that the tenant must carry, what leasehold improvements will be performed by the tenant and what will be provided by the landlord. Operating hours, sign require-

This lease, entered into this _____ day of _____ , 19 ____ , between the Landlord and the Tenant hereinafter named.

ARTICLE 1. Definitions and Certain Basic Provisions. 1.1

(a) "Landlord": Smith Development Co. _____

(b) Landlord's address ___ 120 Main Street
Springfield, Ill. 22573 _____

(c) "Tenant": ___ Mr. John Doe DBA Gard Town _____

(d) Tenant's mailing address ___ 32 Washington Ave.
Springfield, Ill 22513 _____

(e) Tenant's trade name. _____

(f) Tenant's address in Shopping Center ___ A-8

(g) "Demised Premises": approximately ___ 1200 ___ square feet in Building ___ A ___ (computed from measurements to the exterior of outside walls of the building and to the center of interior walls) having approximate dimensions of __25__ feet x __50__ feet such premises being shown and outlined on the plan attached hereto as Exhibit A, and being part of the Shopping Center situated upon the property described in Exhibit B attached hereto. "Shopping Center" shall refer to the property described in Exhibit B, together with such additions and other changes as Landlord may from time to time designate as included within the Shopping Center.

(h) Lease term Commencing on the "Commencement Date" as hereinafter defined and ending ___ Thirty Six (36) ___ months thereafter except that in the event the Commencement Date is a date other than the first day of a calendar month, said term shall extend for said number of days in addition to the remainder of the calendar month following the Commencement Date.

(i) "Estimated Completion Date": day of ___ October 15. 19XX

(j) Minimum Guaranteed Rental: $ __729.17*__ per month, payable in advance.

(k) Percentage Rental: ___ 6 ___ % of gross sales in excess of $ __146,000.00__ per month during the calendar year, payable on or before the 10th day of each following month subject to Article IV, Section 4.3 below.

(l) Initial Common Area Maintenance charge per month: $ _____ 52.08

(m) Initial Insurance Escrow Payment per month: $ _____ 10.42

(n) Initial Tax Escrow Payment per month: $ _____ 62.50

(o) "Security Deposit" $1,793.76 _____ , refundable upon expiration of term less any damages for unusual wear and tear or charges necessary to restore the Demised Premises to satisfactory condition.

(p) Permitted use: ___ Hallmark store — retail sale of cards and gifts

1.2 The sum of:

Minimum Guaranteed Rental as set forth in Article I, Section 1.1 (j); and	729.17*
Initial Common Area Maintenance charge, as set forth in Article I, Section 1.1 (l); and	52.08
Initial Insurance Escrow Payment as set forth in Article I, Section 1.1 (m)	10.42
Initial Tax Escrow Payment as set forth in Article I, Section 1.1 (n)	62.50
Initial Base Sales Tax Payment as set forth in Article I, Section 1.3	42.71
MONTHLY PAYMENT TOTAL	896.88

1.3 In addition to its obligation to pay the Monthly Payment Total, adjusted from time to time as provided herein, Tenant shall pay simultaneously therewith any sales tax, tax on rentals and any other charges, taxes and/or impositions now in existence or hereafter imposed by any governmental authority based upon the privilege of renting the Demised Premises or upon the amount of rent collected thereof. All payments provided for herein shall be in lawful (legal tender for public or private debt) money for the United States of America.

Figure 7.1. Lease cover sheet.

ments, what will be sold, and which party is responsible for the mainte-nance of exterior versus interior of the facility are all spelled out. Also the procedures that are to be followed to assure timely rent payment and the tenant's and landlord's right to abandon property.

A lease can be quite complex and you must be familiar with both terminology and intent. It is important to understand that leases in most situations are very negotiable, depending on supply and demand. Even in a totally occupied commercial center, if the landlord needs your type of business to offer a better tenant mix, you can negotiate terms to fit your budget. Very seldom would you agree to the first offer of lease conditions.

Chapter Summary

In many businesses, particularly retail, the site selection may be the most important decision the new business owner makes. The business must be perceived as convenient to the customer. Convenience results in greater sales.

The choice of the particular location will depend on where the busi-ness's customers are. Retailers may choose from four different types of shopping centers—neighborhood, community, regional, or a downtown area if all conditions are right. Businesses who are dependent on strong drive-by traffic might chose to have a free-standing building. Industrial marketers should look at community industrial parks and incubators. With improved access to modern office technology, many businesses are choos-ing to be home-based if client visits are not required.

If a business is to lease space, the owner must become familiar with leasing terminology and the many different clauses in standard leases.

The Next Step

Visit local shopping centers, realtors, commercial office complexes, or industrial parks and request a copy of their standard lease agreement. Review it closely and discuss questions with your resources or an attorney.

When you have zeroed in on desirable locations compare walk-by or drive-by traffic with comparable locations if it is a consumer business. If it is an industrial site make sure that transportation facilities are available for shipping your goods and services.

Review Questions

1. *What is your goal in choosing a location?*
2. *How does convenience translate into greed?*
3. *What are three types of retail shopping centers?*
4. *What are some of the danger signs of a downtown location?*
5. *What businesses can survive in stand-alone locations?*
6. *What is an industrial park?*
7. *What is an incubator?*
8. *Why have home-based business become so commonplace?*
9. *Name three additional rent charges that are commonplace in retail shopping centers.*
10. *Why is a sublease clause important?*
11. *What is a percentage rent clause?*
12. *Why should new businesses consider leasing property as opposed to buying?*

8

Creating a Marketing Plan

Objectives

1. Understand how marketing mix can influence the customer's needs, attitudes, motivations and perceptions.
2. Learn marketing strategies to enhance product acceptance.
3. Learn the communication process.
4. Understand the various stages of the consumer and business life cycle.

Key Terms

Four Ps	Noise factors
Encoding	Consumer life stages
Decoding	Business life cycle

In order to create a successful marketing plan the entrepreneur must fully understand how the four Ps of the marketing mix—product, price, place, and promotion—affect the needs, attitudes, motivations, and perceptions of the potential customer.

Product	Needs
Price	Attitudes
Place	Motivations
Promotion	Perceptions

The Four Ps

The Product

The product is the package of need satisfiers that the customer purchases. It is the tangible (a physical item) or intangible (a service) representation of what will satisfy an unsatisfied need. The product must be designed and marketed to clearly demonstrate how it will satisfy. The total product includes its purpose, design, packaging, identification, and physical characteristics of size, weight, etc. The entrepreneur must understand how it will satisfy needs, what elements will enhance the customers' attitudes, what features, advantages, and benefits (FAB) will create the tensions to motivate, and how its presentation can influence a customer's perception.

In marketing a product, no effort should be spared to assure that the customer clearly identifies its purpose. The marketing strategy should show its resourcefulness, practicality, time conservation features, and anyway that it will improve a customer's lifestyle. Questions such as adding a warranty or guarantee need to be answered in creating the final total product.

Price

Determining the price is more than a financial decision, it has a direct bearing on intensifying the customers' motivations to satisfy the need if it is perceived as worthy of the exchange of values. The entrepreneur must be able to understand how a price will influence the motivation to purchase or to select a substitute product.

Marketers refer to this as *utility satisfaction*. The customer must decide on the most satisfying way to bring satisfaction from the exchange of a utility, in most cases, money. The entrepreneur who is selling an intangible product, such as entertainment, may have to compete directly with an entrepreneur selling a tangible product.

For instance, a young man deciding whether to spend $15 on a date or to use the money to purchase something for himself will be influenced by his perceptions to the best value. A sale at a record store offering two CDs for the price of one may persuade him to purchase the CDs as opposed to taking a date to a movie. The price will alter his perception as to which course of action will offer the greatest utility satisfaction from his $15. Price will have a direct bearing on the motivation to satisfy the need as well as influence the customer's attitude in building confidence in making the decision.

Place

How difficult an item is to purchase and how much time is needed to obtain it will either enhance or deplete the urgency of the customer's need factor. Inconvenience certainly will change the perception of a substitute product to satisfy the need. Having created a motivation to eat can be satisfied in many different manners. Is the motivation for pizza strong enough to bypass the hamburger stand on the way to the pizza parlor? It will depend on if the attitude of the customer towards a particular type of pizza is strong enough to sacrifice the time necessary to acquire it.

Promotion

What is the most effective strategy for influencing the needs, motivations, perceptions, and attitudes through communications? In this era of modern communication technology, the entrepreneur has a wide array of choices in making this decision. The entrepreneur must know the lifestyles of the potential customer if he or she expects to accurately reach and persuade them. Promotion is how we draw attention to the superiority of our product or service. It can be accomplished through advertising, promotional events, selling techniques, publicity, or through word of mouth. The entrepreneur must know what form of promotion will best produce the desired results.

Ways to Enhance the Four Ps

There are numerous tools available to create an effective marketing strategy.

Packaging

How well your product or service is presented will determine the initial consumer acceptance or rejection. Packaging does more than protect your product from damage, it expresses a strategy. Effective package design has an impact on all the four Ps as well as influence all the customer senses. It tells the features, advantages, and benefits of the product. It creates a perceived use. Packaging influences price perception. It can determine how the product is placed and merchandised. Its image can enhance or distract from the customer's attitude. In service businesses, packaging includes the signing and exterior of the business which attracts the customer to the location. This final presentation of what you sell is an extremely powerful statement that can greatly influence the target market.

A simple product, such as a puzzle, creates its market by its packaging. An expensive imaginative puzzle package creates the perception that it is a gift for a special occasion and can be sold for $10 to $15. By simplifying the package and showing the puzzle as a simple item for personal consumption or as an entertainment value for a sick child, the product changes target markets. It is now a pick-up item and should be priced in the $3 to $5 range. The same product using different packaging strategies appeals to different target markets, each with a different perception of value and each willing to pay a different exchange for its value. So different packages designed for different needs can create different perceptions, attract different motivations, and can be placed in different locations. The entrepreneur must decide which path he or she will follow in forming a marketing strategy.

Brand Names

Selling a brand name with a recognizable trademark is a strategy aimed at building positive attitudes. The entrepreneur must decide the importance of customer confidence in brand affiliation before deciding which to sell. Brand name selling also has significant influence on price perception. A strategy must be decided as to whether the target customer will pay the added expense of buying an identifiable brand name or, if price is the more important motivator, a generic name might produce greater profits.

Guarantees and Warranties

By offering guarantees or warranties to the customer, the entrepreneur is creating positive attitudes towards his or her business and product. Customer satisfaction guarantees heighten the perception of utility satisfaction. At the same time, guarantees can influence price acceptability.

Price Discounting and Sales

Offering discounts, or markdowns, will change the value perception of the exchange. Brand names versus generic labeling can help determine how great the influence of this strategy will be. Marking items down or putting them "on sale" can add to cash flow, however, if sales are overused, the strategy can detract from the customer's attitude towards the product. It is difficult to regain the original product value if the customer perceives it as a marked down imitation.

Distribution

How the entrepreneur decides to get the product or service to the market will alter the *place* variable of the four Ps. Over distribution leads to greater convenience but can also alter the perception of the differential advantage to the product. Many products hold their place in the market due to the type of business where they can be found. If a specialty good is overly distributed for convenience reasons, it will lose its perception as a specialty good and thereby adversely affect the customer's price perception.

These are some of the basic decisions to be made by the entrepreneur in devising a marketing strategy. You will have to weigh each decision carefully as to how it affects your target market. The strategy you use for implementing the four Ps must be made in consideration with your customers' needs, perceptions, attitudes, and motivations.

Communication Strategies

Once you feel confident of your marketing approach, you must incorporate a communications plan into the strategy. But first, you must understand how the communication channel works if you are to be successful.

The Communication Channel

Effective communications are elusive. For a small business owner a poor strategy of transmitting a message can prove very expensive. To effectively transmit a message the entrepreneur must understand the danger of *noise factors* in the communication process.

All messages begin with a sender. The sender processes, in his or her mind, the message to be sent. This process of selecting what is believed to be the best way to express the message is called *encoding*. Once determined, the sender then selects the message vehicle to send the message. The message vehicle might be verbal, written, or visual. The receiver is alerted to the incoming message and proceeds to decode it. Decoding refers to how the receiver translates the message in reference to the knowledge and conditions within the framework of their mental make-up. Once the sender encodes the message, chooses a message vehicle, and the receiver decodes the message, the sender awaits feedback from the receiver. In marketing, this feedback is often the sale or response to an advertising or sales enticing message. The breakdown that occurs in the communication process is from the noise factors that frequently interfere with the decoding and the feedback. Noise factors are any inhibitors that get in the way of the receiver misinterpreting or not receiving the message as intended. A simple example of this breakdown in the communication channel is illustrated by the game of "telephone." The game is played by whispering a message around a circle of people to see how the ending message differs from the original. Fig. 8.1 illustrates the communication process.

You must create your marketing strategies with the recognition that noise factors will interrupt the communication process. This is why we are constantly and consistently exposed to the same commercial over and over; the sender is trying to break through the various noise factors that prevent us from clearly hearing the message the first time. In determining a successful marketing strategy, you will need to be consistent and often repetitious in sending out messages to be an effective communicator with your target market.

Understanding Consumer and Industrial Stages

To properly position your product or service's marketing strategy, you must be acutely aware of where your target market stands in its life cycle. An individual's or business's position in its life cycle determines need levels.

Consumer Life Cycle

Sociologists have identified nine stages in the consumer life cycle.

1. *Bachelor stage.* This is the time of life with fewest financial burdens and obligations. This group is the largest group of fashion and recreation buyers.

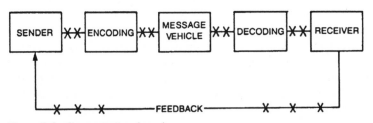

Figure 8.1. Communication channel.

2. *Newly married with no children.* Their highest needs are for big ticket purchases such as cars, appliances, and furniture.

3. *Full nest 1 with youngest child under six.* This group is characterized by first-time homebuyers, baby needs, washers, dryers, etc.

4. *Full nest 2 with youngest child over six.* Their financial position is improving. Both spouses work and are able to make larger purchases.

5. *Full nest 3 are older couples with dependent children.* They are financially strong, although frequently burdened with college expenses. As a group, they are hard to influence with advertising.

6. *Empty nest 1 are older couples with no dependent children.* Home ownership is greatly emphasized. Resist new products.

7. *Empty nest 2 are older couples.* Income likely to drop. They stay home and are frequent purchasers of medical care products.

8. *Solitary survivor still in work force.* Income level is good, but will likely stay home.

9. *Solitary survivor, retired.* Income drops and medical needs rise.

Entrepreneurs who sell consumer products or services should feel confident of their knowledge as to how their target market spends their money and their time before deciding on a marketing strategy.

Business Life Cycle

Businesses have life stages as well as individuals. The entrepreneur selling to an industrial market must be aware of where his or her customers are in their development.

1. *The introductory stage.* Businesses normally in their first year of operation have needs for products and services that will accelerate their development. Start-up equipment and heavy promotional services are in demand.

2. *Growth stage.* Once established, the business enters a period of heavy growth and often cash flow problems. They are seeking better equipment and financial services.

3. *Maturity stage.* Having obtained an acceptable market share, a business must purchase whatever is necessary to maintain and improve its position. These businesses are very concerned with customer services and improved efficiency.

4. *Decline stage.* Threatened with new market entries and technology, the business is hanging on in hopes of adding a new stimulus. Looking for

technological developments to replace obsolete equipment and new ideas to generate new interest.

Since industrial entrepreneurs often sell to an industry comprised of members at different stages in their life cycle, their market strategy must be flexible enough to appeal to the individual needs of its members.

The marketing strategy for a business must be tailored to the needs of its target market. A business must approach its market with a distinct identity and image. Creating the proper marketing strategy will give the business a differential advantage over its competition.

Chapter Summary

An entrepreneur must be keenly aware of the influence of each of the four Ps of the marketing mix—product, place, price, and promotion—has on the customer's needs, motivations, attitudes, and perceptions. By understanding these influences, the business owner can create a marketing strategy that is tailored to his or her target market. This strategy takes into account distribution, pricing, discounting, guarantees, packaging, and the use of brand names.

A marketing strategy will not be effective without understanding the dangers of noise factors in the communication channel. Proper communication will be enhanced if the entrepreneur is aware of the life cycle stage of the potential customer.

The Next Step

Through discussions with members of your proposed target market, analyze where they stand in regards to their life stage and how you can best appeal to their needs. Develop an outline for a marketing strategy for your business to follow. Consider each of the four Ps separately as they relate to your target market.

Review Questions

1. *Describe the four Ps of the marketing mix.*

2. *How do the four Ps affect the needs, motivations, perceptions, and attitudes of potential customers?*

3. *What marketing strategies can influence customer need levels?*

4. *How can price affect a customer's product perception?*
5. *What strategies are available to reinforce customer attitudes towards a product or service?*
6. *How does a distribution strategy affect customer motivation?*
7. *Describe the communication channel.*
8. *What is the best method to overcome noise factor inhibitors?*
9. *What are the stages of the consumer life cycle?*
10. *What are the stages of the business life cycle?*

9

Determining Prices

Objectives

1. Understand the complete purpose of pricing
2. Learn to calculate a break-even point.
3. Understand markup and markdown strategies and reasoning.
4. Learn various pricing strategies.

Key Terms

Cost plus	Market penetration
Break-even point	Price skimming
Markup	Price lining
Markdown	Loss leading
Economies of scale	Status quo pricing

The price component of the marketing mix is the determinant as to how much profit is to be made by an entrepreneur. This price determines the profit margin of the business. If the margin is too low, the business is destined for failure. Many small businesses fail because they do not adequately protect their profit margin. As entrepreneurs we are confident that the products and services we provide our customers are superior to the larger businesses because we know our customers' needs better than big business. If this is true, the small business owner deserves to receive a fair profit margin. Too many small businesses do not have the necessary confidence to ask for fair prices and end up competing, price-wise, with larger companies. This can be disastrous to their future.

The Purpose of the Price

The price serves numerous functions:

1. It should cover the cost of goods, receiving, and shipping.
2. It must cover the overhead expenses of the business. Overhead expenses are those that apply to operations (i.e., rent, utilities, salaries, insurance, etc.).
3. It must pay the owner a fair salary, if he or she works in the business.
4. It should pay back the owner(s), over a period of time, any monies invested in the business.
5. It should provide enough profit margin to insure a contribution to the long run stability of the business.
6. It should act as a marketing tool that attracts a customer seeking a fair exchange for the product or service.

If the determined price is not accomplishing all of these functions, it is incorrectly set and will eventually lead to the downfall of the enterprise.

Small businesses in competitive markets must protect their profit margin. For example, suggested retail pricing for many retailers would breakdown on average as follows for each dollar sold:

Revenue (after sales tax)	$1.00
Cost of good (including shipping)	−.54
Gross profit	$0.46
Operating expenses	−.34
Net profit	$0.12

For each dollar sold, the owner will receive a 12 cents profit. The $1 price has covered the cost of goods and the overhead costs. The net profit must cover the owner's salary, any principal debt repayment, a contribution to the long run stability of the business (possibly increase inventory or keep as retained earnings for future use), and a repayment on money invested. The net profit must go a long way. Imagine what happens when the price is reduced. In small retail businesses, most of the expenses are fixed (constant) because the retailer is supplied by an outside source and most of the operating expenses such as rent, utilities, or insurance do not vary due to the number of units sold. Any reduction in price will reduce the already slim profit margin, making it impossible for the business to realize all of the price objectives.

Determining Break-Even

Remember basic economics?

1. As price falls, demand increases for elastic products.
2. In a free economy the marketplace eventually determines the price.

Certainly you can drop your price and increase the demand, however, if you drop it below your comfortable profit margin it will be just a short run, cash flow raising strategy that will put you out of business.

In the long run, the customers will tell you what they are willing to pay for your goods or service. However, as a new market entry you must make the initial stab at finding that point. This is not always easy and if done improperly can damage your image to your customer. The starting place is determining what your break-even point is going to be and then adjust prices upward until demand corresponds to your desired profit objective.

Industrial Pricing

Determine your cost per unit and add your profit. You have two types of costs—fixed and variable. *Fixed costs* are easy to calculate, they are the costs that will remain constant no matter if you sell one widget or 5000 widgets. Examples of fixed costs are rent, utilities, and other operating expenses that are ongoing. For most small start-up operations, most of these operating expenses are relatively fixed.

Variable costs are those that change due to production and sales. The largest variable cost will be the cost of goods or materials. The more you sell, the more you will have to buy to replace what is sold. Payroll and advertising costs are also variable in that they have a correlation as to the level of sales.

Cost-plus pricing is breaking down the fixed and variable cost to a per unit cost and adding the needed profit. As you can see from the break-even

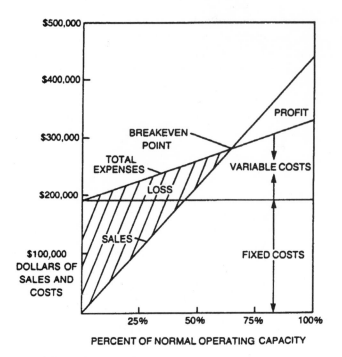

Figure 9.1. Break-even graph.

graph (Fig. 9.1), as more units are sold past the break-even point the profit margin continually widens.

The more the industrial supplier manufactures, the less the unit cost to make. This is referred to as *economies of scale*. To set your initial price you must carefully gauge your demand and your capacity to produce in order to make sure that you can produce and sell at an acceptable profit. Many entrepreneurs create products that might have high demand but because of lack of cost effective production capabilities, they cannot enter the market.

Retail Pricing

Retail pricing is easier to calculate. The cost of goods is derived from the supplier's invoice. Also, unless you are selling a totally unique product, competition has set a precedent. However in order to allow the proper profit margin, the retail entrepreneur must become familiar with markup and markdown calculations.

Markup

The difference between the cost of the item and the selling price, if higher, is the *markup*. Different retail industries use different average markup percentages ranging from 20 percent for discounters to over 50 percent for specialty retailers. After calculating the operating expenses for your business, you can determine what markup percentage you must achieve to be profitable. Retail markups are normally expressed as a percent of the retail selling price. The following are examples of methods used to calculate retail markups:

1. A $10 retail item which carries a 50 percent markup costs the retailer $5 ($10 × .50), or a $5 cost item which you wish to markup 50 percent can be calculated $5/.50 = $10.

2. A $10 retail item which carries a 40 percent markup costs the retailer $6 ($10 × .40 = $4, $10 − $4 = $6), or to calculate the $6 cost item to gain a 40 percent markup divide the cost by the reciprocal of the desired markup ($6/.60 = $10).

3. If you wish to know the markup percentage and you know the cost and the retail price, divide the difference by the retail price ($10 retail, $5 cost, $10 − $5 = $5/$10 =.50 or 50 percent markup).

Many retailers use a chart, or calculator, to quickly calculate the desired mark up. Experience will eventually make determining the desired mark up quite simple.

The important thing is to make sure that your average markup for the business as a whole assures the desired profit margin. If the retailer must gain an average margin of 46 percent to pay operating expenses of 34 percent and leave a 12 percent net profit, he or she must sell some items for more than 50 percent markup in order to compensate for items sold at sale prices, stolen merchandise, and damaged goods.

Markdowns

Taking a markdown, lowering the price from the initial retail price, is part of retailing. No retailer can expect to receive a full markup on everything he or she sells. Slow selling merchandise must be sold in order to bring in better selling merchandise. Obsolete merchandise, such as seasonal items, must be sold to make room for the new seasonal merchandise. Leftover merchandise from a selection must be reduced since it no longer has the initial appeal it held when the selection was complete. Damaged goods cannot be sold at full price. Often "sales" can be an effective customer relations strategy. For these reasons the retailer must incorporate in their pricing strategies a method of assuring that the overall markup objective can be obtained.

If, on average, 10 percent of their inventory is sold on a cost basis to improve their inventory turnover rate (the number of times the average inventory sells in a given period of time) the buyer must plan this into his or her purchase plan and markup strategy. (Inventory control plans will be discussed in detail in Chap. 15.)

Industrial producers also take markdowns for similar reasons. A product may be produced with a new design, therefore, the old must be reduced to make room. Wholesalers often offer markdowns to their customers in order to clear out an old line for the addition of a new one.

Pricing for Professional Services

A service which sells the time and ability of its personnel must calculate fees for time. The fees must cover the salary of the service provider plus any overhead expenses. Calculating the overhead expenses varies depending on whether the business is home-based or uses commercial office space.

Often these businesses charge by the hour or the project. Make sure that in determining the fee you cover the cost of downtime and the self-employment taxes due. If you are a consultant, you will not be able to bill for all of your working hours as you will spend considerable time doing administrative and marketing tasks as well. The fees you charge must cover this time.

For example, if you are able to bill 20 hours of consulting time per week you must charge enough to pay yourself a full week's salary. Charging $50 per hour will gross $1000 per week. After paying overhead expenses of perhaps $150 per week and approximately 15 percent for self-employment taxes on $850 ($127.50) your pay would be $722.50, before income taxes. If that is suitable, your plan must assure the 20 hours per week average, after deducting any vacation or sick time. If you are uncertain as to your ability to average 20 hours per week, your fees must increase to realize your objective. Of course, the fees will have to be competitive with others doing the same service.

Beware of Discounting Your Prices

Do not attempt to compete in price with larger discount-oriented businesses. You should not have to if your business offers superior products and services. If you do take on large competitors in the area of pricing you will find yourself in trouble. Big businesses work on smaller profit margins. While you are fighting to make a 12 percent profit, their stockholders might be delighted with a 5 percent profit on a multi-million dollar revenue base. They have the capital behind them to offer lower prices.

For example, small retailers who offer a 20 percent discount from their normal markup are giving up their profit margin. Since most of their overhead is fixed and they are not able to buy in large enough quantities from their suppliers to qualify for quantity discounts, their cost of goods remain the same as well. If you could offer a 20 percent discount against the normal 46 percent profit margin and sell 100 percent more units, you will not increase your profits once additional operating expenses for payroll and suppliers are included to handle the increased demand.

	Before Discount	After Discount
Sales	$500,000 (1000 units × $500 per unit) less (−)	$800,000 (2000 units × $400)
Goods	270,000 (1000 × $270–54%) equals (=)	540,000 (2000 × $270)
Gross	230,000 less (−)	260,000
Expenses	170,000 (34% of sales) equals (=)	272,000 (34% of sales)
Net	$60,000	($12,000)

To be successful at discounting, a business must have a large market, buy at substantial discounts, and make a sizable investment in inventory. The risks are high as is the investment. Unless the entrepreneur has substantial capital, he or she is better off selling quality and good service for a fair value exchange.

Pricing Strategies

There are a number of pricing strategies the business owner can consider using when entering a market.

1. *Market penetration: Initially offering a low price to gain the attention of the marketplace and secure a foothold into market share. After an introductory period, prices will have to increase to be profitable. Sometimes this escalating price strategy is referred to as snowballing.* As long as the initial price discounting is calculated into the business plan and the customer realizes the prices are for introductory reasons, this idea can be effective.

2. *Price skimming: Entering the market with high end prices to see what the market will bear. This can work with new technology and new ideas, however, it can backfire as it threatens your customer relations. Many fad products can be priced in this manner as the market life cycle is predicted to be short. Do you remember the infamous Pet Rock? It was a common garden stone that sold for $6.95. Its life cycle was approximately eight very profitable weeks.*

3. *Price lining: Simplifying pricing by grouping similar products at one price (i.e., all ties $9.99). Some of the group will attain higher than needed markup percentage, others lower, but the average will be the desired percentage. This makes the buying decision easier for the customers and less work for the entrepreneur.*

4. *Status quo pricing: Setting and maintaining prices at the competitive level. This is the dominant strategy in established markets.*

5. *Loss leading:* Usually a strategy used by larger businesses where prices of a certain percentage of products are sold at below actual cost in order to entice customers to the business with the hope of selling them other items at a full markup. This strategy is often seen at drugstores, supermarkets, and large outlets featuring many product lines. Not usually a good idea for smaller businesses.

Chapter Summary

Price setting determines the entrepreneur's profit margin. It is extremely important to protect the profit margin to insure that all costs are covered, a profit for the owner is assured, a fair return on investment is received, and a contribution is made back into the business to assure long-term growth and stability.

The industrial goods provider must accurately calculate a break-even point per unit sold. The retailer must become familiar with markup and markdown strategies for his or her industry. The service provider must take into consideration time spent on administrative and marketing tasks.

Small businesses must be aware of the dangers of discounting their prices in order to compete with larger businesses.

There are numerous strategies that can be used. Before choosing a strategy, the business owner must be alert to the perceptions of the customer. In the long run, the customer will determine the value of the product or service.

The Next Step

Closely scrutinize the prices of your competition. You can add or subtract from that price depending on what you plan to offer as a differential advantage. Review your initial pricing strategy with your resource and support group to receive their opinions.

Review Questions

1. *What are the functions of price?*
2. *What is meant by cost-plus pricing?*
3. *How do you calculate a break-even point?*
4. *What are the laws of supply and demand?*
5. *What is markup? Mark down?*
6. *How is markup expressed?*
7. *How do you figure the markup when you know the cost of an item and wish to calculate its retail price?*
8. *What are good reasons for taking markdowns?*
9. *What is the danger of discounting?*
10. *How should a professional service provider calculate fees?*
11. *What is market penetration pricing?*
12. *What is price skimming?*
13. *What is price lining?*
14. *What is loss leading?*
15. *What is status quo pricing?*

10
Effective Promotional Strategies

Objectives

1. Learn the components of the promotional mix.
2. Understand the various advertising alternatives.
3. Learn the principles of creating effective advertising copy.
4. Learn the components of the selling process.
5. Understand the value of publicity and word-of-mouth referrals.

Key Terms

Promotional mix	KISS
Advertising	FAB
AIDA	Opinion leaders

For many entrepreneurs the excitement of selling is the most fun part of the whole experience. Selling is the lifeblood of all businesses. Without revenue-producing customers there can be no business.

The Promotional Mix

The *promotional mix* consists of all the methods used to persuade a customer to buy—advertising, promotional events, personal selling, publicity, and word-of-mouth referral.

Advertising

Advertising is defined as an impersonal presentation of a sales enticing message. By its own definition it does fit the objectives of the small business owner. The emphasis of a small business should always be personalization, not impersonalization. Therefore, unless the entrepreneur can design advertising to have a personal appeal he or she should not use it. The large businesses are suited for reaching large audiences in an impersonal manner, but small business owners must reach small niches of customers in a more personal manner. Many of the medias used for advertising are not suitable to the start-up entrepreneur.

The most common mistake small business owners make in advertising is overreaching their perspective markets. Advertising rates are determined by the number of people a media reaches or is exposed to. If the media is reaching people that are not part of your market, you pay the same to reach them as those who are part of your market. Therefore, in deciding on an advertising media pay close attention to exactly who is exposed to a particular media.

Newspapers

The cost of newspapers and other print media is determined by the newspapers published circulation numbers. Circulation numbers do not mean readers and readers do not necessarily mean advertiser readers. A Starch Marketing survey of 6400 newspaper readers showed that on average 31 percent of readers noted advertisements and only 11 percent read them. It also showed that 50 percent more women noticed and read ads than men. Since the advertising rate of a newspaper can be quite high for a single exposure, the advertiser must be very confident that their particular market reads that particular newspaper. It does not make sense for the small business with a single location to use larger newspapers with wide circulation unless they are certain that their product or service is powerful enough to attract the reader from miles away. This is seldom the case. Most small businesses should leave the larger newspapers to the chain retailers, banks, and franchises that have multiple locations in the circulation area and whose product or service has a general appeal. Small businesses are better off considering smaller, more local newspapers who circulate directly to their surrounding market. Don't overreach your market, and if your product or service is very specialized, don't use newspapers to advertise.

Newspapers charge by the column inch. Most newspapers are six columns wide and measure a vertical inch as 56 lines. If the charge is $20 per column inch and your ad is 4 columns wide and 4 column inches deep, the charge for the ad will be $320 (16 column inches × $20).

Television

With the continued expansion of cable TV to local and targeted markets, television advertising has become a usable media for some small businesses. Cable has added many stations with definitely defined markets that can appeal to advertisers to those special markets. For example, a retailer of sports equipment for community sports teams might do well advertising on the local high school game of the week. By so doing, the business can be in touch with its target market in a very effective visual format. If your market is not so easily defined that local television programming would overreach it, television should not be considered due to its expense. Although the cost per advertising spot for many local stations is not out of the question, the advertiser must also pay the production cost which is high unless amortized over the times the spot is run.

Television station audience viewership is determined through the Nielsen ratings and should be available by asking the station advertising sales representative.

Radio

Radio is the preferred choice for many small businesses because of its perception as affordable. It does allow you to choose your particular market as stations clearly market to different age groups and taste. Also when presenting a message to a solitary listener, it offers a more personal presentation format than newspaper or television.

Radio advertising fees are determined by surveys conducted by the Arbitron Company, similar to the Nielsen ratings for television. These surveys should be readily available from the station sales representatives and will show you exactly what age group listens to what station when. If your product or service has a direct tie-in with a particular listening audience (i.e., a record store with a teen audience or a western wear store for a country western audience), radio advertising should be considered.

There is no separate production charge. You can determine a budget since stations offer different charges depending on the air time of day and number of spots. If properly written and produced, there can be an element of personalization in the advertisement. However, if the audience cannot directly be defined as your target market, you will be overreaching and paying too much to reach those who have no interest in your product or service.

Direct Mail

For many small businesses, a well-designed direct mail advertising program is the most effective form of advertising. When properly pre-pared, it has the important element of personalization. It offers the advertiser the opportunity to have your potential customer's singular attention focused on your letter or brochure. The trick, of course, is to make sure the customer pays attention to your message in a time of mail boxes filled with advertising messages. Once accomplished, you can deliver a message in a personal manner for only the cost of mailing and printing. Compared to the cost of the other medias, direct mail is a bargain.

Direct mail for start-up businesses may require renting a mailing list from a mailing house listed in your yellow pages. You can request very targeted mailing lists. Mailing houses often collect names from magazine subscription lists (i.e., *Field and Stream, Gourmet Magazine*, etc.), so they can supply you with names by interest markets. They also supply names by geographical and demographical description (i.e., certain areas of town, particular education or income levels, etc.). The lists are rented on a one-time use basis. Placed in the lists will be dummy names whose addresses are directed back to the mailing house to make sure the list renter does not send a second mailing without paying for the list use. Normally, you rent lists by a fee per thousand of names.

Eventually, you'll want to build your own mailing list from customers and leads that you are able to generate on your own. A company database of customers is a very valuable marketing tool. It allows you to keep in touch with those whom you have previously served and who are also your greatest assets in regards to word-of-mouth advertising.

Billboards, Yellow Pages, and Other Alternatives

Lack of communication vehicles is not a problem. In addition to newspa-per, television, radio, and direct mail there are many other sources available to send a message.

Billboards are effective for businesses appealing to drive-by traffic. Restaurants, motels, and tourist services are examples of businesses that extensively use billboards. The cost and effectiveness depend on their location, the design, and whether they are lighted. The charges are determined by the number of drive-by cars. The contracts are for a specific period of time at a monthly charge which will normally include printing, design, and painting fees.

Consumer businesses must be in the yellow pages because most present-day customers expect to find them there. The fee is added to your monthly phone bill and will be determined by size of ad, number of classifications used, and the number of telephone books distributed. In the days before telephone deregulation, it was simpler as there was only one yellow pages; now there is competition. Frequently, the small business owner must be in more than one directory to assure coverage. Yellow page advertising can be a costly, yet very essential advertising media. Be cautious as to the classification you decide to use as there are many crossovers and you will not be able to afford to display in all. Choose the one or two with direct appeal to your target market.

Depending on your business, other advertising alternatives include transit billboards on trucks or buses, computer modem advertising, sky writing or airplane banners, and flyer distribution. Continual scrutiny and narrowing of your target market description will allow you to make the right decisions.

Creating Advertising Copy

Creating the image you wish to express concerning your business is an important customer relations tool. The entrepreneur must perform this responsibility as it is his or her image and not someone else's. The various media—newspaper, magazines, television, radio—have art and production departments that can assist, however, they should not be the ones creating the message, that is the entrepreneur's job. It is not as difficult as you might think, just remember two acronyms AIDA and KISS.

AIDA

Attention, interest, desire, and action statements should be in all advertising messages. *Attention* must be there or else the reader or viewer will not become aware of your message. Attention comes through effective use of headlines in print media or opening statements for verbal media. *Interest* should build from the supporting statement of the headline or opening statement. *Desire* should grow as the customer or receiver receives the body of the message. *Action statements* are needed to get the receiver to respond. Since the receiver is exposed to so many messages in any given day, the action statement is very important as most individuals will retain the message for a very short period of time and if they do not act immediately the message will be lost.

Just as any good salesman knows that asking for a sale is an essential part of a sales presentation, the advertiser must appreciate the importance of asking the receiver to respond in some manner. Examples of action statements are "come in today," "send now," "call immediately," "come visit us today."

KISS

The other important acronym, KISS, stands for Keep It Simple Stupid. Advertisements must be clear, easy to understand, and uncluttered. Receivers should not be expected to take time to read detail or understand technology. Exposure is brief, the message should be concise, and the call for action immediate.

When creating your advertisements, post these two acronyms close by your work pad and make sure that you adhere to both. You know your product best, you should create its message. Once your idea is on paper, take it to the media representative or print shop and let them add the professional touches to make it special.

The following is a list of suggestions for various media:

1. Newsprint copy should be clear—when possible use white space to draw attention.

2. The dominant or largest advertisement on a newspaper page will receive the highest notation. Do not place minuscule ads—they get lost.

3. Television advertisements should contain action. Still shots are for the newspaper.

4. Radio copy must be written to sound as personal as possible. A professional spokesperson will sound as if he or she is speaking directly to the consumer.

5. In using direct mail, when possible use photos to draw attention. Particularly using photographs with people in them will draw attention as readers have a natural curiosity about other people.

6. Direct mail pieces can use charts to break the monotony of a letter and also to show credibility.

7. Direct mail must be addressed to a person, not an address. Use personal copy such as words like "thank you" or referrals to industry members or acquaintances (i.e., "Don Johnson of XYZ company has been using...").

Evaluating Advertising

Unfortunately the effectiveness of an advertising program is difficult to evaluate immediately in terms of sales results. Rarely will the immediate sales returns support the expense of an advertising expenditure. The entrepreneur must realize that advertising does more than create immediate product sales. It has a residual effect in regards to image creation, reminding customers of your existence, and creating allied and future sales of other products customers are exposed to as a result of visiting a business as the result of an advertisement.

Deciding how much to spend on advertising will vary depending on your industry. Usually it is budgeted as a percent of annual sales. For example many retailers spend between 1½ to 3 percent of their projected annual sales on advertising. If the sales projection is for $300,000, the budget might be $9000 annually spread out to insure a consistent program. You can find these recommended percentages in a number of published industry reports at your local library.

Staging a Promotion

The best promotional events are those that are designed to entertain. Many entrepreneurs find out early that part of their marketing efforts should be aimed at creating goodwill which creates additional sales. The purpose of advertising is to bring attention to the superiority of your products and services. Promotions give emphasis to the advantages and benefits of dealing with your company. They can be as simple as giving away inscribed ballpoint pens or as elaborate as grand opening events that award lavish prizes. Promotions should be included in your promotional mix.

Promotions do not have to be expensive. The retailer who gives away a gift certificate for guessing the number of jelly beans in a bowl spends very little, however, the impact can be very significant. Suppose 1000 people enter a store contest. If it is a contest for children, 1000 children will visit the store with a parent or parents, substantially multiplying the number of visitors to that business. That can translate into thousands of possible sales for a very small investment. In addition the entrees are having fun which reflects well on the business.

The most important promotion a business can have is their grand opening. It serves as an announcement that you are open and you like to have fun. Ribbon cuttings, prize drawings, refreshments, and entertainment are all ways to dramatically announce your market entry. Budget money separately for your grand opening promotional event and don't hold back. First impressions are important. Besides you can't sell unless people know that you are in business.

Whatever your promotion plan always take into consideration what your clientele will enjoy. An added by product of a good promotion is your employee involvement. They also pick up the sense of excitement. Just as in advertising, promotional events should be planned well in advance and staged in a consistent manner.

Developing Your Sales Philosophy

Selling is not difficult if those who are doing it fully believe in their product. If sales people thoroughly believe that the customer will be better off because of a purchase, they can be very persuasive.

Good selling comes from having confidence in the *features, advantages, and benefits* (FAB) of a product. You and your sales people must be knowledgeable as to what you sell. As the leader you must make sure the knowledge is there. Once again, small businesses are successful because they know their customer and their product better than their larger competition. How many times have you turned away from making a purchase because the sales person could not answer all of your questions to satisfaction. You must transmit the knowledge and then make sure the business is able to back up your statements and guarantees. If an industrial salesperson promises a customer a certain delivery date, the company must deliver or risk losing the customer forever.

Selling is comprised of six steps:

1. *Prospecting*—Getting good leads or attracting customers with unsatisfied needs and the ability to purchase.

2. *Making an approach*—Using the most effective manner to attract the attention of the customer.

3. *The presentation*—The demonstration or explanation of the features, advantages, and benefits of what you sell.

4. *Handling objections*—There are always going to be reservations. Make sure that your sales team can anticipate these objections by turning them into a question that benefits the customer. For example, objection "the price is too high"—answer "if we can show you how this purchase will save you money, would you be interested?"

5. *Making a trail close*—A trail close is normally a question aimed at discovering where the customer stands in the decision process. For example, "Do you believe this carpet will look nice in your living room?"

6. *The close or asking for the order*—If you don't ask, the customer will not buy. You and your salespeople must understand the proper ways to ask for the order for your particular product.

These steps can be learned through sales and product training. A sales training program must be part of your business strategy. Either through yourself or an outside sales training source, make sure your people understand the rudiments of effective selling. It is also important to understand that sales training is motivational. Without regular exposure to good selling techniques, sales people will lose their edge and motivation and fall prey to poor and careless habits.

Telemarketing

Don't let the initial response of "oh those obnoxious people" dissuade you from considering what has become a very effective selling tool for small businesses. The right plan can produce for many entrepreneurs. It must be one that takes the customer's lifestyle into consideration. Do not sell in a manner that your particular customer finds objectionable. Use common sense but don't be afraid of using your telephone.

The most effective telemarketing plans are tied to direct mail advertising. Use the telephone as a courteous follow up to a mailing piece. In many instances tell the direct mail recipient that you will be in touch by telephone shortly to answer any questions they might have. By using a tactful approach and being conscious of the timing of your call, you can turn the telephone into a personal, one on one situation, that can effectively sell. Telemarketers must know the product, have attractive telephone voices, and be prepared to handle objections.

You must design a sales training program that fits the needs of your target market. How do they expect to be sold? Is it a low-key sales strategy or can you use higher pressure sales tactics. As the owner attend sales seminars to see how others do it.

Publicity

The best type of media marketing is free—publicity. There is no reason that your business cannot gain some free help. All businesses have a story to tell or a differential advantage that has some community interest. Newspaper reporters, particularly for small town dailies, are constantly looking for new stories. Your business can most likely be one. A grand opening is news, new fashion looks are news, contests are news. The many variations of what people do for a living are good news copy. Not only are publicity articles free, they are frequently more effective than paid advertisements. They tell a story, expose your product or service, and create goodwill. Develop in your promotional mix schemes to receive media coverage.

In addition to the business being in the news, the owner should be in the news as well. The event does not necessarily have to be business-related to act as publicity. If you are the chairman of the local YMCA Board of Directors, you will be normally referred to as John Doe, owner of ..., in any news articles about the YMCA. This notation brings attention to the business, creates goodwill, and, in the long run, creates more business. Community involvement and service is not only good for the soul, it is also good for your business image.

Word of Mouth

By far, the most effective marketing tool is customer referrals. Customers telling acquaintances of good products and service is the best method of gaining new customers. Unfortunately, it is the slowest form of marketing. You can enhance this marketing tool with a plan that assures customer satisfaction with effective salesmanship. Good selling requires leaving a favorable attitude with a customer whether a particular sale is successful or not.

Instill within your business strong customer service policies. Although not always right, your customer should *feel* that they are always right. Do not lose a customer because of a minor disagreement. Customers must be viewed as to their total contribution to a business over a lifetime, not just on one occasion. You have spent time and money attracting that customer, do not waste it by being confrontational. A dissatisfied customer tells friends and creates a negative referral situation that can be disastrous.

Knowing the importance of gaining customers from referrals will lead to success by selling to community or industry opinion leaders. In every community or industry there are members whose opinion carries great weight. If you are successful in selling to an opinion leader, your word-of-mouth referral program will be accelerated. Selling carpeting and pleasing a bank president may lead to selling carpeting to many of his or her business associates. The circle of customers will continually widen as these people are active in their respective arenas and have a network of people who seek their opinions and advice. Fashion and fad merchandisers try to sell to those who are imitated. If a fashion is worn by a leader in a group, others will follow until the leader changes to another fashion and then they will change to that look as well.

Chapter Summary

The entrepreneur must decide the most effective means of implementing the promotional mix of advertising, promotions, personal selling, publicity, and word-of-mouth referral to assure product acceptance.

Advertising choices are many, however, the business owner should seek those vehicles that allow, as much as possible, an affordable and personal approach. For many, the use of direct mail meets these requirements. The business owner should be directly involved with creating any advertising copy as it reflects the business's image.

Promotional planning and selling techniques should be tailored to the expectations of the target market and in consideration of the goodwill enhancement of the business. Publicity and word-of-mouth referrals also create goodwill and result from a strong customer relations program.

The Next Step

Visit local advertising media sources to discover rates and exposure. Determine if your target market is served by these medias. If applicable do a rough draft of a mailing piece for your intended business. Also check your resources to find the industry average percent of annual gross sales spent on advertising. Develop your ideas for a grand opening promotion or announcement.

Check with your chamber of commerce or local college to find out when the next sales training program is scheduled. You should attend and take any possible associates with you.

Review Questions

1. *What is included in the promotional mix?*
2. *What is the purpose of advertising?*
3. *List the advantages and disadvantages of newspaper, radio, and television advertising.*
4. *What makes direct mail advertising appealing to small business owners?*

5. *How does a promotional event enhance a business's goodwill?*
6. *Why is a grand opening promotional event important?*
7. *What are the parts of a sale?*
8. *Is sales training necessary? What does it accomplish?*
9. *How can you generate publicity?*
10. *How can you accelerate your word-of-mouth advertising program?*

Part 2 Case Study—Delicate Decisions

Pedro and Beatrice had a product but did not have a business. They were faced with some difficult decisions that would determine the fate of their promising idea.

Two months prior, Beatrice had come to her friend Pedro with what appeared to be a wonderful idea. She had created a table top game that was a combination of Scrabble™ and Trivial Pursuit™. Her friends loved it and urged her to market it. She had come to Pedro, a long-time friend who owned a small packaging manufacturing business, for assistance in designing and producing the game for distribution.

Once Pedro saw how the game worked, he shared Beatrice's enthusiasm and optimism for developing the product. They formed a partnership, each contributing $2500, to begin the production and marketing of a game called Trabble.

They now sat admiring the final prototype of the product and were trying to determine what to do with it. It was a difficult since whatever they were to do would require additional investment.

The final cost of designing and creating the prototype was $1500. The cost of an initial test market production run of 200 games would be close to $5000 or $25 per game. Add to that significant marketing costs and it was quite apparent that the initial $5000 was just the tip of the iceberg. Neither of the partners were prepared to ante up any sizable additional contribution.

The first question that had to be answered was whether or not there was a market and at what price? Pedro suggested a test market through mail order. He had researched consumer magazines and had found three magazines directly targeted for leisure time activities that he believed would be suitable. If they ran a small 2 × 2 column inch ad with a photo in each, the total advertising cost would be approximately $1600. Added to the $1500 already spent and the $5000 for the production run, the partners would have $8100 at risk. Since it was a test, the objective would not be profit, it would be market research. So the selling price was set at cost, $25, plus shipping and handling charges. The hope was that if the demand could be proven, unit production cost, because of economies of scale, could be reduced over 50 percent to $12 if manufactured in quantities of 5000. They went for it and spent some sleepless nights.

Six weeks later—success! They received orders for over 150 games and received approximately $3750. What was just as promising was the response received from the consumer questionnaires that had been included with the games. There seemed to be no doubt that they had discovered an unsatisfied market need.

The partners were ecstatic, but also confused in regards to the next step. There was multiple directions they could go—all involved increased risk.

1. They could manufacture a production run of 5000 and expand the mail order circulation to two other magazines which served the same market. Working on a $13 per unit gross profit, they could project a profit of approximately $50,000. However, it would probably take over two years to sell through their inventory and they couldn't be sure that their idea wouldn't be copied. A patent attorney had told them it could be patented at a cost of $10,000, however it required an additional investment and there were still no guarantees that one of the big game companies wouldn't come up with a pretty close substitute. The 5000 unit production run would cost $60,000. Each partner would have to borrow against the equity in their homes to raise the money. Both had reservations.

2. They could run the 5000 and take it to retailers at a wholesale price of $18 per unit which would retail at $30. The gross margin of $6 per unit would return less than $30,000 to the partners. However, if this meant turning the inventory in six months, they could produce another 5000 units for the following six months and produce a $60,000 profit in the first year. They still faced the same investment risks.

3. They could attempt to sell the entire run on an exclusive basis to a large national toy discount store. However, they could not expect as high of a wholesale price and might have to sell at a profit margin as low as $3 per unit which would produce less than a $15,000 profit—maybe not worth the investment risk.

4. They could proceed with obtaining a patent with the hope of selling the idea to one of the large toy and game manufacturers. In all likelihood they would receive an upfront payment that would cover the cost of the patent and a small royalty on future sales of the game. This would certainly lower the risk and investment, but also severely limit the profit potential.

Case Questions

1. Which of the alternatives would you choose?
2. Are there other alternatives?
3. Create a marketing strategy for Pedro and Beatrice that would allow them to seek the profits at a minimum risk.

PART 3
Financing a Small Business

It is difficult to begin without borrowing, but perhaps it is the most generous course thus to permit your fellowmen to have an interest in your enterprise.

HENRY DAVID THOREAU

11
Initial Capitalization

Objectives

1. Learn how to make a capital needs statement.
2. Understand what personal assets can be used for business investment.
3. Learn the financing sources available to small business owners.

Key Terms

Capital needs statement   Limited partner

Personal financial statement   Joint venture capitalist

SBA loans

Finding the money to seek the dream is the most difficult part of becoming an entrepreneur. How much do you need? How much do you have? Where is it going to come from? These are the three questions that haunt any aspiring entrepreneur.

Determining Capital Needs

To find the answer to how much you will need, start with your sales projection and your break-even point. The sales projection, although it may be somewhat rough at this point, tells what is needed to achieve the objective. If you have forecasted that $250,000 in revenues is what you must receive to make the under taking of a venture worthwhile, you must decide what must be bought and how you must operate to make sure that you receive sales of $250,000. The following questions must be answered.

How much inventory will be required?

What type of equipment is needed and at what cost?

What supplies are needed to support operations?

How large of a facility is needed to house the operation?

What must be done to it to make it operational?

How many employees are needed to serve the target market?

What type of insurance must be carried?

How much must you spend on advertising?

Answering these questions determines the capital that you'll be required.

Creating a Capital Needs Statement

The most important source of information for initial capitalization will be industry sources. They have the experience to guide you. Make sure you find reliable sources. They can guide you in determining the amount of inventory, equipment, and fixtures that will be necessary to reach your goal.

If you have done your homework up to this point, you'll know who your target market is and where they can be found. You should have a location in mind. How much will it cost?

If you know the size, you can project the utility cost of the operation. Check with your utility companies for a monthly estimate. Find out what deposits are required.

Discussions with the landlord on the condition of the property will determine how much work must be done to the premises and who is to pay for what to make it presentable to your customers. Call around for free estimates on the planned leasehold improvements. If purchasing the property, it will be neceassary to negotiate the downpayment and calculate all closing costs.

Hopefully you have investigated advertising medias and have developed a strategy. What percent of sales does it require? What are your plans for a grand opening? Cost the grand opening expense out as a one-time expense and budget separately from your advertising forecast.

In determining the initial sales projection you must determine how many people it will take to serve the projected market adequately. Having surveyed the competition you should be able to estimate how much you should pay employees either hourly or salary.

Review your plan with an insurance agent to receive an insurance estimate.

Visit an accountant and determine the extent you will need his or her service. Inquire as to what should be budgeted for payroll taxes.

Call city hall or the county courthouse to find out about licenses required and costs.

If you use heavy equipment, including automobiles, what do the experts tell you in regards to annual maintenance expenses?

What supplies are needed to serve the customer. Shipping boxes, shopping bags, and office supplies all must be budgeted.

Do you need petty cash on hand or a cash register bank? This is usually separate from operating cash reserve.

Answering these questions allows you to fill in the missing blanks of a capital needs statement. The capital needs statement answers two questions—how much must be spent to get the business opened and how much should be set aside to cover initial operating expenses. The sample shown in Fig. 11.1 has a column to calculate each and then combines the two to show the total capitalization required.

As you can see, the example recommends three months of operating cash in reserve. A cash reserve allows you to spend your time creating sales and attracting customers, instead of worrying how to pay the bills in the critical first months of being open. Some businesses, particularly those with a high percentage of accounts receivable, may require more in reserves.

Determining How Much You Have

Of course there is another side to the equation—how much do you have? In order to determine what you have available for a business investment you should determine your net worth on a personal financial statement (see Fig. 11.2). Your net worth is the difference between what you own and what you owe. On one side of the personal financial statement list all of your assets, on the other all of your liabilities. Subtract the difference and enter that figure into the equity space at the bottom.

Once you've listed your asset and liability figures, your equity must undergo a close scrutiny to determine what can be used and what cannot

Start-Up Business Plan				
Estimated Monthly Expense		Months	Operating Cash Reserve	Total Year's Expense	
Item	Column I	×	= Column II	Column I × 12	
Owner's salary		3			
Other salary		3			
*Rent		3			
Advertising		3			
Supplies		3			
Telephone–utilities		3			
Accounting		3			
Insurance		3			
Loan principal and interest		3			
Taxes		3			
Miscellaneous		3			
Total Month Expense					← Total Year Expense
Starting Cost Paid Only Once		Start-up expenses ↑	Start-Up Capital:	
Fixtures and equipment			Start-up expense	$_____
Decorating–remodeling			Only once expense	$_____
Installation cost			Total Cash Needed	$_____
Starting inventory			1st Year Income and Expense	
Utility deposits			Total retail sales	$_____
Legal fees and others			Cost of sales	$_____
Opening promotion			Gross profit	$_____
Cash on hand			Total year expense $_____	
Other			Total Only Once $_____	$
Total Paid Only Once Expense			Net Profit	$_____

*Figuring Rent:
Store is 20 ft × 70 ft = 1400 sq. ft.
Rent is charged by the square foot. If the rent is $10 per sq. ft. per year, 1400 sq. ft. × $10 per sq. ft. = $14,000 per year.
$14,000 per year ÷ 12 = $1166.67 per month.

Figure 11.1. Capital needs statement.

Personal Financial Statement

Assets		Liabilities	
Cash on hand and in bank	$_____	Notes payable to bank	$_____
Government securities	$_____	Notes payable to others	$_____
Stocks and/or bonds	$_____	Accounts and bills due	$
Accounts and notes receivable	$_____	Real estate mortgage	$
Real estate owned home	$_____	Home	$
Auto	$_____	Other	$
Other	$_____	Other debts	$
Cash surrender value	$_____		$
Life insurance	$_____		$
Total Assets	$_____	Total Liabilities	$

Net Worth Calculations

Total assets	$_____
Less: Total liabilities	$_____
Equals capital surplus	$_____
Amount of capital willing to risk	$_____

Figure 11.2. Personal financial statement.

be used. This depends on what can be liquidated (turned into cash) or used as loan collateral. Cash, savings, stocks, and bonds are usable, other assets may or may not be. If you have a whole life insurance policy, any cash value that has accrued can be borrowed against at an attractive interest rate from the insurance company. Automobiles are not usually liquidable as they are needed for transportation. Retirement accounts can be liquidable, in most instances, however the expense of doing so and the risk of using these monies makes this choice difficult. The IRS imposes a 10 percent tax penalty on early withdrawals from a tax-deferred retirement investment fund before the age of 55. Added to the income taxes you must pay on this money, the cost might be as high as 43 percent of the total withdrawn.

Risking your retirement money on a business investment will be discussed further in Chap. 12. Other assets are personal belongings such as furniture, jewelry, etc. which, in most cases, are not available for immediate liquidation.

For many, the largest asset is their home. If you have substantial equity in your home, the difference between the home value and any home mortgages, it can be converted into cash through a home equity loan. Many will use this as a source of funds. Of course, your home will be at risk in the event of business failure. Give careful consideration to this if it causes anxiety.

The liability side of the statement gives an indication as to whether or not this is a good time to consider business ownership. Too much immediate debt for credit cards, college expenses, medical bills must be taken into account. Too much debt will be an obstacle to borrowing money for business use as well.

For most the amount available is that sum of cash convertible assets and possibly a percentage of real estate equity. Unfortunately, often the amount available, as opposed to the amount needed, is not enough. There are sources of help for you to consider if you find yourself in that predicament.

Where to Find Money

Personal Sources, Family, and Friends

The majority of new business start-ups rely primarily on the personal contributions of the entrepreneur and any support he or she can receive from family and friends in gathering seed money. There are two ways of looking at family and friend support. One is the negative view of asking for help, the other is the positive view that these are the people you most want to share in your success as an entrepreneur.

Borrowing from your personal sources should be considered if it is volunteered, not coerced. A friend or relative, who senses your enthusiasm and has confidence in your proposal, may wish to become part of it either through investment or loans. Whatever the case, it should be documented as any business transaction. Any lender should receive a fair interest rate, any investor a fair dividend on profits. Loose knit arrangements between friends and relatives often backfire on all parties.

Banks and Lending Institutions

If you haven't heard, lending institutions do not like to loan money to start-up business operations. The reason is very simple, they are aware of the published failure rates of small businesses and they are not risk takers. So no matter what you see on television advertisements do not be surprised at their negative response to your request for a loan. Lending institutions will only loan seed money for businesses if the loan is secured fully by liquid assets. Once you are established and profitable, the banks will become important allies, but for now the amount of assistance they will offer is minimal.

SBA Loans

In an effort to foster small business development, the Small Business Administration, an agency of the federal government, offers loan assistance to start-up businesses. Originally, small business owners could receive direct, low interest loans from the government, however, the program has been changed to one of loan guarantees to banks. Almost 99 percent of SBA loans are made as guarantees to the lending institution that the government will pay up to 90 percent of the loan balance if the borrower defaults.

The procedure for qualifying for an SBA loan starts at the participating bank or lending institution. Some banks do SBA loans, others do not like to fool with the necessary bureaucratic procedures involved. The closest SBA or SBDC office can direct you to participating banks. To qualify you must be turned down for a conventional bank loan. Once the bank says no, you should inquire as to whether they would be willing to make the loan if it was SBA guaranteed. If your business plan is sound and your personal financial statement has enough collateral, the bank will act as the loan processor.

SBA loans are not for everyone. Normally the bank and SBA look for loans in excess of $150,000 to make it worth their efforts. The process can be lengthy, often three to six months. Just as in a regular bank loan, the borrower must secure the loan with all personal assets, including their house. The loan is treated as a bank loan since the bank is the lender. Because there is little risk, the interest rate is usually the same as a fully secured loan. The bank will charge an originator's fee to cover their administrative work on processing an SBA loan. The greatest advantages of SBA loans are the length of term, often up to 15 years and even longer on real estate loans.

There are some SBA programs available to some disadvantaged groups such as disabled Vietnam vets and the handicapped. If you think you might qualify for special assistance call the SBA or an SBDC office for information.

The SBA has recently inaugurated a program of assistance for businesses with smaller needs. Although initially poorly funded, this program could help many business owners. There is growing pressure on the SBA to help create more opportunities. Take the time to investigate SBA loan programs.

Taking a Partner

One way of increasing assets is to add the assets of a partner(s). This can add to your cash or collateral value. Partnerships give two heads and also two personal financial statements. Forming a partnership will be discussed in Chap. 18.

Taking a partner is not a decision to be taken lightly as partnerships often ruin relationships if formed for the wrong reason. However, if taking a partner provides the necessary financial support it is certainly worth consideration.

If taking a partner is strictly for gaining financial support, you might wish to find a limited partner. A *limited partner* is an investor with no formal direct voice in management and who's financial obligation does not exceed the amount invested. This allows control to remain in the hands of the general partner(s).

Taking Investors

If your capital needs are greater than the support you can gain from adding a partner you might wish to add investors through selling stock in your corporation. Incorporating procedures, advantages and disadvantages, will be discussed in Chap. 18. Raising capital through selling stock gives the entrepreneur cash without debt. A stock prospectus can be written that spells out the investment opportunity and explained to groups of interested investors at meetings. The entrepreneur's responsibility will be to share profits, but not management. A simple stock prospectus is shown in Chap. 12.

Joint Venture Capitalists

There are joint venture companies that represent groups of wealthy investors looking for speculative opportunities. These companies normally are interested in high technology development that can create considerable profits in the future. They are interested in start up companies that have the potential to develop into multi-million dollar operations. They do not invest lightly, normally in excess of $5 million, and they often require a controlling interest in management. *Joint venture capitalists* are for those start-up businesses requiring substantial capital who are willing to give up some control. The high tech entrepreneur who is willing to accept 40 percent of a lot, as opposed to 100 percent of nothing, since there may be no other way to raise the capital, might consider finding a joint capital company. They are found in larger metropolitan areas. Bankers, lawyers, and community business leaders can put you in touch with them.

Trade Credit

In most industries, short-term credit is available through suppliers. Although inventory purchasing terms are normally too short to consider as start-up assistance, equipment and fixture financing is often available on longer terms and can be written into the initial capitalization plan. Unlike the banks which do not consider equipment as suitable collateral, equipment manufacturers do since they have a market to resell the equipment in the event they must foreclose on a loan. Chapter 12 will examine ways to put a financial plan together and how to weigh the risk behind your decisions.

Chapter Summary

The entrepreneur must determine how much money is needed, how much is available, and from where the money will come. The process starts with making a capital needs statement. This statement shows the amount needed to get the operation open and the amount of operating cash that should be available for the initial stage of operations.

The entrepreneur should make a personal financial statement showing all personal assets and liabilities. This will show what assets can be converted to business use.

In many instances, the needs will be greater than the means. There are numerous sources available for raising needed capital. The aspiring business owner must investigate the various sources to determine what financing options are available for his or her particular business.

The Next Step

Contact industry sources to assist you in putting together a capital needs statement. Fill out a personal financial statement to determine your net worth and what you own that can be used for business investment. If financing is required, visit with the various sources available to discuss your idea and receive their opinions as to its feasibility. Although you are not prepared at this point to make a formal proposal with your business plan, it is not inappropriate to hold preliminary discussions with financing sources to show your enthusiasm and update them on your progress.

Review Questions

1. *What is a capital needs statement?*
2. *What are the two parts of the capital needs statement?*
3. *What is a personal financial statement?*
4. *What personal assets are normally convertible to business investment?*
5. *What procedure should you follow in obtaining an SBA loan?*
6. *Why do banks avoid start-up business loans?*
7. *What is a limited partner?*
8. *How would you seek investors?*
9. *What type of businesses appeal to joint venture capitalists?*
10. *What type of industry trade credit can be used for initial capitalization?*

12

Understanding Investment Risk

Objectives

1. Learn ways to minimize financial risk exposure.
2. Learn to think creatively in developing a business capitalization and financial plan.
3. Learn methods of attracting investors.
4. Understand how to measure investment advisability.

Key Terms

Creative financing   Stock prospectus
Limited partner   Personal cash flow

Once you've identified the amount of money that you need for start-up investment you must develop confidence in a plan that minimizes the risk. This is the "gut check." If your anxiety level is too great, the idea should be set aside or revamped. Once implemented, there will be no turning back. This chapter will give some ideas and methods to consider in raising capital and cutting down personal risk.

Creative Financing

Too many get to this point and then quit out of desperation. They look at their capital needs statement and then at their personal financial statement and decide there is no way to put it together. However, for those who really believe in their idea, there is usually a way, if the determination is there. Let's create some scenarios based on what we learned in Chap. 11.

Suppose the capital needs statement asks for a $50,000 one-time, start-up investment and $25,000 operating reserve cash for a total capital needed $75,000. The entrepreneur has found only $35,000 available from his or her personal financial statement leaving a $40,000 deficit. A visit with a couple of banks and it quickly becomes apparent that banks do not loan to start-up businesses without easily liquidable personal collateral securing the loan. Since the entrepreneur is planning on selling any personal collateral to raise the $35,000 there appears to be no bank assistance. The banker also tells the prospective borrower that there is no suitable collateral to do an SBA guaranteed loan and that $40,000 is too small of a package for SBA consideration. The entrepreneur will have to rely on his or her own initiative to piece together the missing money.

The search starts with the industry. Of the $50,000 needed to open, $25,000 is for equipment to be purchased from a large manufacturer. Although the bank is afraid of an equipment loan for fear that they might end up owning equipment that they have no use or market for, the manufacturer will work out an installment payment plan after an initial downpayment of perhaps 50 percent. They may give the buyer a three-year, low-interest loan of $12,500 using the equipment as collateral. The deficit is now $40,000 – $12,500 or $27,500.

More than half way to the goal, the entrepreneur describes the venture to family and friends with great enthusiasm. An interested friend and a loving aunt each offer $5000 in the form of a three-year note with an attractive interest rate of two percentage points higher than what they are receiving from the bank. They also want the assurance that if the business takes off, they have first option to buy any stock offered for sale at a later date. The deficit is now $40,000 – $12,500 – $10,000 = $17,500.

Getting closer, the entrepreneur looks to a source not originally considered due to high interest rates—credit cards. Admittedly the interest is too high, however a $5000 cash advance will only represent 10 percent of totaled borrowed money and the extra 5 percent interest on just that fraction of the debt may be acceptable. The deficit is now $12,500.

The entrepreneur looks harder. He or she finds a personal possession that can be sold to raise $2500. Perhaps it comes from trading down in automobiles or selling a collectible item that has been saved for just such an occasion. The deficit now stands at $10,000.

The money is now there to get the business opened and the operating reserve now covers perhaps the first 40 days of operation expenses. With a business plan in hand, the entrepreneur may now go back to the bank with a slightly different posture. It is no longer an idea, he or she has definitely decided to open this business. Now it must be decided where the revenues will be deposited on a daily basis. The banker has more interest since the sales projection may indicate $200,000 or $300,000 of possible deposits. The new business owner can now request a $5000 line of credit to be used only if needed in exchange for the deposits. If the borrower has a clear credit record, the request is now small enough that the banker can approve it without going through a loan committee.

The entrepreneur has put together all but $5000 of needed capital. Although slightly short of the original goal, he or she can count on confidence and possibly short-term industry trade terms, which will give 30-, 60-, or 90-day payment terms on inventory to take the risk and open the business. The plan has been pieced together through five different sources and the risk has been spread beyond just the entrepreneur.

Giving Up Equity

Two common ways of attracting money from outside sources is by offering them equity, or ownership, in the business enterprise. Depending on what is at risk, this may or may not be a good idea. Your desire to be a totally independent entrepreneur may blind you to the advantages of giving up some control in exchange for badly needed capital.

Taking a Partner

There are two valid reasons to take a partner(s). If there is a void of knowledge that can only be secured by adding a partner, or if there is a capital need that can only be raised by offering a partnership. Partnerships should never be created because of friendship or family. They constitute entirely different relationships, based on profits, and can seriously damage personal relationships.

If your capital needs cannot be pieced together on your own and there is an individual(s) whose determination matches yours, you may wish to consider forming a partnership. Ideally this individual also brings a piece of missing knowledge into the business as well. The addition of this person or persons multiplies your net worth considerably as his or her personal assets are now available to liquidate or borrow against.

There are general partners and limited partners. The procedures and tax considerations in forming a partnership will be discussed in Chap. 18. *General partners* all share proportionately in the management and financial activities of the business. *Limited partners* only share proportionately in the financial activities of the business. There is a big difference because if you take a limited partner all management control remains with you as the general partner. Ideally if you are faced with a $50,000 deficit in creating a business, and you decide to take a partner, you would find a limited partner to come up with the $50,000 in exchange for a percent of profits and not a voice in management. Although profits must be shared, control remains with you. This is preferable particularly if the individual is not able to offer knowledge that would assist in the management of the operation. In doing so, the risk has been shared to more than one individual.

Selling Stock

The other method of attracting capital is to sell stock by forming a corporation. Buying stock represents ownership rights, not management rights. As long as you own 51 percent of the stock, you will be the majority stockholder and have full control of the management decisions. Selling stock in a small enterprise is no different than selling stock on the New York Stock Exchange, the price is determined by profit potential, not asset value. It is the law of supply and demand. If individuals believe they will make an attractive return on their investment, they will buy stock at whatever price they feel is a good investment. You become a salesman for investment potential. Stock sales receipts become the property of the corporation and can be used for whatever management considers appropriate to gain profits. Instead of incurring debt, you have given away equity. The risk has been spread to many as opposed to one person. As long as the entrepreneur keeps control of the business, this can be the preferable avenue to take.

To sell stock, you must share your business plan with interested investors. In addition to the business plan, you will need to show them a stock prospectus that tells how the stock is to be sold and how the money will be used to achieve the objectives of the business plan. Figure 12.1 is an abbreviated illustration of a stock prospectus. If you seek more than just investors from your immediate circle of family and friends, you should conduct meetings for work colleagues and church or other organization acquaintances to discuss your plans and to sell stock. Initially, you will set a stock offering price that reflects an attractive return, however once investors start buying you can raise or lower the price dependent on the level of demand.

Another group of prospective investors is the employees of the business. Many successful businesses are attributing their success to the fact that

Number _____.   Offeree _____

PRIVATE PLACEMENT MEMORANDUM

THE LINGERIE SHOP, INC.
A Georgia Corporation
20,000 shares of common stock
$5.00 per share

THESE ARE SPECULATIVE SECURITIES. SEE "RISK FACTORS." THE
SECURITIES ARE SUBJECT TO CERTAIN RESTRICTIONS ON TRANSFER.
THERE IS NO MARKET FOR THEM AND NOMARKET IS LIKELY TO DEVELOP.
CONSEQUENTLY, THEY WILL NOT BE READILY TRANSFERABLE.

	Price to Purchaser[1]	Proceeds to Corporation[2]
Per Share	$5.00	$5.00
Total	$100,000.00	$100,000.00

[1]There will be a minimum investment required of Five Thousand
Dollars ($5,000.00), per purchaser and any amount thereafter
in increments of $1,000.00. The Corporation reserves the
right to refuse any offers to purchase the securities
.described herein for any reason.

[2]A portion of such proceeds will be applied to the payment of
expenses incurred in connection with the formation of the
Corporation and other start-up expenses. See "Use of Proceeds."

THESE SECURITIES ARE OFFERED ONLY TO A LIMITED NUMBER OF
QUALIFIED PERSONS (35) WHO PURCHASE FOR THE PURPOSE OF
INVESTMENT AND NOT FOR RESALE. THESE SECURITIES ARE EXEMPT
FROM REGISTRATION PURSUANT TO REGULATION D, RULE 505
THEREUNDER, AND THEREFORE HAVE NOT BEEN REGISTERED WITH THE
SECURITIES AND EXCHANGE COMMISSION AND NOT BEEN APPROVED NOR
DISAPPROVED BY SUCH COMMISSION.

THE SALE TO GEORGIA RESIDENTS (NOT TO EXCEED FIFTEEN (15) IN
NUMBER) UNDER THIS OFFERING IS BEING MADE IN RELIANCE ON THE
EXEMPTION FROM REGISTRATION SET FORTH IN SECTION 9(m) OF THE
GEORGIA SECURITIES ACT OF 1973, AS AMENDED.

THIS PRIVATE PLACEMENT MEMORANDUM DOES NOT CONSTITUTE AN
OFFER TO ANY PERSON OTHER THAN THE PERSON WHOSE NAME APPEARS
IN THE UPPER RIGHTHAND CORNER HEREOF. REPRODUCTION OF THIS
PRIVATE PLACEMENT MEMORANDUM IS STRICTLY PROHIBITED.

ISSUER

Figure 12.1. Small business stock prospectus.

they are employee owned. This provides more incentive for hard work and also allows management to trade off pay increases for stock ownership. It has become an effective way to control employee operating expenses. Although not usually a source for start-up capital needs, it is an effective management and capital tool after the business has become operational.

Calculating Your Investment Risks

The goal is to minimize risks and maximize profit potential. It is not possible to eliminate risks. If the business owner is not prepared to put his or her assets at risk, he or she should not expect others to show interest in investing. The idea of starting businesses using only outside capital, and none of your own, is not realistic nor particularly ethically responsible. The owners investment is a confidence indicator. Would you invest or loan money to a business in which the principals had no risk if the business failed?

You must determine how much you wish and are able to risk. It should not be all that you own. No matter how good the plan or how high the level of confidence, there are unforeseen things that can happen to sink even the strongest of business enterprises. Therefore, there must be a personal reserve for you to fall back on in the event the worst happens. Personal circumstance and time of life will have a direct bearing.

The best time to take risks is when your personal financial obligations are low. Often this is for the 25 to 35 age group who have been in the workforce 5 to 10 years, have developed some savings, and are not faced with college or medical expense obligations. At this age, there is still plenty of time to recoup if the business does not develop as planned.

The older the individual, the less time to build a business, and the less time to rebound from a business failure. On the other hand, older individuals often have more capital and knowledge. It is not recommended that those over 55 use their retirement savings for business investment as it will not be possible to start to build a new retirement program if the investment fails.

Each entrepreneur must gauge his or her circumstance individually. A personal cash flow budget should be worked through to make sure that all financial obligations are accounted for and that their is a contingency plan to meet them (Fig. 12.2). Basic financial obligations such as food and shelter do not disappear and must be accounted for properly. Many married entrepreneurs make sure that their spouse is gainfully employed with regular paychecks that cover the basic obligations.

Current Year Expense	Expense Items	Year 1 19__ at __%	Year 2 19__ at __%	Year 3 19__ at __%	Year 4 19__ at __%
	Housing				
	Rent or mortgage				
	Real estate taxes				
	Repairs and maintenance				
	Home improvements				
	Home insurance				
	Total Housing Cost				
	Utilities				
	Electric				
	Gas				
	Telephone				
	Water, sewer, garbage				
	Total Utilities				
	Personal				
	Food				
	Restaurant				
	Clothing				
	Dry cleaning, laundry				
	Hobbies				
	Vacation				
	Total Personal				
	Health Care				
	Medical (including insurance)				
	Dental (including insurance)				
	Drugs				
	Total Health				

Figure 12.2. Personal cash flow budget.

The size of the investment must be in consideration with the projected return on investment. As discussed, in buying an existing business, the original business investment should be returned over a period of time to the owner plus any salary for work. If your plan does not realistically allow you to recapture the money that you have decided you can invest over a five- to seven-year period, you should reconsider going ahead with the plan.

For some, the idea of selling off good investments in stocks or bonds is disagreeable. In many instances, it is preferable to use these investments as loan collateral as opposed to selling. Although the bank takes physical possession of these securities, the owner still receives the dividends and interest that accrues. Since business interest paid is deductible, the cost of the debt is not as high in consideration of the off setting interest and dividends received. Banks will normally loan 70 percent of the current market value of securities. They will loan as high as 100 percent on CDs on deposit with their bank. By borrowing against securities or CDs, you will be establishing a credit record with the bank and as the debt decreases, you can gradually receive your collateral back.

There is no standard rule as to how much you should have in debt as opposed to equity. Banks like to see ratios of 2:1 equity to debt, although in some industries a ratio of 1:1 may be acceptable. Borrowing more than your equity is risky, but often done. As a new entrepreneur a conservative approach should be emphasized until experience can be your guide.

Chapter Summary

Financial risk cannot be avoided in creating a business. The entrepreneur must understand the risk to be undertaken and the methods available to minimize that risk. Seldom is the financing for a business readily available. The entrepreneur must study ways of creatively putting the financing together, including the possibility of taking in partners or selling stock to investors.

It is essential to have a sound understanding of all financial obligations before proceeding with a business implementation. Creating a personal cash flow analysis will identify how much income must be made available to the owner to meet personal financial obligations.

The Next Step

Devise a plan for financing the business if necessary. Consider all possible sources of funds including the idea of finding investors or partners. Do a cash flow analysis of your personal financial obligations and develop a contingency plan for meeting these obligations.

Review Questions

1. *In addition to lending institutions, name other sources available to help put together a financial capitalization plan.*

2. *When would you consider taking a partner?*

3. *What is the difference between general and limited partners?*
4. *How would you sell stock to investors?*
5. *How is the initial stock price determined?*
6. *What is a stock prospectus?*
7. *Why sell only 49 percent of your stock to outsiders?*
8. *Why should you do a personal cash flow analysis?*
9. *Why should you not use retirement savings for business investment?*
10. *Is a 1:2 equity to debt ratio too risky?*

13

Financial Statements

Objectives

1. Learn how to create and state the purpose of pro forma income statements.
2. Learn how to create and state the purpose of pro forma balance sheets.
3. Learn how to create and state the purpose of a pro forma cash flow analysis.

Key Terms

Pro forma income statement
Pro forma balance sheet
Current assets
Long-term liabilities

Fixed assets
Cash flow analysis
Current liabilities

The business plan requires three projected (pro forma) financial statements—the income statement, balance sheet, and cash flow analysis. Each should project the first three years of operation in order to give a complete picture of how the business's financial objectives will be reached.

The Pro Forma
Income Statement

The *pro forma income statement,* also known as the *profit and loss statement,* shows the expected profits or losses of a business over a particular period of time, normally one year. It serves as an illustration of expected revenues, gross profits, operating expenses, and net profits or losses. Figure 13.1 shows a simplified income statement.

To create a pro forma income statement, start with the projected revenues from sales activities. All costs and deletions against sales are shown as a percentage of this figure.

Revenues minus the cost of goods or materials represents the *gross profit* of the business. Gross profits are the monies that are available for operational expenses, debt reduction, and investment return. As the example illustrates, the cost of goods or materials and the gross profit is shown as a percent of the total revenues. Consult with industry sources or secondary information to determine the average cost of goods or materials for your industry.

Gross profits minus all operating expenses will equal the net profit before taxes of the business. The dollar figures recorded on the capital needs statement to determine the operating cash reserve needed can be

---

Pro Forma Income Statement (Simplified)

Company Name
Income Statement
For Year Ending December 31, 19__

Sales	$_____	
Cost of goods sold (% of sales)	_____	
Gross profit		
Operating expenses		$_____
Payroll %	_____	
Rent %	_____	
Maintenance and repairs %	_____	
Operating supplies %	_____	
Taxes and licenses %	_____	
Utilities %	_____	
Advertising %	_____	
Insurance %	_____	
Accounting and legal %	_____	
Miscellaneous %	_____	
Total operating expenses %		$_____
Net profit		$_____

Figure 13.1. Pro forma income statement.

used to calculate the first year's operating expense totals. The operating expenses are listed individually and also shown as a percent of gross revenues. If the owner is an employee, as in the case of a corporation or some partnerships, the salary paid him or her can be included in the payroll operating expenses. However, if the business is a proprietorship, any money withdrawn by the owner will be treated as a deduction from the assets of the business, therefore, it is not listed as an expense of the business. A proprietor's draw comes from the net profits of the business.

The net profit is the money earned by the business. It may be used to pay the owner (if a proprietorship), for any principal paid on debt, for income taxes owed, or kept in the business as retained earnings. It is important to note that although principal debt reduction is paid from net profits, any interest expense attributed to debt is considered an operational expense and is deducted before determining net profits.

Since the pro forma income statement shows the anticipated net income of business operations, do not include the one-time opening expenditures for capital assets as operating expenses. They are considered investments and will be shown on the balance sheet, not the income statement.

The pro forma income statement shows the anticipated profits for a year's period of time, however, it does not show when the profits or losses were actually received. That is done in the cash flow analysis to be discussed later in this chapter.

Once you have formed the initial year's pro forma income statement you can easily project years two and three. Normally this shows an improving projection as the upcoming years should show additional sales from continued operation. Many businesses that show a loss, or minimal profit, the first year will show great improvement during the second and third year as the business matures.

Anticipate the future sales growth by what you expect to receive from repeat business and by inquiring as to the annual growth percentage of the industry. Review the expense budgets for any foreseen changes such as additional payroll or increased advertising and factor these changes plus inflation into the projected total operating expense. If sales are expected to grow with maturity and expenses are controlled, years two and three of the pro forma income statements will show a healthy increase in net profits.

The formal business plan that you would show an investor or lender should show a projection that can be well validated by your research. For your personal business plan you should also create a worst case scenario income statement to make sure you are prepared to handle any situation. It can also be motivational to project a best case scenario that reflects the potential for the business as well.

Pro Forma Balance Sheet

The *pro forma balance sheet*, also known as the *statement of condition*, is created to show the financial strength or weakness of a new business. Similar to your personal financial statement, it shows how much property the business will own as opposed to how much it will owe, which when subtracted will show the net worth, or equity, of the business. Figure 13.2 is an example of a simplified balance sheet.

You can use the dollar estimates for one-time opening expenditures from the capital needs statement to determine the assets for the opening day pro forma balance sheet.

The asset side of the balance sheet lists current assets and fixed assets. *Current assets* are those that will normally turn into cash or be used up during the next 12 months. Cash, inventory, operating supplies, and accounts receivables are examples of current assets. *Fixed assets* are those that are used to support the long-term activities of the business. Property, equipment, fixtures, and leasehold improvements are examples of fixed assets. These assets are not as easily converted to cash and can be depreciated over their lifetime. A formal balance sheet will show the accumulated depreciation of equipment to date and subtract that total from the original purchase value to show its remaining book value. Also any deposits in escrow by utility companies or landlords are considered fixed assets as they are not available as cash until the business closes or terminates a lease. Adding the current assets to the fixed assets gives the value of all capital holdings of the business.

Pro Forma Balance Sheet (Simplified)

Company Name
Date _ _ _
Balance Sheet

Assets		Liabilities and Owner's Equity	
Current assets		Current liabilities	
Cash	$_____	Accounts payable	$_____
Inventory	_____	Current portion of	
Total current assets	_____	long-term debt	
Fixed assets	_____	Long-term liabilities	
Total assets	$_____	Total liabilities	_____
		Owner's equity	
		Total liabilities and owner's equity	$_____

Figure 13.2. Pro forma balance sheet.

The right side of the balance sheet is used to show all liabilities, or debts, of the business. Liabilities can be either current or long term. *Current liabilities* are those that are due to be paid during the next 12 months. Normally account payable, short-term notes payable, unpaid taxes, and any portion of long-term debt to be paid in the next 12 months are considered current liabilities. *Long-term liabilities* are those which come due after 12 months. Any portion of equipment or lending institution loans which are not due in the next year would be listed as long-term liabilities. Since lease payments are listed as operating expenses, it is not necessary to list the future lease obligations as liabilities.

The difference between what is owned and what is owed is the *net worth* of the company. It may be listed as *stockholder's equity* in a corporation.

Your business plan should show an estimate as to its statement of condition on the day it opens, one year, two years, and three years after opening. The assets will include the estimated opening inventory on hand, anticipated equipment, fixture or property acquisitions, the operating cash reserve, and any required deposits. Liabilities must show any short- and long-term notes to be incurred and any accounts payable to suppliers for inventory or supplies bought on credit terms.

To estimate the pro forma balance for the end of year one, two, and three, apply any profits or losses from the pro forma income statements. You will need to determine how these profits, or losses, will be accounted for. For example at the end of year one, a $10,000 projected first-year profit might show up on the pro forma balance sheet as a $10,000 reduction in long-term debt or a $10,000 increase in inventory. Distribute the profits in whatever manner you believe is in the best interest of the business.

Pro Forma Cash Flow Statement

The *pro forma cash flow statement* and analysis explains when money cycles in and out of the business on a monthly basis. The income statement will show how much profit or loss a business incurs over a specific period of time, but the cash flow analysis tells the reader exactly when those gains or losses happen.

You probably do a cash flow analysis on your personal budget every month. When you sit down and appropriate how and when to spend your paycheck you are doing a cash flow analysis. You deposit your check to a checking account and record the beginning balance. You schedule bill payments when they become due and then appropriate monies available for daily living expenses. Hopefully, there is money left at the end of the month, your ending balance. In some months you anticipate extra money coming from insurance payments or tax refunds and when the check does not arrive on time, it may change your plan of action. It is the same for a business.

Start with a beginning balance of your cash reserve from the capital needs statement, add in anticipated revenues to be received the first month, subtract the projected expenses to be paid out that month, and project the ending monthly balance which will be the next month's beginning balance. By doing this you create a plan based on money in versus money out, which is different than sales versus accrued expenses. The cash flow analysis speaks in terms of actual dollars. Particularly if your business has accounts receivables and payment trade credit terms for accounts payables there is a big difference as opposed to a monthly income statement.

For example, a business opens with a cash reserve beginning balance of $1500 and a first month sales projection of $10,000, however, only 50 percent of sales are collected during month one and 50 percent are not collected until month two.

Beginning balance	$1500
Cash receipts	5000
Cash available	6500

The business operates on a 46 percent gross margin, however, it has 30-day payment terms, meaning the first month's cost of goods are not paid until month two.

Purchases	$0

Operating expenses are incurred on a regular monthly activity basis.

Rent	$2000
Payroll	1800
Utilities	450
Supplies	150
Insurance	150
Advertising	200
Other	1200
Total operating expense	$5950

The cash flow for the first month of activity will be:

Beginning balance	$1500
Cash receipts	5000
Cash available	6500
Less: Purchases	0
Less: Operating Expenses	
Rent	2000
Payroll	1800
Utilities	450
Insurance	150
Supplies	150
Advertising	200
Other	1200
Total paid out	5950
Ending balance	$ 550

The ending balance is moved to the second month's column as the beginning balance, followed by the cash receipts of 50 percent of the current month's sales plus 50 percent of the preceding month's sales, minus the purchases paid for of the first month's sales (54 percent of $10,000) and the operating expenses paid as incurred. Presuming second month's sales improved to $12,000, the second column looks as follows:

Beginning balance	$ 550	
Cash receipts	11,000	(50% 10K, 50% 12K)
Cash available	16,550	
Less: Purchases	5,400	(54% 10K)
Less: Operating expenses		
Rent	2,000	
Payroll	1,800	
Utilities	450	
Supplies	150	
Insurance	150	
Advertising	240	
Other	1,400	
Total paid out	11,590	
Ending balance	$ 4,950	

It is essential that the entrepreneur run a cash flow analysis to receive a true reflection of how the business will operate financially. The cash flow analysis will show the effects of accounts receivable, accounts payable, and seasonal fluctuations of a business. It will show the months of excess cash inflow and months when there will be deficits. It is a control and planning tool that can be used to borrow short term money to smoothly operate the business. Any retailer who makes their greatest profits in December understands the wisdom of planning a course of action to weather the summer doldrums that precede the Christmas harvest. Rarely are there businesses that do not have fluctuations that must be taken into account.

Businesses that run extensive accounts receivables must be very careful to keep their clients paying on time or run the risk of not being able to pay their own bills. If a business has collection problems, they may be forced out of business no matter how good the sales. A cash flow analysis should be run for a minimum of the first 12 months of operation and preferably for the first 36 months. Figure 13.3 illustrates a cash flow worksheet.

The cash flow analysis can also be used to accurately estimate the amount of operating cash reserves that will be required to get a business started. If you begin your cash flow projection with a beginning balance of $0 you can track the month's receipt and paid out projections to determine how much money must be available until a positive cash flow is reached for the new business. For instance:

Month 1	($7,500) ending balance
Month 2	(12,500) ending balance
Month 3	(12,500) ending balance
Month 4	(10,000) ending balance

This business would require the owner to have a minimum of $12,500 in reserve in order to reach month 4, the first month of positive cash flow.

Chapter Summary

The business plan should contain pro forma income statements, pro forma balance sheets, and a pro forma cash flow analysis for its projected first three years of operation.

The income statements will show the anticipated annual profits or losses of the new business. The balance sheet will show the financial strength of the operation. The cash flow analysis illustrates how the business receives and pays out its revenues.

The Next Step

Using your capital needs statement as a starting point, create pro forma income statements and balance sheets for the first three years of operation. For your own assurance do a worst case, best case, and realistic assessment of your future.

After an in depth discussion with industry sources regarding payment terms, seasonal fluctuations, and accounts receivables make a spreadsheet of cash flow for 36 months of operation. Review all three of these financial tools with your financial advisor for opinions.

Review Questions

1. *What financial information must be included in a business plan?*
2. *What does an income statement show?*
3. *What is the purpose of a balance sheet?*
4. *What is a business' net worth?*
5. *What is the difference between current and fixed assets? current and long-term liabilities?*
6. *What is the starting point for the information needed for the pro forma income statements and balance sheets?*
7. *Why do you need three years of pro formas?*
8. *What is the purpose of the cash flow analysis?*
9. *How can accounts receivables, seasonal fluctuations, and accounts payable credit terms affect the business operation?*
10. *How can you use a cash flow analysis to predict your initial operating cash reserve?*

MONTHLY CASH FLOW FORECAST
3-F-1/9A REV 12-84

CASH FLOW ITEMS	January	February	March	April	May	
BEGINNING CASH BALANCE						
CASH INFLOW						
SALES						
LOAN PROCEEDS						
TOTAL INFLOW						
CASH OUTFLOW						
PURCHASES						
RENT						
PAYROLL						
UTILITIES						
SUPPLIES						
ADVERTISING						
INSURANCE						
MAINTENANCE						
TAXES						
MISCELLANEOUS						
DEBT SERVICE (PRINCIPAL & INTEREST)						
INCOME TAXES						
TOTAL OUTFLOW						
NET CASH FLOW						
CUMULATIVE CASH FLOW (optional if using the beginning cash balance line)						
ENDING CASH BALANCE						

Figure 13.3. Cash flow worksheet.

DATE							

MONTH							TOTAL
June	July	August	September	October	November	December	

Part 3 Case Study—The Loan Officer

Holmes Norling, a loan officer with Valley Central Bank, was reviewing a small business loan application from Paula Doran. Paula was requesting consideration for a five-year $100,000 loan to start a restaurant. The business plan that accompanied the application was very well done and its financial projections supported the request with room to spare. Unfortunately, the amount of collateral to secure the loan was not enough.

This was the type of loan application that had frustrated Holmes many times during his seven years with the bank. Paula had always kept a good personal account with the bank and had paid all obligations, such as her car loans, promptly. Her personal credit record was impeccable. However, Holmes was well aware of the bank's attitude toward start-up business loans—if you can't fully collateralize it, you can't have it.

It was Holmes's job to make recommendations to the loan committee for loan approval or rejection. He knew that if he presented Paula's loan request as it was, it was sure to be rejected. Paula's personal financial statement showed $40,000 of liquid collateral to secure the loan. In addition, she had $60,000 of equity in her home and a $9000 cash value in a life insurance policy.

Personal Financial Statement—Paula Doran			
Assets		**Liabilities**	
Cash (CDs)	$ 15,000	Accounts/bills payable	$ 4,200
Stocks, bonds	25,000	Real estate mortgage	65,000
Real estate	125,000	Total liabilities	69,200
Automobile	11,500		
Life insurance cash value	9,000	Net worth	$151,300
Personal assets	35,000		
Total assets	$220,500	Total net worth/liability	$ 69,200

Paula was hoping that the assets to be used in her business could make up any deficit in personal collateral. Being a restauranteur, her planned assets were principally in equipment ($50,000) and leasehold improvements ($25,000).

Holmes knew that the proposed restaurant assets would have no value with the loan committee. What would the bank do with restaurant equipment, or leasehold improvements, in the event of a loan default. Maybe they could get 10 cents on the dollar from a salvage company on the equipment, or $5000. In addition, the mortality rate for new restaurants was higher than new small businesses in general.

Holmes scratched out some ideas on a notepad to present to Paula. He picked up the phone to invite her in for a consultation to discuss ways she could proceed to finance her package.

Case Questions

1. What can Holmes recommend?
2. What other financing methods can Paula pursue?
3. What would you do if you were Paula?

PART 4

Managing Your Small Business

Sam Walton's 10 rules for managing a business* are:

Rule 1. Commit to your business.

Rule 2. Share your profits with your associates, and treat them as partners.

Rule 3. Motivate your partners.

Rule 4. Communicate everything you possibly can to your partners.

Rule 5. Appreciate everything your associates do for the business.

Rule 6. Celebrate your successes.

Rule 7. Listen to everyone in your company.

Rule 8. Exceed your customer's expectations.

Rule 9. Control your expenses better than your competition.

Rule 10. Swim upstream. Go the other way.

*Sam Walton: Made in Ameica, Sam Walton with John Huey, Doubleday, 1992.

14

Controlling Your Enterprise

Objectives

1. Understand the management functions of a small business.
2. Learn the importance of properly managing and controlling inventory levels.
3. Learn the importance of effective cash management.
4. Understand the importance of determining an effective management philosophy for a small business.

Key Terms

Planning	Staffing
Organizing	Just-in-time inventory
Directing	Management by objectives
Controlling	Total quality management

Managing a small business requires using the same management principles as in a large organization—planning, organizing directing, controlling, and staffing.

Planning, Organizing, Directing, Controlling, and Staffing

Planning

The planning function of looking into the future often gets lost in the strenuous day-to-day operations of a small business. The entrepreneur differs from the corporate manager in that he or she must participate in all business activities, not just in a specialized role. As such, the days are full and the duties are many. Time must be found for financial planning, marketing strategizing, personnel responsibilities, maintenance routines, and administrative duties. Often the time needed to plan into the future six months, one year, and further is difficult to find, however, if the business is to be successful proper planning is essential.

Entrepreneurs should discipline themselves to find a way of divorcing themselves from the operating activities on a regular basis to plan. Some may set aside a period of time each day to remove themselves from the premises, or close their office door, in order to set future objectives and map out a course of action to reach them. Others may take weekend retreats. Regardless of how it is accomplished, taking the time to look at where you are headed is imperative.

The enterprise has not been created for just a day or a month. It is expected to perform productively over many years. Management activities such as purchasing, advertising, financing, and personnel recruitment must be planned well in advance if long-term growth and profits are to be obtained.

Organizing

Organizing is the decision making of how to use resources to get objectives accomplished. Who will do what, or what plan should be prioritized, are decisions that determine the responsiveness of a business. Small businesses survive and prosper because they are able to respond quickly and personally to their customers' needs. Properly organizing the activities of the business assure that all jobs get done properly and on time.

Directing

Directing the enterprise is the leader's job. Directing is guiding and effective directing comes from good listening. Giving effective instruction and setting fair policy and procedures is gained through understanding the strengths and weaknesses of your organization. Learning these requires listening to your customers, employees, and suppliers. Be willing to hear what you may not want to hear. The egotist, who is not willing to accept criticism and admit errors, will not be an effective small business manager.

As the leader, the entrepreneur must stay abreast of new ways to do things. Continuing education in regards to the industry developments, management techniques, marketing strategies, and financial planning, should be built into the entrepreneur's work schedule. Attend trade shows, take courses, and participate in seminars to keep current.

Controlling

Controlling is setting procedures to stay on top of progress. There are many ways to keep an eye on how the business is doing. Setting the objectives is one function, but making sure they are achieved is just as important. The small business manager must decide on timetables to meet goals and devise methods to check for progress or problems. Effective observation is the key.

Entrepreneurs must be flexible in devising the means to reach the goals. If progress is slow, new ways to get where you want can be instituted quickly. It is another area the small business owner has an advantage over his or her corporate counterpart. Methods can be changed without committee meetings or waiting for bureaucratic approval procedures. Be equipped with methods to detect problems. Employee meetings, keeping on top of the numbers on a daily basis, evaluating the results of marketing strategies, and closely observing the competition, will allow you to detect when changes are required. Creating contingency plans in advance for best and worst case scenarios will allow you to take swift action.

Staffing

Staffing your business is critical to efficiency and customer relations. The people who work for you can make or break a business. The small business owner should always be looking for ways to fill weaknesses through staffing. Recognize your deficiencies and hire to fortify. Project employee needs for the future to assure enough time to recruit the right personnel. Building team morale and hiring properly will be discussed in the next chapter.

Managing Inventory

With the exception of service businesses, the cost of goods or materials is the largest single expense factor of operating a business. In our earlier discussion of protecting profit margins, we emphasized that by controlling a cost and reducing its percent to sales, a greater profit goes to the owner. Cost of goods or materials in many businesses is over 50 percent of gross revenues and, in some cases, it may be 70 or 80 percent. If a business operates on a 13 percent of sales profit target and its cost of goods is 54 percent of sales, a drop of 2 percent in cost of goods increases the profit to 15 percent—a 14 percent pay increase for the owner. The goal is to receive maximum profit from minimum investment. Effectively controlling the percentage of cost of goods investment dollars to sales is the single most important management function of many small businesses. To be successful at inventory control the owner must plan, organize and control the methods used to make purchase decisions.

Just-in-time inventory control methods should be used in today's competitive markets. "Just in time" means having the right amount of inventory arrive just in time for sale or use. If you are able to time your purchases and delivery accurately, you will not tie up money in unnecessary stockroom inventory and you will be able to convert the materials or goods into dollars in the shortest possible period of time. Often this can mean selling before having to pay. To be successful it requires great cooperation from suppliers and great discipline as a buyer.

Businesses should maintain a well thought out purchase plan. Purchasing is not done compulsively. All purchases must be planned in advance and all factors affecting inventory levels should be monitored closely. There must be contingency plans in place to deal with changes in the marketplace. Figure 14.1 is an illustrated six-month purchase plan for a retail operation.

The plan starts with projecting the desired level of ending inventory for the purchase period. By stating ending inventory objectives, the business owner will be deciding the future growth of the business. New businesses are often wishing to increase inventory levels during the growth stage in order to increase market share. Mature businesses may wish to maintain inventory levels that have proven profitable. Starting with a beginning inventory figure, the buyer inserts the projected monthly sales figure and calculates the purchase amount needed to assure reaching the sales estimate, and then adds or subtracts from that amount to reach a desired ending inventory level for the month. The ending inventory becomes the beginning inventory for the next month. The inventory level for each beginning of the month in the plan must accommodate the projected sales for that month after adding anticipated purchases to be received, and subtracting any markdowns during that period. The purchase formula is:

Beginning inventory + purchases − sales − markdowns = ending inventory

	July	August	September	October	November	December	Total
Beg. Inventory	$50,000	$52,500	$55,000	$55,000	$62,000	$75,000	
+ Purchases	$19,000	$21,750	$22,000	$29,500	$42,750	$24,000	$159,000
(−) Sales	$15,000	$17,500	$20,000	$20,000	$27,500	$40,000	$ 40,000
= End Inventory	$52,500	$55,000	$55,000	$62,500	$75,000	$55,000	

Figure 14.1. Purchase plan.

The key to success is making sure the needed purchases arrive on time and being flexible enough to make adjustments in the event that actual sales are different than planned sales. The illustration shows a business that has peak sales in November and December. The inventory should build to handle these months and then reduce sharply at the end of the Christmas selling season. Properly planning the arrival of merchandise prevents the inventory needed for December arriving in August and having to be paid for in September, if the trade credit terms are only 30 days.

The buyer must arrange for the manufacturer to ship on a schedule that allows just in time arrival. The buyer must also have flexibility in the plan that allows a change in inventory arrivals, plus or minus, in the event the business does not operate as projected. If sales in September are 25 percent higher than originally planned, the business will not have enough inventory on hand to start October if a plan is not flexible enough to add purchases quickly. Purchasers must leave an "open to buy" margin that allows quick additions to orders and deliveries in the event sales are running ahead of pace. Conversely, if sales are below expectations, the buyer will have too much inventory on hand at the beginning of a month. There should also be suitable arrangements with suppliers that allow the cancellation, or rescheduling, of orders in this event.

The biggest handicap the new business owner must face is the lack of sales history and experience in planning inventory purchases. Initial purchase plans will often be out of line and will tie up money in unneeded inventory or run the risk of selling out too quickly. Too much inventory ties up money and also restricts the amount and type of purchases the buyer can make for the next selling season. Selling out, or too low of an inventory level, causes lost profits due to not being able to satisfy the customer and also carries the threat of losing the customer to the competition. Experience will alleviate this problem, however, initially there should be allowances for fluctuating inventory levels that are bound to cost the new entrepreneur money.

Much of the purchasing function is done at trade shows or through sales representatives who come to the business. The buyer must buy from a plan or run the risk of being too greatly influenced by new products or pressure sales tactics. Seasoned buyers often fill out their own orders in privacy after reviewing the goods with suppliers' sales representatives.

New business owners should use caution when buying fad items. Fad items have a short life cycle and can be adversely affected by late delivery or the market entry of another fad product. Buying seasonal merchandise is risky in that what is not sold during the season will either have to be sold at mark down prices or carried as stockroom inventory for a year. Too many markdowns on seasonal items destroys the profit margin made on the seasonal goods sold at the original intended price.

The informed small business owner always knows the inventory situation. Income tax filing requires business owners to report inventory annually. This is done by taking a physical inventory—counting each and every unit of inventory owned. This assures you of an accurate counting once per year that has been correctly adjusted for spoilage and theft. Using this figure as the starting base, the entrepreneur should keep this adjusted throughout the year by using a perpetual inventory system. A perpetual inventory count is a running and changing figure based on purchases minus sales for any given time period. If the physical inventory is $15,000 on January 1 and you sell $400 that day, after the inventory count, the inventory level is $14,600, not counting any theft or spoilage. However if $600 of purchases arrived that day, the inventory level at the end of the day would be $15,200, $15,000 + $600 − $400 = $15,200. A daily tabulation should be kept on hand to keep track of the inventory status.

Controlling Cash

We have discussed the purpose of a cash flow analysis. The smart entrepreneur quickly learns control tools to dramatically alter cash flow.

Just like keeping track of inventory levels, cash flow cycles can be done on a daily or monthly basis. Plotting the month's cash flow on a daily basis keeps the owner informed as to any cash surpluses or deficits that may occur during the month. It may allow him or her to make arrangements to pay a bill earlier, and receive a larger discount, or to arrange holding off a bill for a later payment date.

Almost all industries have payment terms from supplier to buyer. Knowing how to use these terms to your advantage can save considerable money and substantially improve cash flow.

Suppliers often give discounts on invoices if paid early. This is their tool to assure speedy collection. If taken advantage of, it can make a difference in the buyer's net profit. A business that buys in an industry that gives a 2 percent discount for early pay, can improve their profit margin by making sure they receive the discounts. For example, a business that buys $150,000 per year would receive a discount of $3000 ($150,000 × .02) during the year on purchases if all were paid promptly. If the business was making a $30,000 per year profit before figuring the discount, the owner would be receiving a 10 percent raise for taking the discount. In addition, the business will be maintaining an excellent credit record and will be given preferable treatment by the supplier. Conversely paying invoices late will result in late charges, reducing net profits and adversely affecting the business's credit record.

As a business owner you must be aware of the payment terms when you buy. As an effective manager you will want to find as many ways as possible to improve those terms. The longer you have to pay and the bigger the discount that you can receive, the better your cash flow and net profit. Suppliers will negotiate with good customers who buy regularly and pay their bills on time. Once again building sound relationships pays off. If you are on good terms with suppliers ask for an extra 30 or 60 days on particular invoices and you may very well get it. Imagine how much easier that can make your cash flow. Goods that arrive in October can be paid in January instead of November and still receive a discount. If sold in November the buyer has the use of the sale proceeds for two months. This money could be invested, used to buy new goods, to accelerate debt payoff, or for the owner's personal reasons. This is one of the reasons to start a business with a cash reserve so that you can take advantage of discounts and build credit relationships immediately.

The same holds true of improving collection techniques from those who owe you. If you accelerate collections 20 days by offering a discount if paid within 10 days of receipt of goods, it will give you more cash to conduct your business and more flexibility in negotiating your purchases from your suppliers.

When the economy goes into a tail spin, cash flow cycles are interrupted throughout industries. Vendors are slow paying suppliers, who must slow down ordering from manufacturers and everyone suffers.

Study the cash flow cycle for your business. Learn who to pay first to get the best discounts and use the money saved to increase your flexibility with other vendors.

Management Philosophies

One of the reasons that entrepreneurs start businesses is to gain the right to do things the way they think things should be done. They are tired of working under another's management style. This is the opportunity to manage a business the way they believe a business should be managed.

Part of management is getting goals accomplished through the efforts of others. As the manager you are the leader, coach, advisor, and listener of your employees. It is important that you create a management philosophy that stimulates action from employees and serves the needs of your customers.

There are a number of management gurus who espouse management theories and philosophies. As an aspiring entrepreneur you should become familiar with contemporary management practices and then adopt a management philosophy that is agreeable to your personal style and best suits your customers.

Many small business owners will incorporate some form of *management by objectives* (MBO). MBO creates objectives for employees and holds them accountable for progress in reaching them. Setting objectives is one management function, deciding how to hold an employee accountable is another. The difference between MBO in large corporations versus the small business, is the entrepreneur's personal involvement. Since the entrepreneur is so closely involved as a participant in the operation of the business, rarely is an employee solely responsible for specific outcomes. This being the case, the entrepreneur must share the responsibility and accountability with the employee. MBO can be used successfully in a small business if this sharing of accountability is recognized. Successful small business managers understand the importance of setting the objectives with the employee's input and approval because it creates a shared objective.

Tom Peter's book, *In Search of Excellence*, brought the management philosophy of Total Quality Management (TQM) to the attention of business managers, owners, and teachers. TQM is a management philosophy based on customer satisfaction. All decisions should be centered on what is best for the customer. The basic premise of TQM is very much in line with effective small business management. Entrepreneurs should become familiar with the TQM approach to management.

As you design your business, give thought to your management style. This is an opportunity for you to manage your way. If you don't like committee meetings, you don't have to have committee meetings. If you like weekly staff meetings, you should have weekly staff meetings. You are in control, just make sure that you place customer satisfaction foremost in your decision on how best to manage the business.

Customer satisfaction, in the long run, will determine the success of any business. Always be aware of the importance of repeat business. A business must do all that it can afford to do to please the customer. It is essential to view each customer in regards to the total contribution the customer makes to the business over its lifetime. A decision that drives a customer to the competitor will possibly lose the customer not for one sale, but for the entire purchasing future of that customer. Keep in mind that it is less expensive to retain a present customer than attract a new one.

Entrepreneurs often do not make good administrative managers. The very nature of the personal characteristics of creativity is in conflict with administrative management. If you believe this to be the case with your background, recognize it as a potential danger. Administrative management is part of any business and plays an important role in operating a business smoothly. It might require self-discipline on the part of the entrepreneur or assistance might be hired to overcome this obstacle.

Chapter Summary

The management functions of planning, organizing, directing, controlling, and staffing are the entrepreneur's responsibility. Good management practices must be in place to reach business objectives, particularly in regards to inventory and cash management practices. Planning and controlling theses two vital areas of a business operation are critical to the bottom line success of the business. The entrepreneur must study inventory and cash flow cycles to achieve the maximum profit from the minimum investment goal of a small business.

Entrepreneurs must devise a management philosophy that allows them to incorporate their personal style in a manner that best serves the customer. Small business owners should read and become familiar with contemporary management theories. Good listening skills allow the entrepreneur to stay close to employee and customer needs.

The Next Step

Using a form similar to Fig. 14.1, plan anticipated purchases and inventory levels for the first year of operation. Determine a perpetual inventory system to keep track of daily inventory levels. Discuss trade credit terms with your suppliers and compare.

Write out a management philosophy that is comfortable for you. Visit the library and bookstores to read and learn contemporary management philosophies that fit your planned business.

Review Questions

1. *What are the five functions of management?*
2. *Why is the planning function so critical to business success?*
3. *What is "just-in-time" inventory planning?*
4. *What is the starting point for an inventory purchase plan?*
5. *What is the purchase formula?*
6. *Explain how to maintain a perpetual inventory system.*
7. *How can a change in accounts receivables and payables affect your cash flow plan?*
8. *Why do suppliers offer a discount for early payment?*
9. *What is management by objectives?*
10. *What is the basis of the philosophy of Total Quality Management?*

15
Managing Small Business Personnel

Objectives

1. Learn how to recruit employees into a small enterprise.
2. Learn where to find applicants.
3. Understand how to create an effective compensation package.
4. Learn effective personnel management principles to follow.
5. Understand the importance of properly training personnel.

Key Terms

Theory X and Y managers   Simplified employee pension plans

Entrepreneurs quickly learn the importance of their human resources to the overall success of their operation. The people who work for you represent your business and its image. The ramifications of poor personnel representation is disastrous to a business enterprise.

Human Resource Management

Forming a winning team in a small business is a rewarding and continuous job. The goal is to create an atmosphere of trust, loyalty, and involvement for all involved. The entrepreneur as the leader must carefully evaluate all decisions involving personnel to prevent any disruption to the mission of the business.

It starts with the attitude of the owner towards the people who work for the business. Please note the reference "who work for the business" as opposed to "who work for the owner." There are managers whose management style is based on authority inherited through position. These authoritative individuals often have little regard for employees and believe that they must be motivated through fear tactics and strictly financial incentives. They assume that employees come to work through necessity and not for personal satisfaction. In management theory, this type of management is referred to as a *Theory X management style.*

Theory X doesn't work for small businesses. Small businesses are personalized not only to customers, but employees as well. There are many people who prefer working for small businesses because they desire a greater feeling of belonging and self-actualization than they receive from a larger organization. The entrepreneur who is not able to design a personnel management philosophy that embraces these need levels will find it very difficult to recruit and retain good employees. Managers who recognize the importance of providing intrinsic motivators to employees are regarded as *Theory Y* managers. They are very much human relations-oriented and work to achieve the harmony and comraderie among employees that is so very important to a small enterprise.

It is important to understand the difference between what is expected as opposed to what motivates in a work place. Employees expect to be paid and work in a safe and comfortable environment. These are extrinsic components of a job and do not motivate. Motivation comes from an individual's desire to improve and achieve. Giving challenge and responsibility creates self-esteem and provides self-actualization. Be aware that by allowing employees to be a direct participant in the mission of the business, they will be motivated through their own sense of achievement. This is why small business employees are normally harder workers.

Recruiting Good Employees

In recruiting employees, small businesses are often at a financial disadvantage. Rarely is the money available to compete with larger businesses in regards to pay and benefit programs. The entrepreneur must use the personal advantages of belonging to successfully compete.

Important decisions must be made from short application interviews. The entrepreneur must be confident as to what he or she is looking for in advance of the interview. In most instances, the most important qualifications for working in a small business environment is enthusiasm, ambition, and cooperativeness. If these characteristics are evident, can the skills be taught? If the answer is yes, hire with the emphasis on personal characteristics as opposed to skill level. You can train and teach, however, you will not be able to change the personal characteristics.

To successfully recruit, the entrepreneur must sell the applicant on the values of working in his or her business. This can be done through an honest expression of why you want this person and the challenges that will be offered. Do not recruit strictly on a financial basis as it is not a strength. The strength is that the employee can grow with the organization. If the business does well, those who are there should prosper. As an employee of a small enterprise they will not be encumbered with red tape bureaucracy. Offer flexibility in scheduling, discounts on the product sold if applicable, and a family type of environment. Share your values and management philosophies with the applicant. Allow them to see the human advantage of a small business as opposed to the financial advantage of a large corporation.

Always keep in mind that you are building or adding on to a team. A team that must have teamwork. A bad attitude can ruin the morale of the team. Creating the proper environment for employee comraderie pays off in many ways.

1. Customers form attitudes and images from the feeling they receive from a business's employees.
2. The group works to win, not just to get paid. They realize that if the business is successful, they gain success through financial incentives and job security.
3. Loyalty builds honesty. Many businesses are victimized by employee theft. If comraderie and caring is built into the business, employees will safeguard the business from theft by reporting any violations of employees to the owner.
4. An employee who believes they are an integral part of a business will give 100 percent effort.

Where to Find Employees

The number of applicants for a position will vary depending upon the number of skills required. As the employer you wish to generate the greatest number of applicants possible since it will allow you the greatest selectivity. Applicants can be recruited from the following sources:

1. *Classified newspaper advertising.* The most common place for applicants to look. The cost to the employer is not high and a large number of applicants is all but guaranteed.

2. *Window signs.* Signs have limited exposure, but will surely create walk-in curiosity seekers. Window signs are often used for low-skilled and lower-pay positions.

3. *Employment agencies.* Using employment agencies saves time as they will perform the initial screening of applicants. However someone, either the employer or employee, must pay for their services.

4. *College placement offices.* For either full-time professionally trained applicants or part-time college students, college placement offices are a no charge source for qualified job seekers.

5. *Employee referrals.* Those who currently work in your business may know other qualified people looking for an opportunity. Since you have confidence in those you employ, their references should be listened to.

You as the Boss

There is no ivory tower for a small business owner. The owner is a participating manager. He or she works along side employees. Employees are associates, not workers. There are no staff positions as everyone works in a line capacity in jobs directly related to the success of the operation. They work together and sometimes play together. The family environment should carryover into outside events such as bridal and baby showers, weddings, baptisms, and other important occasions. The relationship is based as much on friendship as just employer-employee.

Compensation

A business should pay its employees what it can afford to pay. It must be competitive with similar businesses, but does not have to be higher, if the proper environment is evident. Find out what the competition is paying and then build a program that works well for the business. There are many ideas to consider in forming an employee compensation package.

1. Offer savings on the product or service of the business if applicable. In many instances, this can amount to an out-of-pocket savings that improves the net earnings and disposable income of the employee.

2. Add any benefits that are affordable and appropriate. Certainly full-time employees should receive paid vacation time and a basic paid sick

leave policy. Employer aided health insurance plans are becoming mandated for larger small businesses.

3. Consider bonus programs to improve earnings. Bonus programs serve as motivators that are not commitments for the long term. Bonuses are also a method of rewarding present efforts. Paychecks represent compensation for work done in the past. Pay raises are long-term commitments. A good bonus program creates excitement and can be instituted when the business can afford to pay rewards. Pay raises are long-term commitments. Many businesses will offer prizes versus money as reward bonuses. Prizes have a tendency to be regarded as gifts and are often more appreciated, provided the prizes are meaningful and desired.

4. If the business employs sales personnel, base pay plus commission pay plans should be considered. It is important to offer a base pay, no matter how low, to insure that the individual feels part of the business and not independent from it. It also protects the employee from being without during times of personal or business hardship. The added commission incentive has advantages to the employer and the sales person. For the owner, commission pay protects against slow sales periods. For the sales person, commission pay increases the pay potential of the job.

5. Consider benefit programs that offer ownership either in the business or a pension plan. There are a number of pension programs that have been designed for the small business owner and employees.

A *simplified employee pension* (SEP) allows employers to contribute up to 15 percent of an employee's annual pay, not to exceed $30,000, to a retirement account and treat the contribution as a deductible business expense. For instance, for an employee earning a salary of $20,000, the employer may contribute $3000 into a pension plan and deduct the $3000 as an operating expense against net profits. The employee does not have to declare the contribution as income until it is withdrawn from the pension account.

For the small corporation, employees can participate in a 401K plan which operates with the same limits of the simplified employee pension.

The business owner should consider an employee pension plan after consulting with a financial planner. Pension programs can be arranged for special categories of employees based on seniority and contribution. You will not be able to afford to make all employees immediately eligible for a pension plan upon employment, therefore, you must learn what is best for your particular situation.

For certain key employees, you may wish to offer them an opportunity to buy into, or earn, actual ownership in your business. This is a very motivational strategy which can pay handsome dividends in the long run. It creates direct involvement from employees and ties compensation to business earnings.

Evaluating Performance

Employees deserve to know how their performance measures up against expectations, whether in a large or small business. The small business owner can personalize the procedure and receive a great benefit for all parties in the process.

The performance evaluation in most large organizations is a dreaded process for the manager and the subordinate. Due to inflexible procedures and fears of hierarchy repercussions, the system is often self-defeating in purpose.

The purpose of an employee performance evaluation is to measure progress toward goals and to receive valuable employee input regarding improvements to the work place. In a small business, there is no reason for ranking or assigning numerical representation to employee performance. The owner should be very familiar with the employee since he or she works with the individual on a daily basis. Evaluations should be direct and personal with the purpose of clarifying any misunderstandings, recognizing achievements, redirecting efforts where necessary, and to set new objectives for the future.

It is important that evaluations are done on a regular six-month or annual basis. Normally, they can be conducted over a cup of coffee away from the business. It is not necessary to have a standard form, however, the entrepreneur should plan in advance what should be accomplished from the evaluation. A checklist of goals and questions should be brought along. A good discussion using good listening skills is the only requirement. After the conversation, the owner should be able to summarize the conclusions and agreements in a concise written report that is shared with the employee and used to set future objectives.

Evaluations are the time to discuss plans of the future and analyze them with those who make goals possible. It is a constructive time and should not be destroyed with discussions centered on minor criticisms. Procedural corrections or work habit deficiencies should be addressed when they occur, not held back until a performance review.

Organization Chart

Any business that employs more than four should have an organization chart. The purpose of an organization chart is to illustrate where each individual stands in the overall picture of the business. It shows opportunities for advancement and includes job descriptions which describe the responsibilities of positions. The job descriptions are more general than large organizations because small business employees wear many hats and are often called upon to assist others in their work.

Employee Handbook

If the business employs more than 10, the owner should consider writing a simple manual addressing basic policies and procedures of the operation. Its content does not have to be specific as the flexible nature of small businesses means a minimum of hard and fast rules and procedures. The manual is more for the purpose of describing benefits and the long-term goals of the business.

Training Employees

Since small businesses have difficulty competing financially for employees, they often must hire less skilled personnel. This puts an increased training burden on the employer. In many cases, this can work to the employer's advantage.

Because small enterprises are specialized, the skills needed to work in one should be tailored as much as possible to the particular business. Although training a less experienced person for a position takes longer, having the opportunity to work with a fresh and unbiased attitude may make a better employee in the long run.

Most small business training is on the job. Seldom is the capital available to send employees to expensive skill development or education programs. If the owner is involved with the on the job training the employee, at least theoretically, is working with the best and learning exactly what is expected.

Developing a sound training program is essential to the success of the operation. The entrepreneur must properly plan what and how employees will learn. The customers must be served by competent people who know the product and the business thoroughly. Often the customer motivation for coming to the small business to buy is the belief that the employees of larger businesses cannot answer their questions nor back up the sale with service.

There are published training programs—written, audio, and visual—that can be used to supplement the training program. Employers should investigate which of these programs are best suited for their business and create a library of resources. Many of these programs are available through industry sources and some may be found at the local library or bookstore. The good programs motivate as well as teach.

There is often low-cost classroom and hands-on training through the industry. Trade shows sometimes offer training seminars during the shows in which both owners and employees can take advantage. Local community colleges offer continuing education programs that will complement training at affordable prices.

Building a knowledgeable team of employees is also protection from the threat of the entrepreneur becoming sick or disabled. The owner must be sure that the business can carry on in the event he or she is temporarily unavailable. As the business grows the owner must learn to delegate certain responsibilities if the growth is to continue. Delegation cannot be effective if employees have not been prepared to assume responsibilities. It all starts with the initial training.

Chapter Summary

Small businesses are often at a financial disadvantage in recruiting qualified personnel. They must rely on offering a human advantage of belonging to an organization that fosters participation, challenge, and self-actualization. The owner must search for any benefits programs that are affordable to the business, including ownership sharing and pension plans, to further motivate performance.

The owner is a participant who works along side of employees, not above them. A Theory Y, human relations, approach to personnel management should be adhered to in creating an environment that promotes trust and comraderie.

Effective personnel management requires performance evaluations based on building on strengths, not weaknesses. Many small businesses should use organization charts and employee handbooks to assure good communications. Proper training of employees is an important responsibility of the small business owner.

The Next Step

Describe the positions your business will require and research the competition and industry for the competitive pay scale. Write out the characteristics you would like your employees to have and prepare sample interview questions.

Contact applicant sources to discover cost and procedure to follow. Discuss benefit programs with a financial advisor to see if there are programs your business can afford to offer. Talk to industry representatives regarding possible training programs that would fit your business.

Review Questions

1. *How can the small business owner compete with larger businesses in recruiting qualified personnel?*
2. *How does a Theory Y manager operate?*
3. *Make a list of motivators for working in a small business.*
4. *How can you find job applicants?*
5. *What benefits can a small business offer?*
6. *What is a simplified employee pension plan? What is the contribution limitation?*
7. *What are ways to improve employee compensation?*
8. *How should small business owners conduct performance evaluations?*
9. *What is the purpose of an organization chart?*
10. *Why is the training function so vital to a small business?*

16

Computer Applications

Objectives

1. Learn the bookkeeping uses for a business personal computer.
2. Learn how the computer can be used as a communication tool.
3. Learn what hardware and software is available for the small business owner.

Key Terms

Cash receipts journal   Customer data base
Cash disbursements journal

Personal computers have become commonplace in small businesses during the past 10 years. Prices have fallen to the point of affordability for all but the smallest of business enterprises. They have given the entrepreneur an effective control and organization tool to better operate his or her business. PC's greatest use is as a bookkeeping tool freeing up time for the owner and cutting down the cost of accounting services.

Bookkeeping Systems

The basic bookkeeping chores for a small business are neither complicated nor time consuming. It is the owner's responsibility to either maintain or oversee the process of recording the financial activities of the business. Accountants should not be used for bookkeeping services—their fees are expensive and not in the best interest of the business. Entrepreneurs who use accountants to handle all financial tasks, including basic bookkeeping, are often out of touch with the financial status of the business, which can lead to decision-making errors. There are five parts to an accounting system which can be taken care of manually or with the help of a computer.

Cash Receipts

A simple entry into a computer or manual bookkeeping system is required to keep track of revenues received. Posted daily on a monthly ledger sheet, it should show monies received and deposited. Any adjustments as to what was actually received as opposed to what was reported such as refunds, shortages, or miscellaneous disbursements, must be reconciled. When totaled the cash receipts register shows the cash receipts collected and deposited for the month incurred.

Cash Disbursements

Keeping a record of cash disbursements is simply a detailed checking account register. All checks are recorded as to date, number, amount, to whom, and then classified in an expense category. In most computer software programs, expense classifications are designated by a number. By posting to the number, the business owner has an up-to-date record of how much has been expended to each type of expense. The disbursement journal is maintained daily and totaled monthly.

If the cash receipts and disbursement journals are posted correctly, the business owner has a monthly operating income statement with the push of a button on a personal computer. He or she will always be informed as to the financial condition of the operation.

Payroll

If a business employs more than three employees, doing payroll on a computer is a tremendous time-saving device. The computer will automatically calculate all deductions for taxes, social security, insurance, and any other money to be withheld. Some programs will even write the paychecks. At the same time, the computer will store a running year-to-date tabulation for all employees individually. Keeping a manual record of payroll activity requires posting to separate payroll sheets for each employee and can become quite laborious.

Accounts Payable

When an invoice arrives it should be posted to the accounts payable ledger. The posting will include date received, early pay discount information, net due date, and a running total as to all activity from the particular supplier. When the invoice is paid it should be posted as to date, check number, and any discrepancy to the amount owed. The computer will store the information by account number and also supply a running total as to total owed for all accounts.

The same records are kept for any notes payable. Notes payable records should show any interest paid and an up-to-date account of unpaid principal.

Accounts Receivable

If the business offers payment terms, a complete register must be maintained for each account showing amount owed, date due, and past performance of the account. A computer allows a quick referral to how much money is owed the business and is broken down into current versus past due amounts. The owner can keep track of any changes in account collection activity before a serious problem arises.

Capital Assets Ledger

The purchase of any fixed assets must be recorded separately in order to keep an accurate record for depreciation allowances. Posting capital asset purchases by date allows the item to be immediately calculated into depreciation expense deductions. An accountant can advise as to the most beneficial depreciation schedule to use. This can be entered into the computer memory. Once entered, the computer can easily calculate depreciation on an up-to-date monthly basis.

Perpetual Inventory

As discussed in Chap. 14, purchase decisions must be made in consideration of current and planned inventory levels. Since the owner cannot do a physical inventory on a regular basis, a system must be in place that tracks a perpetual inventory. Maintaining a sales versus purchase record on a daily basis and following a physical inventory provides this information. The type of business will dictate the complexity of this program depending on various inventory classifications. There are software programs available ranging from simple summary calculations to minute, item-by-item detail.

If the business maintains an accurate accounts payable, accounts receivable, capital assets and inventory ledgers, the computer can easily produce an operating balance sheet after bank statements are reconciled for available cash.

A computerized bookkeeping system is not intended to replace the use of an accountant. However it will cut down on the amount of time an accountant is used and will keep the owner adequately informed for decision-making purposes.

Using the Computer as a Communications Tool

There are many word processing software programs available to allow the business to look as professional as the larger organizations.

Correspondence

Letters and memos on attractive letterhead can be quickly produced and permanently stored in the computer for future reference. Direct mail letters to customers will look professional and can be produced at considerable savings as opposed to using secretarial or printing services. Since printers can make copies, the computer can serve as a copy machine for times when a limited number of copies are needed.

Presentations

Word processing software programs can create graphic illustrations to use for demonstrations and clarifications. The small business salesperson can be equipped with professional presentation packages when calling on clients. Graphs, curves, charts, in color or black and white, can be created quickly and professionally.

Advertising

The small business owner can create his or her camera ready advertisements with the proper software. Whether the ad is for newsprint reproduction or for a mail out flyer or announcement, many programs are equipped with art work and illustrations. Learning how to use this type of software allows the small business to create advertisements quickly for immediate distribution, as opposed to waiting for a printing service to complete the assignment.

Keeping a Customer Data Base

A very important key to the success of a business is keeping in touch with present and former customers. These are people that you have pleased in the past and can be more easily enticed to buy than new customers. They also represent your word of mouth referral advertising program. There must be a method of keeping in touch with them on a regular basis.

Many businesses will install a computer data base program that keeps a directory of former and future customer contacts. A data base program will store these references but also categorize them. The entrepreneur may retrieve the names alphabetically, by age, location, per capita income, or by any manner needed once properly entered into the computer. The same program will create mailing labels.

Keeping an up-to-date customer data base can be used to send regular newsletters or announcements to customers to keep them informed of what is new with your business. Maintaining a regular contact program insures good customer relations and promotes repeat sales.

Choosing Software
and Hardware

If the entrepreneur is starting fresh without previous purchased equipment, he or she should choose the most appropriate software first and then choose the hardware that best accommodates that software. The software choices are many.

Popular word processing programs that are compatible with most hardware include Word Perfect™, Micro Soft™, Wordstar™, and Multimate™. Quicken™ and Quick Books™ are popular compatible accounting software programs. Lotus 1-2-3™ is a financial spreadsheet program that will keep a cash flow analysis up to date. Keeping a complete customer listing can be done on a D Base™ system or Paradox™ software. There are many more good programs available that may or may not be compatible with various hardware manufacturers.

The hardware you choose does not have to be expensive. Many will find suitable used equipment at the fraction of the cost of newer computers quite satisfactory. The more expensive computers are faster and can handle more sophisticated programming, but may not be necessary for the start up business. The most well known names in personal computers include:

IBM and compatibles. There are many brands that are compatible with IBM and can handle appropriate application software.

Apple family computers, including Macintosh. Very popular in the education market, Apple also has software available for business.

Tandy. Radio Shack carries this full line of computers which includes IBM compatibles. Service is very convenient.

Commodore and Atari are commonly associated with computer games, but both also have business software available.

The buyer must also decide on an appropriate printer. The choice will be determined by price, compatibility with hardware, speed, and the appearance of output. Laser printers are the fastest and most professional, but are the most expensive.

The entrepreneur should take the time to shop around and buy for long-term usage. Local colleges and training companies and schools offer courses on computer training. It is a good idea to take theses courses before deciding on the software and hardware needs for your business.

Chapter Summary

Computers have become essential to many small businesses. They have made bookkeeping chores less time-consuming and more complete. The small business owner is able to have in easy reach a record of receipts, disbursements, accounts payable and receivable, payroll, inventory and capital acquisitions. The proper software programs allow up-to-date reports on the financial condition of the business and cuts down on accounting expenditures.

Computers are also invaluable as a communication tool. Word processing allows an efficient and professional means of correspondence and can be used to create advertisements, direct mail pieces, flyers, and newsletters. There is programming available that will keep a complete customer data base for the business owner.

Purchasing proper equipment should be carefully planned after reviewing the needs of the particular business. Choosing the software desired before deciding on the appropriate hardware is advisable when possible.

The Next Step

If you are not computer literate, take the courses available at local colleges or training companies on computer applications. You may wish to discuss your needs with a friend or computer instructor who has a solid computer background.

When you feel confident of your needs, shop computer stores for new, and classified newspaper ads for used, equipment to find the best bargain.

Review Questions

1. *How can a personal computer be used as a management control tool?*
2. *Name seven areas of a bookkeeping system that can be helped by the use of a computer.*
3. *How can a computer create an operating income statement and balance sheet?*
4. *Name the uses for a computer as a communications tool?*
5. *What is the purpose of a customer data base?*
6. *What are ways the business can keep in touch with its customers?*
7. *What software programs are available for financial record keeping?*
8. *What word processing software programs are available?*
9. *What does Lotus 1-2-3™ do?*
10. *Why should you decide on what software is needed before purchasing the hardware?*

17

Management Assistance

Objectives

1. Learn what professional services are available to small business owners.
2. Learn how to create an advisory board.
3. Understand the network of local, state, and federal agencies that have been created to assist small businesses.

Key Terms

Accountants
Attorneys
Financial planners
Chamber of commerce

Small business development centers
Small Business Administration
Department of Commerce

Being an entrepreneur means being self-reliant. A small business owner can sometimes feel isolated because he or she is the one at the head of the enterprise and making all the critical decisions. It is important to have a support system to help alleviate some of the tensions and to be sure there is input from others, before making major decisions. There is assistance available from the local business community and state and federal agencies.

Professional Services

Accountants, attorneys, financial planners, and insurance agents are readily available to help for a fee.

Accountants

Accountants are needed to advise the business owner in financial procedures and tax considerations. They should be used to:

1. Prepare tax reports that require adherence to tax procedure and regulation. There are some simple tax reports such as sales tax reports and employee withholding reports (Form 941), which the business owner can fill out with little knowledge of accounting procedures. However, annual income tax forms may require the use of an accountant to insure all reporting is properly done. In many cases, an accountant's knowledge of tax regulations will save the business owner money.

2. Prepare accurate financial statements for review by lending institutions or investors. The entrepreneur can use a computer to keep informal operating statements for the business on a monthly basis, but the accountant should prepare the more formal reports to insure accuracy and also to add credibility to the financial reports. Financial statements are normally reconciled on a quarterly basis.

3. Set up the initial bookkeeping system for the business operation. Using an accountant to establish the bookkeeping system allows the information to be easily transferred into the formal records of the operation.

4. To act as an advisor regarding major purchase and financing decisions.

An accountant should not be used as a bookkeeper. Some business owners become too dependent on their accountants. They ask the accountant to do all the financial recording of the business which causes delays, is expensive, and does not keep the owner abreast of the day-to-day financial status of the business. It is the entrepreneur's responsibility to stay on top of the financial matters of a business.

The choice to use a Certified Public Accountant (CPA), or an accounting service should be determined by the financial complexity of the business operation. If the business requires significant financing and has complicated tax reporting matters, the use of a CPA, although more expensive, will add credibility in the eyes of lending institutions, investors, and the Internal Revenue Service.

Attorneys

It is advisable to build a relationship with a competent lawyer. In most businesses, legal questions will, at least occasionally, surface. It is comforting to know that help is only a phone call away. Lawyers specialize in particular areas of the law. The small business owner should seek out an attorney well-versed in business and tax law.

A lawyer should be consulted in the start-up phases of a business to draw up a formal organization structure and to assist in reviewing legal documents such as leases and purchase contracts.

Financial Planner/Insurance Agents

Small business owners must prepare for the future, both business-wise and personally. A good financial planner can assist in choosing a retirement plan and other investment options. He or she can help plan business goals and expansion timetables with the proper use of business profits. Often financial planners are also insurance agents. If not, you will need the advice of a good insurance agent as well. Insurance and investment decisions are quite complex and you will need an individual with considerable experience to guide you. Take the time to interview several in order to find the person who can most competently take your situation into account.

Community Sources

Communities have agencies available to assist small business owners. The local Chamber of Commerce is such an organization. The role of the Chamber of Commerce is to assist and promote the community business sector. They do this by making information available to business owners, devising programs to assist in meeting other members of the business community, and offering educational programs. If the entrepreneur is starting a business that will be benefitted through an association with the community's business leaders, he or she should join the chamber and become active in its activities.

Many communities have economic development associations separate from the chamber of commerce. Often subsidized with community and or state funds, these organizations are charged with recruiting businesses into the community. They are an excellent source for demographic information and insight into the future growth patterns of the community. Since the leadership normally comes from the financial sector of the business community, economic development agencies can advise start-up businesses on the most active lending and investor groups.

Local colleges or vocational schools should be willing to assist small business owners with research and direction. The entrepreneur should inquire to staff and faculty personnel regarding business assistance and education programs. Many are now offering entrepreneurship programs of study.

The municipal and county government offices will be able to answer many legal questions regarding permits, licenses, and health and safety regulations. A trip to city hall or the county courthouse should be made early in the planning stages of the business start-up.

Business Advisory Committee

Many business owners have created an advisory board or committee to help them with business decisions. It is an excellent idea if properly comprised.

An effective advisory committee might include members from the professional and community groups just described—the business's accountant, attorney, financial planner, insurance agent, and associates from the Chamber of Commerce or economic development organizations. The idea is to bring this group together on an informal basis when important decisions must be made to seek opinions. Many advisory committees will operate as a round table discussion group, led by the entrepreneur seeking help. Direct questions demanding direct answers and opinions will reveal information to be taken into consideration before making decisions. If the business owner is open and honest about the business, this can be an extremely effective resource. Often the cost to the entrepreneur for this invaluable source of information is only picking up the dinner and drink tab at a local restaurant's meeting room. Even if some advisers request monetary compensation for their time, it is money well spent.

State Sources

The state government has a system of resources to promote and assist business development. Most of these sources are free.

Small Business Development Centers

SBDC offices are in all states. They are funded by state and federal tax dollars and are directed by SBA and state university personnel. They offer, at no charge, one-on-one counseling services and low-cost seminar training. You will normally find them located on college campuses.

The typical SBDC office will have trained personnel to assist in business financing, management, marketing and international trade decisions. They will help you in writing your business plan, making loan applications, and explaining legal requirements. Since there is no charge for these services, an appointment with them should be a must.

Examples of the type of seminars SBDCs offer include:

How to Start a New Business

Developing a Business Plan

Legal Aspects of Owning a Business

Bookkeeping for Small Business

Business Use of the Home

Preparing Loan Proposals

Computer Courses

Small Business Exporting and Importing

Understanding Business Tax Reporting

These and many other topics are designed for the aspiring as well as the experienced business owner, and should be part of the entrepreneur's agenda.

Other State Agencies

There are a number of agencies in each state that have been created to spur economic development. Normally, they are coordinated through the Department of Development. They promote the state to out-of-state industries and businesses, and encourage business expansion and start-ups. They provide information regarding labor supply, taxes, markets, and locations. Often they provide job training programs and will give direction as to any financial assistance available through the state. Divisions include Minority Business Development, International Trade, Community Development, Energy, and Marketing and Research.

Also assistance and information is available through The Workers' Compensation Board, the Department of Agriculture and Consumer Protection, State Sales and Use Tax Division, the Department of Labor, the Department of Transportation, and the Office of the Secretary of State.

Federal Assistance

Small Business Administration

There are more than 100 Small Business Administration offices through-out the United States. The SBA was created to assist small businesses development, which in turn creates more jobs and increases federal tax revenues. In addition to supporting the Small Business Development Center program, the SBA:

Helps small businesses secure government contracts.

Acts as a special advocate to small businesses with other federal, state, and private agencies.

Provides financing assistance through the SBA loan program.

Provides no charge counseling services through the Service

Corps of Retired Executives (SCORE).

Publishes information brochures and videotapes available to small business owners at nominal fees.

Other Federal Agencies .

The United States Department of Commerce promotes economic growth, international trade, and technology development through the following bureaus:

The Census Bureau provides statistical demographic information to small business owners.

The Office of Business Liaison serves as the coordinator for all commu-nication between the Department of Commerce and the business community.

The Office of Small and Disadvantaged Business Utilization provides assistance to minority owned and disadvantaged businesses in securing government and private contracts.

The Economic Development Administration is the federal agency charged with providing economic stimulus for business development. It supports state development agencies and also provides loan guarantees for businesses meeting certain criteria in regards to economic development.

The Bureau of Economic Analysis provides published economic statis-tical information to give business owners and managers current eco-nomic analysis.

The International Trade Administration has 47 district offices and 21 branch offices throughout the country to assist businesses in engaging in international trade.

The Federal Trade Commission oversees business activity to insure fairness. It monitors advertising, unfair pricing tactics, credit reporting, fair competition, and generally acts as the government watchdog to protect the small business owner.

The Internal Revenue Service, in addition to collecting taxes, provides assistance to small business owners in understanding tax laws and reporting procedures.

Chapter Summary

The entrepreneur should become familiar with the many avenues available for assistance, locally and through state and federal agencies.

Small business owners should build relationships with an accountant, an attorney, a financial planner, and an insurance agent. Many small businesses create an advisory board of professionals and industry members to assist them in decision making.

There are numerous organizations and government agencies to call on for help. Locally, there is the Chamber of Commerce, colleges, and county government offices. There is also assistance at the state level and federal level including the Small Business Administration.

The Next Step

Visit with accountants, attorneys, financial planners, and insurance agents to find those who are most knowledgeable about your type of business activity. Consider the idea of creating an advisory board and inquire as to potential member availability.

Take the time to learn about local, state, and federal offices that might assist you and where they are located. Start a directory of assistance sources.

Review Questions

1. *What professional services are available to small business owners?*
2. *How should you use an accountant?*
3. *Why do you need a financial planner?*

4. *What is the purpose, and how should you create, an advisory board?*
5. *What is the purpose of a Chamber of Commerce?*
6. *Where is the closest Small Business Development Center?*
7. *What other state agencies can assist entrepreneurs?*
8. *What help is available from the Small Business Administration?*
9. *Describe the various offices of the United States Department of Commerce.*
10. *What is the purpose of the International Trade Administration?*

Part 4 Case Study—
A Problem with Control

Alan Reynolds realized that he had a serious cash flow problem. He was dumbfounded for an answer. Business couldn't be better, but financially he was in desperate states.

He had started his linen supply distribution company three months ago and demand had overwhelmed him. After visiting with potential customers, he launched his business and immediately received orders far surpassing his projections. The first month's sales had been $100,000, followed by $105,000 for the second, and $111,000 for the third. He was increasing orders 5 percent per month and as far as he could tell this trend would continue for the next 12 months. Getting the sales had been easy, collecting the bills had been like pulling teeth.

The business operated on a very low gross profit margin of 20 percent after paying suppliers. The operating expenses were fixed at $20,000 per month. The first month's sales were break even:

Sales	$100,000
Cost of goods	– 80,000
Gross profit	20,000
Operating expenses	– 20,000
Net operating profit	0

Alan had invested and financed the $100,000 to cover the first month's supplies and operation.

The suppliers he purchased from demanded immediate payment since he was new. The problems were arising because he was offering 30 day terms to his customers, the industry norm. This meant paying for supplies before receiving customer payment. The problem was further exasperated because two thirds of his accounts were paying late. The collection pattern was running 33 percent for 30 days from delivery, 33 percent for 60 days, 33 percent for 90 days, 1 percent possibly noncollectable.

Looking at the cash flow for months 2, 3, and projected 4 showed the following:

	Month 2	Month 3	Month 4
Beginning cash balance	0	$ 71,000	$– 103,000
Sales	$105,000	111,000	117,000
Supplies (80%)	– 84,000	– 89,000	– 94,000
Receipts	33,000	67,000	107,000
Operating expense	– 20,000	– 20,000	– 20,000
End cash balance	– 71,000	–103,000	–110,000

He had already used every means he could think of to carry the deficit and now was faced with the very real prospect of having to close the doors despite a booming business.

He had tried to borrow more money to get over the hump but the banker quickly pointed out that borrowing money was only a short-term solution. As long as the business continued its growth rate, it would continually have to pay out more each month for the necessary goods. If receipts were in line with sales this was a very promising business:

Sales	$117,000
Receipts	117,000
Cost of goods	– 94,000
Operating expense	– 20,000
Monthly profit	$ 3,000

In its present position, the more orders received meant a bigger deficit in operation. Alan had to come up with a solution.

Case Questions

1. How could Alan have predicted the problem in his business plan?
2. What suggestions can you give Alan now?
3. What management control tools should be used once a solution is achieved?

PART 5

Legal Considerations

Every social activity, every human enterprise requiring people to act in concert, is impeded when people aren't honest with one another.
WILLIAM J. BENNETT, *The Book of Virtues,* Simon & Schuster, 1993

18

Choosing the Form of Ownership

Objectives

1. Learn the advantages and disadvantages of a sole proprietorship.
2. Learn the advantages and disadvantages of a partnership.
3. Learn the advantages and disadvantages of being a corporation.
4. Learn the procedures to follow in forming business ownership.
5. Understand the tax considerations of the different types of ownership.

Key Terms

Sole proprietorship   Corporation
Partnership   Subchapter S corporation
Limited partnership   Articles of incorporation
Articles of partnership

Business ownership can take the form of a sole proprietorship, partnership, or corporation. Each structure has its advantages and disadvantages and must be studied closely to make sure its features are compatible with your type of business activity.

Sole Proprietorship

The simplest way to start a business is by declaring yourself to be a sole proprietor. As a sole proprietor, the individual will "be doing business as" whatever name is chosen for the business entity (i.e., John Jones doing business as (dba) The Soda Shop). The proprietor is totally responsible for all business transactions. Sole proprietors use their social security number as their taxpayer identification, if there are no employees, or receive an employer's identification number from the IRS if they have a payroll.

Advantages of a Sole Proprietorship

The sole proprietor has total control and responsibility of the enterprise. He or she has the rights to all profits or is responsible for any losses. During the formation stages there are usually tax advantages that can be taken personally. These will be discussed later in the chapter. There is little cost or administrative detail attached to a proprietorship. There is also no arguing with partners on questions which helps quicken the decision-making process.

Disadvantages of the Sole Proprietorship

Being alone means operating with only one person's expertise and pocketbook. The business will be dependent on the knowledge and experience of one, instead of many, in making decisions. The money to start the business comes from only one source as well. Loan collateral will be dependent on the assets of one individual. Since the business is dependent on the efforts and management of one, it will cease to exist in the event of death or disability.

Of greatest concern is that the sole proprietor is personally liable for any adverse business transactions. In the event of business failure or legal action brought against the business, the individual is exposed to great risk. Since he or she is "doing business as," all transactions are performed with the proprietor's personal guarantee. If there are losses, they must be accounted for by the individual whether from the assets of the business or from personal belongings. If there is a legal suit, the plaintiff will sue the proprietor as an individual, not a business. Because the owner has unlimited liability, he or she is at risk of losing all personal assets in the event of a catastrophic adverse legal judgment. Many sole proprietors carry excess personal liability insurance to help alleviate some of the anxiety associated with unlimited liability.

Procedure to Start a Sole Proprietorship

The individual applies for the occupational business license in the community where the business is located. If the business is to operate under a fictitious name that does not identify the owner, the proprietor must have a fictitious name statement published in the local newspaper to identify who is responsible for the activities of the business. In most localities the license is granted immediately and the individual can commence business as soon as approved. If the business does not have a payroll, the owner uses his or her social security number for identification. If the proprietor employs others, he or she should request an employer identification number from the IRS. A married couple can share a proprietorship if they file a joint tax return.

Partnerships

General partnerships are created when two or more individuals join together to conduct business and share proportionately in the responsibilities, risks, and profits and losses incurred.

Advantages of a Partnership

Two or more heads are better than one, two or more personal financial statements have more strength than one. Partnerships are formed to add technical competence and as a way to raise money. They can also protect the business from dissolving in the event that one partner becomes incapacitated or dies. Income or losses from a partnership are treated for tax purposes in the same manner as the proprietorship, therefore, there can be some tax advantages during its formative years.

Disadvantages of Partnerships

Partnerships spread control which can create problems. There can be serious disagreements which can threaten the existence of the business. Often partnerships created from friendship destroy the friendship as well as the business. The entrepreneur must undergo serious consideration before taking a partner as control is normally a very important satisfier to the entrepreneur.

General partners are personally liable for all transactions of the business and run the same unlimited liability risk as proprietors in the event of business failure or catastrophic legal judgments.

Limited Partners

A general partner may elect to take a limited partner. A limited partner is strictly an investor in the partnership. As such he or she has no voice in the management of the business and shares no liability outside of the money invested in the partnership. A limited partner cannot be sued personally for actions of the partnership, only the general partners. Taking a limited partner is a method of raising capital without giving up control.

The only two reasons partnerships should be considered are to either raise capital or add a technical skill that the entrepreneur is missing. It is not advisable to create a partnership in order to simply share responsibility or add a colleague.

Procedure to Start a Partnership

Creating a partnership is more difficult than a proprietorship. The business must register as a partnership with the Internal Revenue Service in order to receive a partnership identification number. The partnership must file a separate income tax return stating profits or losses and how they have been appropriated. The tax return must also show a balance sheet listing assets, liabilities, and partners' equity.

A partnership should also draw up an Articles of Partnership to define all participants contributions, responsibilities, and restrictions. An Articles of Partnership is not legally required, however, if not written there will surely be problems down the road. Figure 18.1 illustrates what should be included in an Articles of Partnership.

Incorporating

By incorporating your business, you will create a separate entity from yourself. The entity you create will have all the business entitlement as you, however, you will become an employee and stockholder, as opposed to a personal owner. The corporation can buy, sell, enter contracts, sue, and be sued. It is responsible for its business activities.

Advantages of Incorporating

Since the corporation is a separate entity, the owner(s) or stockholders, are not personally liable for its decisions and actions. They are granted limited liability. If the corporation fails or is held liable for any judgments from a suit, the corporation is responsible, not the owners. The owners can only lose their financial interests and investment in the business, but not their personal assets. This is the foremost reason for deciding to incorporate—to protect the personal assets of the owners from legal judgments against the business. It acts as a form of insurance. It is not 100 percent perfect as owners can be found to be personally negligent in carrying out business transactions and be named in a suit. It also does not protect against tax claims of the IRS.

Articles of Partnership

- Date of the formation of the partnership.
- Names and addresses of all partners.
- Statement of the business purpose.
- The amount and type of capital invested by each partner.
- The sharing ratios of all profits and losses, including any salary arrangements for working versus non-working partners.
- Provision for the distribution of assets at the time of dissolution. This should be set on an equal basis as to the amount invested. Any personal considerations (such as property on loan from any partner) should be listed separately.
- The specific responsibilities of each partner.
- Any preset conditions to be followed by the partners. This would include any restraints, such as any disbursements, checks or notes that must be endorsed by all partners.
- A provision for the voluntary or involuntary premature withdrawal of any partner. This should specify the responsibilities of the partnership to any partner who wishes to drop out to pursue other interests or the responsibilities involved with terminating a partner.
- Settlement provisions in the event of the death or disability of any partner. This should include a buy sell agreement, normally funded with business life insurance, in amounts equal to the interest of each partner. This assures the survivorship of the business and satisfies the demands of the deceased's estate. Ideally, the agreement should be drawn up by an attorney, signed by all parties, and put in a place for safekeeping.

Figure 18.1. Articles of partnership.

Disadvantages of Incorporating

It costs money to incorporate and requires more paperwork. A small business with limited investors and a simple investment plan can incorporate themselves and save money. The actual cost of incorporating in most states is under $200 and not a difficult procedure. Larger groups of investors with a more complex investment plan should use an attorney to incorporate which will normally cost $500 to $1000.

There is also more reporting for a corporation. The corporation files a separate income tax form which is more complicated than filing for a proprietorship or partnership. In addition the state in which you incorporate will require an annual declaration of stockholders and directors report. There are some tax advantages and disadvantages to incorporating which will be discussed later in the chapter.

Subchapter S Corporations

Smaller corporations may file as subchapter S corporations as long as there are less than 35 investors. This classification of corporations was created to allow small and family-owned businesses to receive the limited liability characteristic of a corporation and at the same time maintain the tax status of a proprietorship or partnership. For some it is the best of both arrangements. This combination gives the smaller corporation some of the rights of a regular corporation, but also has some restrictions as to certain tax deductions to be discussed.

Procedure to Form a Corporation

A business must be incorporated in the state in which it originates. An instruction package should be available at the Office of the Secretary of State. In most states, the following procedure is required:

1. *Name reservation.* The state must approve the name of the corporation to assure that it is not being used by another corporation within the state. Often this can be checked out over the telephone and, if the name is available, it can be reserved until all paperwork is handed in.

2. *You must file an Articles of Incorporation.* Figures 18.2 and 18.3 illustrate what must be included.

The purpose of the Articles of Incorporation is to be correctly registered with the state. It informs who is responsible for the corporation, the location of the business, the business activity planned, and the amount of stock the corporation is authorized to issue. In requesting stock authorization, it is advisable to request a large number. What is important is the amount of stock issued, not the amount authorized. You may issue 100 shares of stock, although authorized for 10,000. The issued stock determines the ownership—the number authorized is strictly for state registration purposes. By requesting a large number of authorized stock the corporation is prepared to issue more stock in the future, if desired, without the approval of the state.

The individual acting as the agent for the corporation is usually the original owner or his or her attorney. The corporation must designate a President and a Treasurer. The Treasurer must be on record with the state as the individual responsible for the financial and administrative report-

PROFIT

THIS IS NOT A FORM. USE ONLY AS A GUIDE.

SAMPLE FORMAT
(Please Type)

ARTICLES OF INCORPORATION

OF

_____

I.

The name of the corporation is " _____ ".

II.
The corporation is organized pursuant to the provisions of the Georgia Business Corporation Code.

III.

The corporation shall have perpetual duration.

IV.

The corporation is a corporation for profit and is organized for the following purposes:
(state the specific purpose for which the corporation will be organized and include the below general purpose clause)
to engage in any lawful business or activities related thereto; and to engage in any lawful act or actitivity for which corporations may be organized under the Georgia Corporation Code.

V.

The corporation shall have authority, acting by its board of directors, to issue not more than _____ shares of a common class having a par value of $ _____ per share. (If the shares are to be without par value, then state no par value.)

VI.

The corporation shall not commence business until it shall have received consideration of not less than $500 in value for the issuance of its shares.

VII.

The shareholders of the corporation shall not have any preemptive rights to acquire any unissued shares of the corporation. (Preemptive rights may be limited or denied.)

VIII.

The address of the initial registered office of the corporation is _____ ,
and the initial registered agent of the corporation at such address is _____ .
(Include street and number, city, county, state and zip code.)

IX.

The initial board of directors shall consist of (number) of member(s), the name and address of each of which is as follows:

X.

The name and address of the incorporator(s) is:
IN WITNESS WHEREOF, the undersigned incorporator has executed these Articles of Incorporation.

This _____ day of _____ , 19 ___.   _____
                                                  (Name of Incorporator or Representative)

*In addition to all of the above which are required statements, the articles of incorporation may, as a matter of election, set forth:

(1) Any provision, not inconsistent with law, for the regulation of the internal affairs of the corporation or for the restriction of the transfer of shares; and
(2) Any provision which under this Code is required or permitted to be set forth in the bylaws; any such provision set forth in the articles of incorporation need not be set forth in the bylaws.
It shall not be necessary to set forth in the articles of incorporation any of the corporate powers enumerated in section 14-2-21 of the Georgia Corporation Code.

*NOTE: Do not include this language in your articles. These are merely notes for further suggested articles which may be included.

FL-Corp.14
7/83

Figure 18.2. Articles of incorporation for profit producing corporations.

NONPROFIT   NONPROFIT

THIS IS NOT A FORM. USE ONLY AS A GUIDE.
(Please Type)

SAMPLE FORMAT

ARTICLES OF INCORPORATION

OF

_____

I.

The name of the corporation is " _____ ".

II.

The corporation is organized pursuant to the provisions of the Georgia Non-Profit Corporation Code.

III.

The corporation shall have perpetual duration.

IV.

The corporation is a non-profit corporation and is organized for the following purposes:
(state the specific purposes for which the corporation will be organized and include the general purpose clause, shown below) to engage in any lawful business or activities related thereto; and to engage in any lawful act or activity for which corporations may be organized under the Georgia Non-Profit Corporation Code.

V.

State the manner in which the directors shall be elected or appointed. In lieu thereof, the articles of incorporation may provide that the method of election of directors be left to the bylaws.

VI.

State any provision, not inconsistent with the Corporation Code or with any other law, limiting in any manner the corporate powers conferred by this Code.

VII.

The address of the initial registered office of the corporation is _____ , and the initial registered agent of the corporation at such address is _____ . (Include street and number, city, county and zip code.

VIII.

The initial board of directors shall consist of three members, the name and address of each of which is as follows:

IX.

The name and address of the incorporator(s) is:
IN WITNESS WHEREOF, the undersigned incorporator(s) has (have) executed these Articles of Incorporation this

_____ day of _____ , 19___ .   _____
                                                          (Name of Incorporator or Representative)

The articles of incorporation may, as a matter of election, also set forth:

(1) Any provisions, not inconsistent with law, for the regulation of the internal affairs of the corporation, including, without limitation, provisions with respect to the relative rights or interest of the members as among themselves or in the property of the corporation; the manner of termination of membership in the corporation; the rights, upon such termination, of the corporation, the terminated member and the remaining members; the transferability or nontransferability of membership; and the distribution of assets on dissolution or final liquidation,

(2) If the corporation is to have one or more classes of members, any provision designating the class or classes of members and stating the qualifications and rights of the members of each class.

(3) The names of any persons or the designations of any groups of persons who are to be the initial members.

(4) A provision to the effect that the corporation shall be subordinate to and subject to the authority of any head or national association, lodge, order, beneficial association, fraternal or beneficial society, foundation, federation or other nonprofit corporation, society, organization or association.

(5) Any provision which under the Corporation Code is required or permitted to be set forth in the bylaws; any such provision set forth in the articles of incorporation need not be set forth in the bylaws.

It shall not be necessary to set forth in the articles of incorporation any of the corporate powers enumerated in Section 14-3-21, Official Code of Georgia Annotated.

Figure 18.3. _Articles of incorporation for nonprofit corporation._

ing of the corporation. For family-held corporations, this may be the spouse of the agent who incorporates.

"Par value of stock" is an antiquated expression that has nothing to do with the perceived or actual value of the stock. Many will state a $1 par value to meet the form requirements. The actual value of stock is based on what people are willing to pay for it.

Just as in the New York or American Stock Exchanges, investors buy stock based on how they believe the company will perform, not on its asset value. Buying and selling stock is determined by supply and demand.

3. *Publication.* All new corporation formations are published in the local newspaper where they reside. The Secretary of State Office will inform you in which paper you will need to publish the corporation announcement as to its purpose, name, and those responsible for carrying out its activities.

4. *The corporation must declare a minimum of $500 of assets.* Although this is all that is required legally to incorporate, the stockholders should draw up and sign a Stockholders Agreement. The Stockholders Agreement is the same as an Articles of Partnership in that it spells out responsibilities and contingency and preformation agreements between the stockholders.

The decision as to whether to operate as a regular or sub chapter S corporation can be declared at the time that you file your initial income tax report. A letter should be included to the IRS with the form and a copy of the letter sent to the Secretary of State where incorporated.

Tax Considerations

Each form of ownership has different tax considerations.

Sole Proprietorship

The sole proprietorship has a very simple tax reporting procedure. The proprietorship attaches a Schedule C to his or her annual 1040 income tax report. The Schedule C is simply a profit and loss statement of business activity. The profit or loss reported is then listed on the Form 1040 as other income from business activity and the taxes are calculated. If a profit, the tax filer must also calculate self-employment taxes in addition to income taxes. The self-employment tax is your social security contribution.

Because a sole proprietor reports all income as personal income, he or she is allowed to take any business deductions personally as well. This can be advantageous to new businesses as certain deductions which are allowed for a business, such as depreciation, will act as personal deductions. For example, the net operating profit of a business might be $30,000, however if the business is entitled to a $10,000 depreciation allowance for use of capital assets, the net profit reported by the owner for tax purposes is $20,000. There are also new investment tax credits available to stimulate business start ups and expansion. The sole proprietor is entitled to take these on a personal basis which in many cases creates a sizable tax savings.

Partnerships

Partnerships income is taxed in the same manner as proprietor income. The partners report their share of business income on a separate line on the 1040. Instead of a Schedule C, the partnership must file a separate Partnership Income Form. This form is more complicated than the Schedule C as it requires an annual reconciliation as to the statement of condition of the business. The IRS wants to know any change in the asset or liability status of the business. Partnership tax forms require a balance sheet report to show the respective investment of all partners. In a partnership, all income or losses are reported in the calendar year of activity, therefore, all depreciation allowances and investment tax credits are deducted against the partners share of net income or losses.

Corporations

The sub chapter S corporation reports income for tax purpose differently than a regular C corporation. A sub chapter S corporation's income or losses are treated the same as a proprietorship or partnership. All profits or losses must be declared and distributed to stockholders in the year in which incurred. There is no provision for deferring taxes on retained earnings. Stockholders declare all earnings either as salary or dividends and the corporation does not pay corporate taxes since all activity is reported through the owners.

The regular corporation pays income taxes separately from owners on profits before dividends. Working owners pay taxes on their salaries and on dividends distributed from corporate profits causing a form of double taxation. The corporate tax rate is presently higher than the individual rate.

However, a regular corporation has more freedom as to how it can use its monies for tax deductible expenses. A corporation can pay the insurance premiums for its employees, including the owner, and take it as a deductible expense. The corporation can deduct greater pension plan contributions for its employees. The corporation may carryover some accrued income and expenses to another tax year and better protect its retained earnings. As a business grows there are more tax reasons to consider converting to a regular corporation.

In making the decision as to form of ownership, the entrepreneur should talk to his or her accountant, attorney, and financial advisor as to how current tax laws can affect the decision.

Chapter Summary

The legal form of ownership of a business should be decided in consideration of liability and tax factors. The sole proprietorship is the simplest form of ownership, is easy to start, and may have some initial tax advantages. However, the owner has unlimited liability and can lose personal assets in the event of a catastrophe.

Partnerships can often turn sour if formed for the wrong reasons. They have the same tax status and unlimited liability factors of the proprietorship, but they must report income, assets, and liabilities on a separate Partnership Tax Form. Some will elect to take a limited partner to raise capital. Limited partners have no voice in the business management and have no personal liability outside of their investment.

Forming a corporation is more difficult and more expensive than starting a proprietorship or partnership, however, it has the advantage of limited liability on the part of the owner. Since a corporation is a separate legal entity, it is legally responsible for its activities and not the owners. Although corporate tax rates are higher than individual rates, there may be tax advantages particularly for the established business operation.

Many small corporations elect to be classified as a sub chapter S corporation which offers the limited liability features of the corporation and the tax reporting basis of the proprietorship or partnership.

The Next Step

Take your pro forma financial statements to an accountant, attorney, or financial advisor to gain their input on the type of legal form of ownership you should choose. Also visit an insurance agent to explain any liability fears you may have in regards to business operations. The insurance agent can discuss various coverages available and warn you of potential dangers in operating your business.

Review Questions

1. *What are the advantages and disadvantages of being a sole proprietor?*

2. *How do you form a sole proprietorship?*

3. *What are the advantages and disadvantages of forming a partnership?*

4. *What is an Articles of Partnership?*

5. *What is a limited partner?*

6. *What are the advantages and disadvantages of incorporating?*

7. *What is limited liability?*

8. *What are the Articles of Incorporation?*

9. *How do you incorporate?*

10. *What is a subchapter S corporation?*

11. *What requirements must be met to qualify to be a subchapter S corporation?*

12. *How does a sole proprietor report his or her income taxes?*

13. *How does a partnership report income or losses?*

14. *How are subchapter S profits taxed as opposed to a regular corporation?*

15. *What tax advantages and disadvantages belong to a regular corporation?*

19

Legal Responsibilities

Objectives

1. Understand the legal reporting responsibilities of a business owner to the Internal Revenue Service.
2. Learn the importance of understanding contracts.
3. Learn the legal implications involved with property acquisition.

Key Terms

STEP

Contract

Real property

Warranty deed

Quitclaim deed

Joint tenancy

Entirety tenancy

Common tenancy

Although the entrepreneur acts independently and is free from supervision, he or she must conduct business being aware of legal responsibilities. Three common legal grounds for all commercial activities are tax laws, contracts, and property acquisition.

Tax Laws

In addition to having access to a good accountant or tax attorney, the entrepreneur should take the time to learn his/her tax responsibilities. In the end, it is the business owner who is responsible for adherence to tax laws, not the accountant or attorney. Failure to comply with tax reporting regulations will be very costly and, in severe cases, can cost the entrepreneur his or her business. The IRS conducts no charge tax education seminars, The Small Business Taxpayers Education Program (STEP) is offered to business owners through the Small Business Development Centers and SBA offices. The program consists of eight, two-hour modules of instruction covering:

1. Business assets—depreciation and selling depreciated property.
2. Business use of the home.
3. Employment taxes and excise taxes.
4. Starting a business—recordkeeping.
5. Schedule C, Schedule SE, and Form 1040.
6. Self-employed retirement plans.
7. The small business as a partnership.
8. Tip reporting and allocation.

It is also recommended that entrepreneurs add an official tax code manual to their libraries. Learning where to look for tax questions can save money paid to an accountant.

Income Taxes

All commercial activity must be reported to the IRS annually, whether there are profits or not. As discussed, the sole proprietor attaches a Schedule C income statement to his or her personal 1040 Form. The partnership files a U.S. Partnership Return of Income or Form 1065. A sub chapter S corporation files form 1120S, and a regular corporation files Form 1120. (See Figs. 19.1 and 19.2) If the proper form is not filed, or is late, the entrepreneur is in violation of tax laws and can be charged severe late filing penalties plus accrued interest charges. If found guilty of avoiding tax payments, the business owner can be convicted of tax evasion and is subject to imprisonment.

Self-Employment Taxes

As a business owner, you must pay 15.3 percent of any profits received from business activity into your social security account. If you are a proprietorship, partnership, or sub chapter S corporation you must file a self-employment tax form (Form SE) with your annual income tax to report your contribution. If the business is incorporated and you are an employee,

SCHEDULE C
(Form 1040)

Department of the Treasury
Internal Revenue Service ⊳ (T)

Profit or Loss From Business
(Sole Proprietorship)

▶ Partnerships, joint ventures, etc., must file Form 1065.

▶ Attach to Form 1040 or Form 1041. ▶ See Instructions for Schedule C (Form 1040).

OMB No. 1545-0074

1993

Attachment
Sequence No. 09

Name of proprietor

Social security number (SSN)

A Principal business or profession, including product or service (see page C-1)

B Enter principal business code
(from page 2) ▶

C Business name

D Employer ID number (Not SSN)

E Business address (including suite or room no.) ▶ ....
City, town or post office, state, and ZIP code

F Accounting method: (1) ☐ Cash (2) ☐ Accrual (3) ☐ Other (specify) ▶ ....

G Method(s) used to value closing inventory: (1) ☐ Cost (2) ☐ Lower of cost or market (3) ☐ Other (attach explanation) (4) ☐ Does not apply (if checked, skip line H) — Yes No

H Was there any change in determining quantities, costs, or valuations between opening and closing inventory? If "Yes," attach explanation

I Did you "materially participate" in the operation of this business during 1992? If "No," see page C-2 for limitations on losses

J Was this business in operation at the end of 1992?

K How many months was this business in operation during 1992? .... ▶

L If this is the first Schedule C filed for this business, check here .... ▶ ☐

Part I Income

1 Gross receipts or sales. Caution: If this income was reported to you on Form W-2 and the "Statutory employee" box on that form was checked, see page C-2 and check here ▶ ☐ | 1
2 Returns and allowances | 2
3 Subtract line 2 from line 1 | 3
4 Cost of goods sold (from line 40 on page 2) | 4
5 Gross profit. Subtract line 4 from line 3 | 5
6 Other income, including Federal and state gasoline or fuel tax credit or refund (see page C-2) | 6
7 Gross income. Add lines 5 and 6 | 7

Part II Expenses (Caution: Do not enter expenses for business use of your home on lines 8–27. Instead, see line 30.)

8 Advertising | 8
9 Bad debts from sales or services (see page C-3) | 9
10 Car and truck expenses (see page C-3—also attach Form 4562) | 10
11 Commissions and fees | 11
12 Depletion | 12
13 Depreciation and section 179 expense deduction (not included in Part III) (see page C-3) | 13
14 Employee benefit programs (other than on line 19) | 14
15 Insurance (other than health) | 15
16 Interest:
a Mortgage (paid to banks, etc.) | 16a
b Other | 16b
17 Legal and professional services | 17
18 Office expense | 18
19 Pension and profit-sharing plans | 19
20 Rent or lease (see page C-4):
a Vehicles, machinery, and equipment | 20a
b Other business property | 20b

21 Repairs and maintenance | 21
22 Supplies (not included in Part III) | 22
23 Taxes and licenses | 23
24 Travel, meals, and entertainment:
a Travel | 24a
b Meals and entertainment
c Enter 20% of line 24b subject to limitations (see page C-4)
d Subtract line 24c from line 24b | 24d
25 Utilities | 25
26 Wages (less jobs credit) | 26
27a Other expenses (list type and amount): ....
....
....
....
27b Total other expenses | 27b

28 Total expenses before expenses for business use of home. Add lines 8 through 27b in columns ▶ | 28
29 Tentative profit (loss). Subtract line 28 from line 7 | 29
30 Expenses for business use of your home. Attach Form 8829 | 30
31 Net profit or (loss). Subtract line 30 from line 29. If a profit, enter here and on Form 1040, line 12. Also, enter the net profit on Schedule SE, line 2 (statutory employees, see page C-5). If a loss, you MUST go on to line 32 (fiduciaries, see page C-5) | 31
32 If you have a loss, you MUST check the box that describes your investment in this activity (see page C-5). If you checked 32a, enter the loss on Form 1040, line 12, and Schedule SE, line 2 (statutory employees, see page C-5). If you checked 32b, you MUST attach Form 6198. | 32a ☐ All investment is at risk. | 32b ☐ Some investment is not at risk.

Cat. No. 11334P

Schedule C (Form 1040) 1992

33

Figure 19.1. Schedule C.

Form **1120**		U.S. Corporation Income Tax Return		OMB No. 1545-0123
Department of the Treasury Internal Revenue Service		For calendar year 1992 or tax year beginning .... , 1992, ending .... , 19 ... ▶ Instructions are separate. See page 1 for Paperwork Reduction Act Notice.		**1992**

A Check if a:
(1) Consolidated return (attach Form 851) ☐
(2) Personal holding co. (attach Sch. PH) ☐
(3) Personal service corp. (as defined in Temporary Regs. sec. 1.441-4T— see instructions) ☐

Use IRS label. Otherwise, please print or type.

Name

Number, street, and room or suite no. (If a P.O. box, see page 6 of instructions.)

City or town, state, and ZIP code

B Employer identification number

C Date incorporated

D Total assets (see Specific Instructions) $

E Check applicable boxes: (1) ☐ Initial return (2) ☐ Final return (3) ☐ Change in address

Income

1a	Gross receipts or sales [____] b Less returns and allowances [____] c Bal ▶	1c	
2	Cost of goods sold (Schedule A, line 8)	2	
3	Gross profit. Subtract line 2 from line 1c	3	
4	Dividends (Schedule C, line 19)	4	
5	Interest	5	
6	Gross rents	6	
7	Gross royalties	7	
8	Capital gain net income (attach Schedule D (Form 1120))	8	
9	Net gain or (loss) from Form 4797, Part II, line 20 (attach Form 4797) . .	9	
10	Other income (see instructions—attach schedule) . . . . ▶	10	
11	Total income. Add lines 3 through 10 . . . . ▶	11	

Deductions (See instructions for limitations on deductions.)

12	Compensation of officers (Schedule E, line 4).	12	
13a	Salaries and wages [____] b Less jobs credit [____] c Balance ▶	13c	
14	Repairs	14	
15	Bad debts	15	
16	Rents	16	
17	Taxes	17	
18	Interest	18	
19	Charitable contributions (see instructions for 10% limitation)	19	
20	Depreciation (attach Form 4562)	20		
21	Less depreciation claimed on Schedule A and elsewhere on return . . .	21a	21b	
22	Depletion	22	
23	Advertising	23	
24	Pension, profit-sharing, etc., plans	24	
25	Employee benefit programs	25	
26	Other deductions (attach schedule)	26	
27	Total deductions. Add lines 12 through 26 . . . . ▶	27	
28	Taxable income before net operating loss deduction and special deductions. Subtract line 27 from line 11	28	
29	Less: a Net operating loss deduction (see instructions)	29a		
	b Special deductions (Schedule C, line 20)	29b	29c	

Tax and Payments

30	Taxable income. Subtract line 29c from line 28	30	
31	Total tax (Schedule J, line 10)	31	
32	Payments: a 1991 overpayment credited to 1992 [32a]		
b	1992 estimated tax payments . . [32b]		
c	Less 1992 refund applied for on Form 4466 [32c]	(d Bal ▶ [32d]	
e	Tax deposited with Form 7004 . . . . [32e]		
f	Credit from regulated investment companies (attach Form 2439) . . . [32f]		
g	Credit for Federal tax on fuels (attach Form 4136). See instructions . [32g]	32h	
33	Estimated tax penalty (see instructions). Check if Form 2220 is attached . . . . . . ▶ ☐	33	
34	Tax due. If line 32h is smaller than the total of lines 31 and 33, enter amount owed	34	
35	Overpayment. If line 32h is larger than the total of lines 31 and 33, enter amount overpaid . . .	35	
36	Enter amount of line 35 you want: Credited to 1993 estimated tax ▶ _____ Refunded ▶	36	

Please Sign Here

Under penalties of perjury, I declare that I have examined this return, including accompanying schedules and statements, and to the best of my knowledge and belief, it is true, correct, and complete. Declaration of preparer (other than taxpayer) is based on all information of which preparer has any knowledge.

▶ Signature of officer   Date   ▶ Title

Paid Preparer's Use Only

Preparer's signature ▶		Date	Check if self-employed ☐	Preparer's social security number
Firm's name (or yours if self-employed) and address ▶				

Figure 19.2. Corporate tax return.

the corporation pays one half (7.65 percent) and the full amount is withheld from your paycheck.

Quarterly Estimated Income Tax Payments

Proprietors, partners, and, in some cases, sub chapter S shareholders, are required to pay estimated income taxes quarterly, if income received from self-employment exceeds 20 percent of total annual income. If all taxes due are delayed until the end of the calendar year, the filer is liable for accrued interest charges and, in some cases, penalties for the income received during the initial nine months of the year.

State Income Taxes

Most states require a separate filing for state income taxes. The business owner faces the same consequences for failure to file state income taxes as he or she does for federal taxes. It may also be necessary to pay estimated quarterly state income taxes.

Payroll Taxes

Business owners who fail to pay employee withholding taxes and social security are in effect keeping hold of money that belongs to employees. It is a serious violation and can be reason for the IRS to close a business. In most cases, employee tax withholdings and social security contributions are deposited monthly by the employer into his or her employer tax account at their local bank. Theses deposits are summarized and reported to the IRS by the employer quarterly on Form 941. (See Fig. 19.3.) Failure to make the deposits or to file the 941 will bring the IRS to the business' doorstep. The penalties for late filing can be as high as 50 percent of the taxes withheld plus accrued interest charges.

Unfortunately this is the area of greatest tax law violation. Business owners who are caught in a financial bind are often tempted to delay this payment in order to pay a more pressing bill. Since it takes the IRS a number of months to catch the violation, the business owner has a false sense of security that he or she can pay the withholding taxes late and use the money for other purposes. It is extremely risky strategy because if the violation is considered extreme, the IRS can place a lien on the bank account of the business and confiscate all assets of the business and its owner(s). The limited liability feature of a corporation does not apply to taxes, therefore the owner(s) is personally liable for all employee taxes withheld.

Form **941** (Rev. October 1985) Department of the Treasury Internal Revenue Service	**Employer's Quarterly Federal Tax Return** ▶ For Paperwork Reduction Act Notice, see page 2. Please type or print

4141

Your name, address, employer identification number, and calendar quarter of return. (If not correct, please change.)	Name (as distinguished from trade name) Date quarter ended	OMB No. 1545-0029 Expires: 8-31-88

Trade name, if any   Employer identification number

Address and ZIP code

T
FF
FD
FP
I
T

If address is ▶ ☐ different from prior return, check here

IRS Use

If you are not liable for returns in the future, write "FINAL". . . . ▶   Date final wages paid . . . . ▶

Complete for First Quarter Only

1a	Number of employees (except household) employed in the pay period that includes March 12th . ▶	1a
b	If you are a subsidiary corporation AND your parent corporation files a consolidated Form 1120, enter parent corporation employer identification number (EIN) . . ▶ 1b –	
2	Total wages and tips subject to withholding, plus other compensation . . . . ▶	2
3	Total income tax withheld from wages, tips, pensions, annuities, sick pay, gambling, etc.. . . ▶	3
4	Adjustment of withheld income tax for preceding quarters of calendar year (see instructions) . . ▶	4
5	Adjusted total of income tax withheld	5
6	Taxable social security wages paid . . . . . $ _____ X 14.3% (.143) .	6
7a	Taxable tips reported . . . . $ _____ X 7.15% (.07 15) .	7a
b	Tips deemed to be wages (see instructions) . . $ _____ X 7. 15% (.07 15) .	7b
8	Total social security taxes (add lines 6, 7a, and 7b)	8
9	Adjustment of social security taxes (see instructions for required explanation)	9
10	Adjusted total of social security taxes (see instructions) . . . . ▶	10
11	Backup withholding . . . . ▶	11
12	Adjustment of backup withholding tax for preceding quarters of calendar year	12
13	Adjusted total of backup withholding	13
14	Total taxes (add lines 5, 10, and 13) . . . . ▶	14
15	Advance earned income credit (EIC) payments, if any (see instructions)	15
16	Net taxes (subtract line 15 from line 14). This must equal line IV below (plus line IV of Schedule A (Form 941) if you have treated backup withholding as a separate liability)	16
17	Total deposits for quarter, including overpayment applied from a prior quarter, from your records . ▶	17
18	Balance due (subtract line 17 from line 16). This should be less than $500. Pay to IRS . . . . ▶	18
19	If line 17 is more than line 16, enter overpayment here ▶ $ _____ and check if to be: ☐ Applied to next return or ☐ Refunded.	

Record of Federal Tax Liability (Complete if line 16 is $500 or more)

See the instructions under rule 4 for details before checking these boxes.

Check only if you made eighth-monthly deposits using the 95% rule ▶ ☐   Check only if you are a first time 3-banking-day depositor ▶ ☐

Date wages paid	Tax liability (Do not show Federal tax deposits here.) First month of quarter		Second month of quarter		Third month of quarter
1st through 3rd	A		I	Q	
4th through 7th	B		J	R	
8th through 11th	C		K	S	
12th through 15th	D		L	T	
16th through 19th	E		M	U	
20th through 22nd	F		N	V	
23rd through 25th	G		O	W	
26th through the last	H		P	X	
Total liability for month	I		II	III	

IV Total for quarter (add lines I, II, and III) . . . . ▶

Under penalties of perjury, I declare that I have examined this return, including accompanying schedules and statements, and to the best of my knowledge and belief it is true, correct, and complete.

Signature ▶   Title ▶   Date ▶

Figure 19.3. Form 941.

In addition to the quarterly 941 Form, employers must file an annual or quarterly 940 Form to pay their share of Federal Unemployment Taxes. The amount of unemployment fund taxes owed is based on a percent of total payroll of the business.

State Sales Tax

If the business sells at retail, it is required to collect sales tax at the point of exchange. These receipts are then sent to the state department of revenue with a report on a monthly basis. As in the case of the employee withholding taxes, sales tax revenues belong to someone else—not the business owner. Failure to pay, or pay late, can result in penalties, accrued interest charges, and legal action against the business. The state has the right to audit your business for accuracy in reporting sales revenues.

Contracts

In all commercial activity, contracts are entered into on a daily basis whether written, verbal, or implied. The entrepreneur should have an understanding of how commitments are viewed in the eyes of the law.

A contract is a promise, or promises, to carry out an obligation. A legally enforceable contract has five parts.

1. An agreement or the acceptance of an offer by another party(ies). The offer must be one that is considered legally binding. It must have definite terms and cannot remain open indefinitely. The offer can end by retraction from the offering party, rejection by the party receiving the offer, or if a counter offer is made by the receiving party. If either party dies or becomes incapacitated the offer is automatically voided. An acceptance of an offer must be clearly demonstrated.

2. It must be lawful. If a contract is entered into that violates a law, it is unenforceable.

3. There must be consideration, or value given and value received, from the parties to be a contract.

4. The parties involved must have the capacity to fully understand the requirements of the contract. They cannot be minors or mentally impaired.

5. There must be a form to the contract. It may be written, oral, expressed, or implied. It must be clearly presented in a reasonable manner.

The entrepreneur should have a clear understanding as to when he or she enters a contract. Many outrageous suits have caught business owners by surprise because they did not realize that their actions constituted a contract. An offer to sell, or an employee benefit announcement, can be an enforceable contract once the accepted by the other party, if it meets the five contractual requirements.

If there is failure to perform in regards to a contractual agreement, the offending party is considered in breach of contract. The injured party has the right to cancel the contract, sue for monetary damages, and make demand for specific performance.

Because the entrepreneur is involved with buying and selling, he or she must feel confident in the knowledge of sales contracts. The sales contract defines the offer, the agreement, and the considerations. Major purchases should be in a written contractual format. Normally the written contract will include the price, the time and place of performance and exchange, the purchaser's right to inspection, any financial responsibility assumed in the event goods are damaged in route to the buyer and any terms in regards to the actual transfer of title to the goods.

In day-to-day operations of a business, invoices, purchase orders, and verbal acceptance of the conditions of a sales offer from a vendor may constitute sales contracts. In retailing the exchange of money for a product represents acceptance of an offer and the money is the consideration. It is important for the business owner to clearly understand the terms and conditions in which he or she buys from vendors and sells to customers. If not, the entrepreneur can be the victim of assuming title to damaged goods, undergo serious cash flow problems due to payment terms, or be sued for misrepresentation of an offer to customers.

Property Acquisition

Decisions must be made as to buying versus leasing real property. Many new businesses will start using leased property with the ultimate goal of owning the property from which the business operates. The entrepreneur should have an understanding of the legal nature of acquiring real property.

Real property consists of land, buildings, and fixtures. Property that is attached to the land (buildings) and that which is attached that property (fixtures) are considered as real property. A written sales contract is required in the purchase of real property. The actual transfer of title is evidenced through a deed. There are two types of deeds—warranty and quitclaim deeds.

A *warranty deed* transfers the title to property with certain warranties. Included in these warranties are:

There are no liens against the property for unpaid claims nor are there any conditions existing which warrant future claims at time of transfer. The seller has the authority to transfer title. The seller ensures that the title is valid.

Quitclaim deeds have no such warranties. Ownership is transferred, including liabilities to the buyer.

A business owner should use a competent attorney to make sure that all facts of the property purchase are exposed and explained. A careless acquisition can result in the buyer assuming problems of the former owner.

Included in the purchase decision is the form of ownership. Partners in a business may elect joint tenancy as the form of ownership which will ensure that ownership will pass to the surviving owners in the event of death. If the owners are husband and wife, they may elect *tenancy by entirety* which ensures that if one of them dies, the other becomes sole owner.

Tenancy in common states that any property ownership passes to heirs in the event of death. Some states have community property laws which state that all property acquired during marriage automatically become jointly owned. Before purchasing real property, the entrepreneur should research what form of ownership is best for the situation and what laws apply.

Property acquisition should be a very intensive buying decision that requires in-depth research. Too often business owners act too quickly in their desire to achieve their goals. The same person who will be very deliberate in the purchase of a home or car does not take the same care in acquiring business property. Business property acquisition has the potential to be a highly appreciable investment. The time should be taken during the initial research to find the right opportunity at the right terms. This cannot be done without an understanding of legal protection and responsibilities.

Chapter Summary

Entrepreneurs must learn the legal responsibilities of operating a business, particularly in regards to taxes, contracts, and property acquisition.

There are severe consequences for tax filing violations. The IRS sponsors an eight-part seminar to explain tax reporting procedures that new business owners should attend.

Buying and selling contracts are constantly entered during everyday business operations. The entrepreneur must be aware of what is considered a legal contract before entering into agreements.

Any business owner considering real property acquisition must understand what should be included in the agreement and the choices of the form of property ownership.

The Next Step

Call the closest Small Business Development Center or SBA office to inquire when the next Small Business Taxpayer's Education Program is to be offered and make plans to attend. Review buying and selling terms with vendors, customers, and your attorney. If property acquisition is planned review what you have learned in this chapter with an attorney.

Review Questions

1. *What is the Small Business Taxpayer's Education Program?*
2. *What is Form 941?*
3. *When is it required to file an estimated quarterly income tax payment form?*
4. *What percentage of income must be paid as self-employment income?*
5. *What are the five parts of a contract?*
6. *What are commonly considered as contracts in everyday business transactions?*
7. *What is real property?*
8. *What is the difference between a warranty deed and a quitclaim deed?*
9. *What should be included in a property sales contract?*
10. *Describe three types of property ownership.*

20
Procedures and Regulations

Objectives

1. Understand the legal procedures that must be followed before opening a business.
2. Learn the role of the Federal Trade Commission.
3. Learn regulations and legislative acts that have been designed to protect consumer and business interests.

Key Terms

Business license

Federal Trade Commission

Express warranty

Implied warranty

Truth-In-Lending Act

Fair Credit Reporting Act

Bait and switch advertising

Sherman Antitrust Act

Clayton Act

Robinson Pactman Act

Having decided the form of organization, the business owner must properly register the business entity with local, state, and federal agencies.

Registration Procedures

Local

All municipal and county governments have a business registration office. It is necessary for all business entities to register and receive a license to operate within the county or city in which the business resides. The purpose of a business license is to keep the local government informed as to who is responsible for the business activities and to make sure that all businesses are in compliance with local zoning ordinances. This is normally a very simple procedure. The owner fills out a simple application and pays an annual license fee. The fee for the license is, in most cases, nominal for a new business and must be renewed each year.

There may be other permits required depending on the type of business. Food processors and servers must pass a health inspection and some businesses require a safety check. If the business is undergoing any structural leasehold improvements, it will be necessary to get a building permit and undergo a clearance check from the local building department before opening the business. The entrepreneur should inquire at the time of registration as to what licenses, permits, and inspections apply to his or her type of business.

State

The Department of Revenue within each state is responsible for the collection of all sales taxes. If the business collects sales taxes at the retail level, it must receive a state identification number. There is a nominal one time fee in most states to register. The application form is available by calling the closest State Department of Revenue office.

Other state registration procedures may need to be followed depending on the type of business activity. The business owner can call the office of the Secretary of State to inquire as to what businesses must have state licenses in order to operate.

Federal

If a business has employees, it must receive a federal identification number for reporting employee tax withholding information. A simple SS-4 form is available through the IRS office nearest you. There is no charge for this registration.

There will be other federal registration requirements for businesses involved with exporting or importing. Discuss your business with an IRS official to determine what registrations apply.

Regulations

There are several basic regulations which the entrepreneur should be aware of. Laws exist that protect both the business and consumer from unethical business practices.

Federal Trade Commission

Unfair business practices come under the scrutiny of the Federal Trade Commission (FTC). The FTC is charged with monitoring business activity involving product warranty and safety, consumer credit reporting, advertising and business competition. This includes:

1. *Product warranty and safety.* The FTC will investigate complaints regarding warranties to make sure what is expressed or implied by product representation is upheld. A warranty is a clearly stated fact regarding the performance or quality of a product.

An express warranty is written and, as such, the warrantor must uphold the declarations of the statement. If a product states "100 percent silk" it must be true. In recent years, the FTC has been busy hunting down violators of fashion designer misrepresentations. A retailer selling designs by a well known designer must be sure that the articles are in fact true representations of the particular designer and not "knock offs," or copies, produced without permission. Similar violations occur in the recording industry in which illegal copies are counterfeited to look like the original recording company's product. A well-known discount operation was cited in 1993 for posting "made in America" signs over imported goods.

An implied warranty is an unwritten warranty that assures the customer that the product will perform in a satisfactory manner under normal use. If a customer buys an appliance, he or she should expect the appliance to perform in the manner intended. If it does not, the seller must provide a remedy or could be found in violation of implied warranty.

The Consumer Product Safety Commission of the FTC investigates claims for unsafe product performance. It is quite common to hear of product recalls by manufacturers for unsafe performance. These recalls are often the result of an FTC investigation.

2. *Consumer credit reporting.* All entrepreneurs who extend credit should be familiar with legislation protecting consumer interests. The Truth-In-Lending Act was enacted to ensure that consumers were aware of the true cost of borrowing. Business owners must disclose the annual interest rate and any finance charges calculated for the use of credit. In the event the business uses credit cards issued by lending institutions, the credit card company is responsible for the disclosure of its terms.

The Fair Credit Reporting Act has been enacted to allow consumers access to their personal credit information. If a consumer is denied credit by a business, the law requires the business to provide the reason along with the name and address of the credit reporting agency used. Under the Equal Credit Opportunity Act a business which decided to offer credit to customers must make it available to all qualified customers.

3. *Advertising.* The FTC is charged with ensuring that information presented and implied in advertising is accurate. If information is presented in a deceptive or false manner, the business can be cited for violation. False advertising lies, deceptive advertising misleads.

Some businesses have been cited for *bait and switch advertising.* Bait and switch occurs when a business advertises a low price item with the intention of selling the consumer a different and higher priced item. This is often done by telling the customer that the advertised product is inferior or, in some cases, out of stock. Although this charge is difficult to prove, enough claims will alert the FTC to what is considered a deceptive practice. The FTC also keeps an eye out for deceptive pricing strategies. The most common is advertising the true price as a "sale" price.

4. *Competition.* The Sherman Antitrust Act, the Clayton Act, and the Robinson Pactman Act were created to protect small businesses against unfair competition. These laws prevent monopolies.

The Sherman Antitrust Act outlaws price fixing. It prohibits industry leaders from acting in collusion to set price levels for the industry.

The Clayton Act prevents agreements that require a customer to purchase one type of product in order to be permitted to purchase another type. A supplier to your business can not force you to buy a certain product in order to have the right to buy the product you desire to buy. The Clayton Act also prohibits companies from mergers that would create a monopoly.

The Robinson Pactman Act outlaws price discrimination. It is illegal to sell to a special interest at prices and terms that are not offered to all.

There are other well known regulations that apply to certain businesses. The Hazardous Substance Labeling Act requires that labels be posted warning customers of any hazards that may arise from using the product. The Occupational Safety and Health Act (OSHA) requires certain safety standards be met at the work place. The National Environmental Policy Act (NEPA) was designed to prevent pollution and reduce noise. The Fair Credit Billing Act protects consumers from unfair and incorrect billing activities.

When creating a business plan, the entrepreneur must take the time to research what laws and regulations apply to his or her business. In an era of devastating lawsuits, business owners must learn the laws that apply.

Chapter Summary

The entrepreneur must follow whatever procedures have been established in his or her locale for registering and licensing business activities. He or she must also learn state and IRS requirements before commencing business operations.

The Federal Trade Commission is the federal agency charged with enforcing regulations to protect business and consumer interests. The new business owner must learn what regulations apply to his or her particular business. There are strict laws in regards to advertising, product safety and warranties, unfair competition, and consumer credit reporting that apply to many business interests.

The Next Step

Inquire to the city or county business registration department to learn the procedure to follow to get your business opened. Make request to your state agencies and the closest IRS office to send all required forms for the purpose of securing identification numbers.

Discuss with industry representatives legislation that applies to your business activities. Visit your library to research the laws and review your status with an attorney.

Review Questions

1. *Why must you register your business activity with the local government?*

2. *What state and IRS registrations may apply?*

3. *What is the Federal Trade Commission?*

4. *What four areas does the FTC oversee?*

5. *What is the difference between express and implied warranties?*

6. *What are three legislative acts that have been enacted to protect consumer credit?*

7. *Give examples of common deceptive and false advertising practices.*

8. *What is an example of a deceptive pricing strategy?*

9. *What legislative acts protect against unfair competition?*

10. *Give an example of a practice that would be in violation of the Occupational Safety and Health Act (OSHA).*

21

Insurance and Risk Management

Objectives

1. Learn the different types of insurance coverage available to small business owners.
2. Learn the guidelines for determining necessary insurance coverage.
3. Understand risk areas that cannot be covered by insurance policies.
4. Learn the value of writing out contingency plans to reduce market and internal risks.

Key Terms

Commercial property insurance   Workman's compensation insurance

Liability insurance   Coinsurance

Risk and entrepreneurship go together. Although you cannot remove the risk element, the successful entrepreneur must learn the tools to reducing that risk factor as much as possible. The risks must first be identified and then a plan formulated to protect against them. Some are insurable, others are preventable but only if you have a plan.

Insurable Risks

For a risk to be insurable, it must meet the following criteria:

1. The risk must be calculable. Insurance companies offer insurance on instances that can be predicted through the use of actuarial tables. Insurance rates are determined by the frequency of an incident occurring, therefore, there must be a basis for calculation.
2. The risk must occur in large numbers. Insurance companies play favorable odds against misfortune. They must cover a sufficient number of similar risks to ensure that the law of averages will work to their advantage.
3. What is insured must have a commercial value. You can not cover sentimental value. The item must have a market related comparative value.
4. The policyholder must have an insurable interest in the person or property insured. You cannot carry insurance on someone else's building. Likewise you cannot have a $100,000 policy on a $50,000 property. You also cannot take out a life insurance policy on an individual who is not related to you or who is not an investor in a business. Insurance protection is for reimbursement and not for the creation of a profit.

Guidelines for Buying Insurance

The entrepreneur should keep in mind that insurance companies are profitable because the odds are in their favor in any calculable insurance risk. This being the case, the business owner should follow five rules for buying insurance coverage.

1. Determine the true needs for protection. You must carry what is legally required and those that can be considered common business risks.
2. Carry insurance only on what the business could not afford to cover in the event of misfortune. Since the probability of something happening is in your favor, it is foolish to pay a premium to cover an incident that if it did happen you could afford to pay for it—probably out of insurance premium savings. Many businesses unnecessarily pay annual premiums of $100 to cover a $300 risk. After three years of payment they will have paid more than if they had replaced the item brand new.
3. Make sure that there is a reasonable correlation of the cost of the coverage to the probability of loss. If the probability of sustaining the loss is extremely low, the premium should be extremely low. A business owner cannot afford to cover every possible incident that can occur.

4. Investigate all possible ways to lower insurance premiums. Implementing measures to reduce risks such as fire walls, security systems and sprinkler systems lower the risk and should lower insurance premiums.

5. Take the time to find an experienced, knowledgeable, and competent insurance agent. The insurance industry has gone through massive changes and the insurance agent has been burdened with many more products to sell. Often this has meant insurance agents who have not received in-depth training in basic insurance policy knowledge. A good insurance agent knows how to write policies that can save the policy holder money. He or she will know how to figure blanket coverage for property coverage or proper ways of classifying worker occupations to save money in workman's compensation coverage. Choosing an insurance agent is often more important than choosing the insurance company.

Types of Insurance

Property Insurance

Commercial property insurance protects against losses associated with damage to or loss of business property. It will cover such incidents as fire, explosion, and acts of nature. Because these incidents can totally ruin a business, basic property coverage is usually considered a must.

In addition to the basic property coverage, additional property insurance policies can also be acquired for a variety of other possible incidents.

1. Business interruption insurance provides protection against a business slowdown or shut down due to mishaps covered through the basic property coverage. This coverage will provide income that is determined to have been lost to the business during recovery or reconstruction.

2. Vandalism insurance will provide protection for a business against any incidents of vandalism or looting.

3. Water sprinkler insurance covers any damaged caused by a faulty water sprinkler system.

4. Dishonesty insurance covers crime and fidelity bonds. Crime insurance protects against theft, robbery, and forgery. Fidelity bonding insures against employees who are in position of trust that may embezzle or steal.

5. Credit insurance can be obtained only by manufacturers and wholesalers who are particularly dependent on the operations of others. A company that receives the majority of its income from supplying a particular business or industry that undergoes insolvency due to cir-

cumstances beyond their control (acts of nature, severe recession, etc.) may be able to purchase insurance against these conditions.

6. Surety bonds. These bonds are a form of insurance which protect a business against the failure of another business or individual to fulfill a contractual obligation. Construction contracts are often covered by surety bonds.

These and other additional coverages should be evaluated individually to determine if they are needed after correlating the probability of loss versus the cost of premium.

Some commercial property policies contain a coinsurance clause. A *coinsurance clause* guarantees insurance only to a specified percentage of property value, typically 80 percent. Coinsuring is a method of reducing premiums. If a building is coinsured at 80 percent of its $100,000 value, the insurance company will pay out $80,000 if the property is a total loss, however, it will pay the full value of any partial loss as long as it does not exceed $80,000.

Liability Insurance

There are two types of liability insurance—employers' liability/workman's compensation and general liability.

Employers Liability/Workman's Compensation.   By law, any business with employees must carry employers' liability and workman's compensation insurance. Employers' liability covers against suits brought against an employer from an employee injured on the job. Workman's compensation covers all employees against injury while on the job. Its premiums are based on the type of work performed and the business's claims history. The more hazardous the work, the higher the premiums. It is charged on a cost per $100 of payroll. The rates are set by the state's insurance commission and may range from less than a dollar per $100 payroll for clerical or retail sales positions to many dollars per $100 for jobs carrying higher accident history, such as construction work. The premiums are billed by the business's insurance carrier as part of the business's comprehensive insurance policy.

General Liability.   General liability insurance protects the business owner from customer injury on the business premise or by the use of a product sold to them. If a business is leasing commercial property, the landlord may require the business to carry general liability insurance for a specified amount. In the event the business owner does not carry general liability insurance, the injured party can bring suit against the property owner.

Key Person Insurance.   Another form of liability insurance is key person insurance. The beneficiary of the policy is the business itself in order to offset the loss of income caused by the death of an income producing individual.

Making a Claim

Times of misfortune are when a business owner finds out how well his or her insurer responds. It is important to understand that it is your insurance company's responsibility to settle claims, not necessarily the offending party. If a roof collapses due to deficient work on part of a roofing company, the business owner should deal with his or her insurance carrier for help—not the roofing company. It is the policyholder's company that should initiate settlement. If it is the roofing company's error, let your insurance company handle a claim against the offending party after you have been satisfied. Too often the insured settles prematurely due to pressures from various parties. In choosing an insurance carrier and agent, check with other policyholders to discover how they have been treated in times of duress.

Common Risks That Are Not Insurable

In any business operation there are numerous *at-risk activities* that are not insured which can be most harmful to the business. Entrepreneurs must build plans to reduce these risks through careful monitoring and creating control tools.

Personnel Risks

Unfortunately, employee dishonesty is not uncommon. Business owners should have clearly stated policies that will help enforce employee honesty. Some businesses will require lie detector tests, others will require package or locker inspection, and others require elaborate sign-in and sign-out regulations. As mentioned earlier, the best prevention of employee dishonesty is through effective interviewing, carefully checking employee references, and building a comraderie that discourages dishonesty.

Some businesses can be hurt from the actions of former employees who share information with a competitor or use trade secrets to start a competing business. One inhibitor to this is to require employees with access to vital information to sign an employment contract that clearly states the employee cannot disclose information for a specified period of time after leaving the organization.

Customer Risks

Shoplifting. For the retailer, shoplifting is an inherent risk. There will be some shoplifting, however, there are steps that can be taken to reduce the exposure to this risk.

1. Carefully place items of highest value and greatest shoplifting appeal under the protection of security cases.
2. When designing the store layout, provide clear visual access to all parts of the store.
3. Provide education to employees on methods of preventing and catching shoplifting. Most municipal police departments will offer no charge training to employees, if requested.
4. Installing monitors and merchandise detectors to discourage and apprehend shoplifters.

Retailers should concentrate on methods to prevent shoplifting as opposed to catching shoplifters. A good and caring staff of employees is the most important element. Employees should be trained to acknowledge all customers as they enter a store in order to give notice to potential thieves that their presence is apparent.

The store owner has the responsibility to prosecute all violators, no matter how minor the item or the age of the shoplifter. There is a grapevine among shoplifters and in a community that quickly gets the word around about what businesses should be avoided by shoplifters because of their reputation for strong action.

Fraud. Credit card fraud has taken the place of counterfeit money as the number one method of fooling the retailer. Store personnel must be trained in how to recognize fraudulent credit cards, how to confirm proper identity, and how to report violations. Police training is available in ways to spot counterfeit money and bad credit cards.

Bad Debts. Customers who do not pay as promised are not profitable relationships and should not be tolerated. Good cash flow depends on adherence to collection policies. The entrepreneur must learn the ins and outs of proper collection techniques. There should be an in-house method of how to handle the slightly tardy accounts and a system, possibly using the services of a professional collection agency, should be in place for problem accounts. All credit relationships should be entered into only after a proper credit check is conducted for all applicants.

Another source of bad debts is uncollectible checks. A check returned to the business marked as insufficient funds or closed account should be acted upon immediately. Sometimes it is an error which is quickly corrected, however, it can also be a deliberate attempt to steal. Employees must be trained on how to validate a check and what information, and why, must be collected before taking a check for payment.

Market Risks

The business owner faces other risks brought on through industry and economic shifts that are difficult to protect against. A company largely dependent on the efforts of other companies must create contingency plans in the event of their failure to perform. Do not become solely dependent on one supplier or one source of customers. Diversify your business to the point that there are options. A bridal store needs a back-up plan in the event the bridal dress manufacturer cannot deliver. The paint supplier to a large business must create alternative markets in the event the prime source becomes insolvent or changes sources. Always write out contingency plans for worst case scenarios.

Times of prolonged recessions or inflationary prices can severely interrupt a business cycle. You cannot control the economy but you must be alert to changes and be able to react. Stay abreast of market conditions and be prepared to change your game plan if necessary. The business that carries product lines that can be quickly and adversely affected by economic cycles should develop allied product lines that will help carry the business through difficult periods.

In the initial stages of development it is difficult to build diversity, however, the business plan should be written to include future possibilities directed at creating a diversified product base.

Chapter Summary

Entrepreneurs, by their very nature, are willing to assume risk. However, many can be reduced through insurance plans and strategic planning.

Insurance should be carried for areas that, if misfortune occurs, would destroy the business. Other coverage must be decided by weighing the probability against the cost of protection, keeping in mind that the odds are always with the insurance companies. Business owners must take the time to learn the various considerations of property and liability insurance coverage.

Many risk elements cannot be covered by insurance policies. To reduce the risks created by personnel and customers, market fluctuations, and economic cycles, strategic plans should be created for worst case scenarios.

The Next Step

Interview several insurance agents to determine the most experienced and competent. Check with policyholders of the various companies to determine their degree of satisfaction. Design a comprehensive insurance policy which protects the long-term future of the business but at the same time does not create an insurance rich, cash poor operation.

Write out strategic plans to deal with worst case situations. Review these plans with others in the industry.

Review Questions

1. *What guidelines can be used to determine if a risk can be insured?*
2. *Why is the choice of an insurance agent important?*
3. *Describe the various types of property insurance coverage.*
4. *Describe the two types of liability insurance coverage.*
5. *Describe the concept of coinsurance.*
6. *What liability insurance is required by law?*
7. *How should you handle making a claim?*
8. *What are risks that are assumed that cannot be covered by insurance?*
9. *How can you reduce customer-centered risks?*
10. *What are ways to reduce personnel risks?*
11. *Describe market risks and plans you can implement to reduce them.*
12. *Are their ways to reduce exposure to risks from shifts in economic cycles?*

Part 5 Case Study— Breaking Up Is Hard to Do

It seemed perfect at the beginning. Joan and Diane were the best of friends. They were long-time friends who shared the same interest, including their love of the latest women's fashions. Joan had proposed to Diane that they should create a partnership and start a ladies clothing boutique. "The Fashion Tree" was opened six months later with an unwritten understanding that all profits and responsibilities would be shared equally.

It was a small operation. Each partner contributed $10,000, which was used for inventory and basic leasehold improvements. Joan contributed some antique pieces to add to the decor.

The business grew at a steady rate, although profits were only $4000 the first year. They both worked the store equally, and neither took a draw the first year. The second year was considerably more profitable. The inventory level doubled and they added to their look with the purchase of $5000 of additional antiques. They managed to pay themselves $10,000 each from profits, although Joan worked more, due to Diane taking some time off to travel.

During the third year, an opportunity arose that Joan was anxious to pursue. A new shopping center had opened and they could get a prime location. The space was double the size of the present operation, as was the rent and general overhead expenses.

Joan was shocked at Diane's negative reaction. Diane was planning to get married and had no interest in increasing her investment or involvement with "The Fashion Tree."

> During a rather heated disagreement, Diane asserted, "Joan why don't you buy me out, then you can do whatever you want."
>
> "Okay, Diane, I'll give you your $10,000 back and we will call it quits."
>
> "What do you mean $10,000!" answered Diane." I want $10,000 plus half the value of all the antiques. I also deserve a share of the future profits for helping to build this business."
>
> "Are you kidding me, Diane, why would I do that, you actually owe me money since you were paid the same as me even though you only have worked half the hours."
>
> "Joan, you pay me $25,000 or else I'll see you in court."

With a slam of the door, the meeting ended, leaving Joan confused and hurt. If she agreed to pay Diane $25,000 she could not consider the new store. However, after this incident she could not stand the thought of continuing this business relationship any longer. She telephoned her lawyer.

Case Questions

1. How could this situation have been avoided?
2. What must be done at this point?
3. Why did this partnership fail?

PART 6

Looking Ahead

22

Your Future as an Entrepreneur

Objectives

1. Learn when you should consider expanding a business operation.
2. Learn when you should consider selling a business.
3. Understand the considerations behind determining family successorship for a family owned business.
4. Understand the importance of preparing for retirement from your business.

Key Terms

Business life cycle   Business successorship

Once the enterprise is launched and performing to expectations, the entrepreneur can look ahead to future opportunities. The tendency to move too fast is dangerous and often too common because of the risk-taking nature of most entrepreneurs. He or she must prepare in advance as to when to explore new opportunities and when to leave a market.

Business Life Cycle

Just as products have a life cycle, so do businesses. All businesses go through an introductory stage, a growth stage, maturity stage, and, eventually, a decline stage. For some, this cycle may last just a matter of months, for others hundreds of years. Single product businesses selling a fad product will enter and exit a market quickly (i.e., the Pet Rocks manufacturer). But even for the giants of industry, the day will come when new technologies or outdated management will force the business to the sidelines. The entrepreneur should devise a strategy that recognizes the lifeline of the business entity. (See Fig. 22.1.)

Different strategic management plans should be used for these various stages, just as different advertising strategies were explained earlier for the stages of the product life cycle. The following questions should be addressed from the outset of the business creation:

1. When is expansion possible ?
2. Under what conditions should the business be sold ?
3. Is the business to be passed on to family members ?
4. When is the entrepreneur going to retire ?

Expansion

Expanding a business is exciting, ego rewarding, and challenging. It is an opportunity to reawaken entrepreneurial creativity. It puts the entrepre-

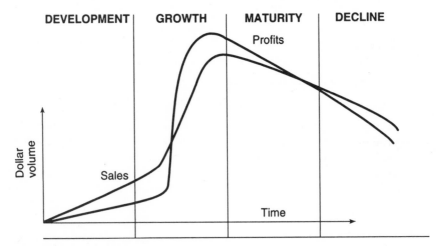

Figure 22.1. Business life cycle.

neur back into the same mode that he or she originally enjoyed when the business was started.

For these reasons, businesses often expand prematurely. Expansions are sometimes made more for ego building reasons than from good common business sense. The entrepreneur must learn the best time to consider an expansion in regards to market opportunity and financial capabilities.

The best time to expand a business is when the business has entered, but not come entrenched in, the maturity stage. By this time the entrepreneur has learned the pitfalls of the market from going through the growth stage. The growth stage has allowed some capital accumulation and eliminated some competition. It is time to apply the experience gained to take the business back into a second growth stage.

For many businesses this time period falls in the three- to five-year stage of development. The owner has usually experienced rapid growth and, for the first time, sees a leveling off of progress. It is important to validate that the leveling off is not just a momentary slow down. One that will pass and put the business back into the chaotic growth period it just came through. Expanding while still in rapid growth can lead to uncontrolled growth, which will surely test the capabilities of the owner and can lead to premature entrance into the decline stage. A business that has grown at a rate of 30 percent per year for two years and then falls to a 20 percent growth rate is probably still in a growth stage. Expansion might be in the mind of the business owner and can be planned for, but should be put off, in many cases, until the 20 percent growth rates falls to 10, or stabilizes at 20 for a long period of time.

Once expansion is considered, it should be tested before making large scale commitments. The retailer who believes it might be time to expand might be able to add more shelves to house more inventory before knocking down a wall and committing to an increased rental obligation. The manufacturer who wants to add new product lines to his or her base, should test market product prototypes to existing customers before buying new equipment. Proper expansions need a business plan, just as new businesses do. Assumptions based on prior experience are historical. Take the time to update your intuitions by researching the market again as you did initially.

Selling a Business

All businesses should be for sale. The business has been created to produce profits. One way of making a large profit might be to sell out. There is a tendency to become so attached to a business that selling opportunities are passed by in order to protect what the originator has developed. It makes little sense to pass up a huge profit because the owner enjoys operating the business. If that is the case, the owner should sell out and take a percentage of the profit and open a new business. Many entrepreneurs have achieved great financial strength by selling out and then starting anew, repeatedly.

There are key times in a business's life cycle when it has achieved its greatest market value. Passing by opportunities to sell at these key times is hazardous as there is no certainty they will return. This is particularly true as the entrepreneur gets older. There have been many instances of business owners who have refused to sell because of unfounded optimism for the future. They turn down the opportunity. The future brings decline and the business loses its value, leaving them with nothing.

The time to sell a business will vary depending on the industry and product itself. If the product is predicted to have a short life cycle, it should be sold midway through the growth stage. A more stable operation with a longer lifeline might reach its highest value midway into its maturity stage.

Passing Along a Family Business

The majority of small businesses are family owned. In many cases, businesses have been handed down from one family generation to the next. It can be a wonderful and rewarding experience or it can be a regretful decision.

There have been many books written, and courses and seminars developed, that explore the experience of passing down a business to a family member. Business successorship is not necessarily easy, particularly when there are decisions to be made concerning who assumes what role. When there are many siblings, the problem is extenuated. How does the owner decide who should inherit what role? There are tough questions that need to be answered:

1. Who has the greatest interest?
2. Who has the greatest capability?
3. What will be the role of those not chosen to lead the operation?
4. What will the impact of these decisions be on the cohesion of the family?
5. How can the answers to these questions be determined?

There must be good communication. There must be clear standards in place to evaluate family members' interest and capabilities. Successorship should be earned, not appointed. In most family business situations, potential successors are exposed to the business at an early age through sharing information and working on a part-time basis. When ready, they should work full-time, in nonmanagerial functions. After learning the functional aspects of the business, they may assume managerial positions. Often they are sent out to work in other businesses to gain a more well-rounded perspective of the industry or business environment. Eventually, they assume the presidency, most likely with the direct consultation of the former president until they and those surrounding them feel confident.

During all stages of succession there should be objectives planned to measure the individual's performance and aptitude. Inherent in any successorship plan should be the recognition that the designated individual or individuals should have the freedom to pursue a career not related to the family business.

Family businesses have many advantages. Family pride and loyalty are the reason they are often more successful than their competitors. The cultural values of the family remain intact from one generation to another. They can serve to keep a family united in seeking objectives and goals. They give the family common ground and mutual interest. They can give employment opportunities to children as they grow, and career opportunities as they mature. The rewards are many, however, they can backfire into an arena of confrontation if not handled properly by the founding member and those who have been passed the authority.

Retiring

No one can work forever, not even entrepreneurs. There will be a time to slow down and reap the rewards of having developed the business. Do not presume that when you are ready to retire that you will sell the business and live happily ever after off the proceeds of the sale. There are too many things that can happen to guarantee that there will be sufficient value in the business to retire on. Part of the business plan should address retirement goals from the outset. Many have retirement plans at their place of work designed to give financial freedom upon retirement. The small business owner has the responsibility to design such a program to insure a financially free retirement and to provide financial security for those left behind after his or her death.

The entrepreneur can choose from the various pension plan programs discussed in Chap. 15. The important element is starting the program immediately in order to get into the habit of contributing and maintaining the discipline to reach the objective. It does not have to be elaborate, nor expensive, to create a worthwhile package over a period of time. Figure 22.2 illustrates the growth of a 20-year plan at $5000 per year that earns 9.5 percent per year.

A financial planner can calculate ending values of different plans based on the length of time of the program. He or she should also direct you to a life insurance plan that assures business continuity in the event of your early departure.

Chapter Summary

The entrepreneur should determine expected business longevity based on the business life cycle. Expansion goals can be planned, but should not be enacted until the business environment reaches predetermined goals.

Selling a business for a profit should be a goal that is determined by opportunity and not a specific timetable. Many entrepreneurs have built their financial strength on profitably selling and then restarting businesses over their career.

20-Year Investment at 9.5 Percent Interest Rate, $5000 per Year	
Year	End-of-year value
1	$ 5,475
2	11,470
3	18,034
4	25,223
5	33,094
6	41,713
7	51,151
8	61,485
9	72,801
10	85,192
11	98,760
12	113,618
13	129,886
14	147,701
15	167,207
16	188,567
17	211,956
18	237,567
19	265,611
20	296,319

Figure 22.2. The growth of a retirement investment.

If passing a business on to future generations of family members is a goal, the originator must learn methods of choosing a successor and the dangers that can arise.

Entrepreneurs must face the reality that someday they will retire. Plans should be made from the outset to assure a financially free retirement and proper insurance provisions.

The Next Step

Include in your business plan a description of expansion possibilities, including projected dates. This should be done in consideration of pro forma income and cash flow statements as to when those points can be reached.

Research the industry to gain an understanding of future market values of similar businesses performing at your expectations. This will give you an idea as to when peak times of business appreciation occur.

Set a retirement timetable and project what you hope to have invested at that time. Review your plan with a financial advisor to determine how much should be budgeted annually to reach your objective.

Review Questions

1. *Describe the business life cycle.*

2. *What is a common problem with many businesses that expand prematurely?*

3. *What is considered a reasonable timetable and stage to consider expansion?*

4. *What steps should be taken before committing to an expansion?*

5. *Why should all businesses be for sale?*

6. *When is the best time to sell a business?*

7. *What are the hazards of passing a business on to family members?*

8. *What questions must be answered in determining who a business should be passed onto?*

9. *Why should you not assume that your retirement can be funded from the sale of your business?*

10. *When should you inaugurate a retirement savings plan?*

23

Small Business Trends

Objectives

1. Acquaint the reader with markets of opportunity.
2. Learn the steps to follow in creating a business involved with international markets.
3. Learn how to benefit from the corporate downsizing trends.

Key Terms

International Trade Administration   Eximbank

The last decade has seen an explosion of service businesses in the small business sector of our economy. Entrepreneurs have developed businesses using their individual talents to better service a market as opposed to creating product based businesses requiring greater financial investment. There has been three primary reasons for this circumstance:

1. The recessionary climate has inhibited our ability and confidence to make large investments in product-based businesses that require large financial commitments.
2. Changes in the American lifestyle, particularly an increase in two-income families, that require us to pay others to do jobs that we use to do when we had more time.

3. The downsizing of corporate America has caused businesses to use temporary and independent services for jobs that used to be performed by employees.

The table shown in Fig. 23.1 validates the increased demand for services. There is nothing in the immediate future that should cause any great changes in this trend, although the government is starting to offer more incentives for business investment through investment credits to small business owners. If these incentives increase, there may be a swing in the pendulum back to more product-based business start-ups.

As we approach the 21st century, some specific areas that should be in the forefront include international business, environmental industry growth, business consulting opportunities, and a continued growth of part-time, home-based businesses.

International Business

Although the growth of the number of small businesses becoming involved with international trade is growing rapidly, they have barely made

---

How They Grew by Industry

1. Fast food/restaurants
2. Maintenance/cleaning
3. Health/fitness
4. Hair cutting
5. Video
6. Real estate
7. Auto maintenance
8. Business services
9. Home decorating
10. Construction
11. Ice cream/yogurt
12. Convenience stores
13. Education
14. Hotel/motel
15. Printing/copying
16. Security systems
17. Travel agencies
18. Rental services
19. Auto rental
20. Retail—miscellaneous
21. Dry cleaning

Figure 23.1. Fastest growing industries, *Inc.* magazine.

a dent in seizing the opportunities available. At one time, the international business market was solely in the hands of large corporations. Now over 25 percent of export and importing activities are in the hands of businesses with less than 100 employees. The opportunities have emerged primarily for two reasons—improved communication technology that is available to smaller businesses and our government's commitment to improve our balance of trade.

Telecommunications technology has given us affordable telephone and fax services so that we can be in touch with foreign-based operations quickly and efficiently. In the past, only the larger businesses had access to these telecommunications tools. Now you can have a fax machine in a home office that allows you to take orders from points on the other side of the world.

Due to a growing imbalance of more imports than exports, the government has become a vital ally in assisting small businesses who engage in international trade. The international market has been identified as having unlimited potential in helping to build a more solid economic base for our country. There has been increased emphasis on government agency support for those who wish to venture into these new markets, particularly the exporter.

Getting Started in International Trade

The International Trade Administration (ITA) of the Department of Commerce has 47 district offices and 21 branch offices throughout the United States. These offices receive and share information gathered from U.S. Foreign Commercial Service offices located in 125 foreign countries. Information gathered includes:

Growth trends in foreign markets.

Which products are in highest demand.

Product standards, regulations, policies and tariff information regarding each country.

Domestic and foreign competition information.

Distribution channels available.

Media evaluations and recommendations within foreign markets.

In addition to providing information, the ITA will assist the international entrepreneur in making contacts through trade shows and seminars. They will assist in doing credit checks, arranging payments, and will offer opinions and advice. They will also direct you to publications available through the Department of Commerce.

Another source of assistance is the Export-Import Bank of the United States (Eximbank). Eximbank provides loan guarantees to banks that extend loans to U.S. exporters. Although these loan guarantees are not available to fund start-up expenditures, they can be used to help finance accounts payable by providing immediate cash on sales contracts to foreign buyers.

Steps to Getting Started as an Exporter

If you believe your product or service has export possibilities, follow these six steps.

1. Contact The Department of Commerce, state development agencies, or any other public or private firms to receive professional counseling.
2. Using these assistance centers, conduct a market research to determine the best foreign markets for what you sell.
3. Plan an export strategy that includes objectives, networking activities, financial planning, and scheduling.
4. Determine a sales strategy. This should include your choice of selling direct through sales representatives and distributors, or indirect using foreign commission agents, country controlled buying agents or export management companies.
5. Arrange financing through Eximbank or other regional and international banks.
6. Learn the best arrangements for receiving payments from foreign buyers.

Viewing the world as your marketplace presents both opportunity and challenge. The changing political climate of Eastern Europe, the Middle East, and even on our own continent has added more urgency for providing goods and services to markets that were not open a short time ago. It is a golden opportunity for entrepreneurs who are willing to take the time to learn the complexities of dealing in international markets.

The Environmental Market

The heightened concern regarding protecting our environment has opened doors of opportunity for many entrepreneurs. As population continues to grow, so will the attention paid to environmental issues and concerns. New industries are popping up to alleviate the fears.

Many entrepreneurs have founded recycling businesses. Some collect and effectively sort recyclables and sell them to material recovery facilities. Aluminum cans, glass, plastic and paper all have recyclable value.

Others turn waste into resalable products, while others remanufacture what was used into something new. There are constant innovations being found to convert waste and obsolescence into profits.

Our landfills are running out of space. More has to be done, therefore, more opportunities can be expected. It may pay to pay attention to environmental issues.

Part-Time, Home-Based Business Opportunities

There are over seven million part-time business operations in America. Most of them operate from homes. There are many ways to turn a small expenditure into an excellent investment. Many of these part-time entrepreneurs are creating home-based incubators from which full-fledged businesses will grow. Others are quite content to subsidize their employment income with extra spending cash.

There are countless ideas—most of which require little investment. Often they are hobbies turned into businesses which are enjoyable to operate. You will find part-time entrepreneurs:

At flea markets and garage sales selling other people's junk.

Manning booths at antique and collectable shows selling hard-to-find items that they took the time to find, and had fun doing it.

Pounding out words on their word processors in the form of newsletters, directories for organizations, or acting as freelance writers.

Creating crafts for sale at craft shows or in mail order catalogs and magazines.

Operating small engine and appliance repair services from their workshops.

Making cakes, selling firewood, taking care of children and many other clever ways to produce a nice profit.

With an uncertain job market and more pressure to find extra income, part-time businesses certainly will continue to grow. They are an industry to themselves which means that they also must be serviced and sold to, thus creating additional entrepreneurial opportunities for entrepreneurs.

Consultants and Temporary Workers

There have never been so many consultants and there has never been so many consulting opportunities. Large businesses would rather hire independent contractors on a project basis, then add employees who require benefit programs. With the new health care program, this market will continue to grow dramatically. The requirement is to know how to do a specialized occupation niche well. Almost any niche will work. It may be computer technology or good secretarial skills. Temporary work agencies cannot find enough people to man the job requests they receive. It is quite possible to market yourself independently of an agency. Make a plan, buy some business cards, and network for contacts in businesses that can use your special services. The pay is often higher than full-time employment as the company does not pay benefits and does have to make a long-term commitment.

This category of entrepreneurship also includes seminar leaders and speakers. Training departments of large businesses have been trimmed to the bone. They would rather hire outsiders, than use full-time personnel in a training function. Many are finding that by doing some research they can quickly become accomplished enough to perform training and teaching at very attractive pay.

Chapter Summary

Entrepreneurs have turned to service businesses in recent years. This trend is expected to continue until governmental assistance programs and improved economic factors provide incentives to develop more product-based enterprises.

Many are exploring opportunities involving international trade. Telecommunications technology and government incentives have allowed small businesses to play a larger part in the global marketplace. Those who take the time to learn the intricacies of dealing with foreign customers should find a world of opportunities.

Others are seeking to create businesses in environmental industries. Recycling and remanufacturing have become big business.

Part-time home-based businesses and independent temporary workers and consultants have created their own industry. Entrepreneurs have discovered ways to fill the void of employees caused from corporate downsizing by taking specialized talents to corporations to hire on a project basis.

The Next Step

Analyze your business idea for its suitability for international trade. If there is a fit, call or visit an office of the U.S. Department of Commerce for assistance in contacting an International Trade Administration official for counseling and information.

Evaluate any ideas that you may have that relate to the environmental industry, part-time home-based business ideas, or independent and temporary work skills that could be hired out on a project basis.

Review Questions

1. *Why have service industries been attractive to entrepreneurs during recent years?*

2. *What must happen to swing the pendulum of business development back to product based business entities?*

3. *Describe the steps to be taken to get started in international business.*

4. *What is the purpose of the International Trade Administration?*

5. *What role has improved telecommunications played in developing small business opportunities for small businesses?*

6. *When would an international company use Eximbank?*

7. *In what areas have entrepreneurs been active in the environmental industry?*

8. *Give five examples of part-time home-based businesses that are considered a good investment.*

9. *What factor has contributed to the increase of opportunities for temporary workers and consultants?*

10. *How will the national health care program affect the market for temporary workers?*

24
Final Thoughts

Objectives

1. Learn how to create a plan of action.
2. Learn the difference between the complete business plan and one that is taken to investors or lenders for financial help.

Key Term

Action plan

There is a final step to be taken before enacting your business plan. The entrepreneur should create a plan of action.

Action Plan

We have discussed creating a map to get you to your goal. Creating objectives and drawing a plan to accomplish them is the purpose of the business plan. Once it is written, it is time to act upon it. But action is different than planning. It asks you to perform specific functions with specific deadlines. The entrepreneur should create a very specific list of what action must be performed, in what order, and at what date in order to get the business opened. This is called a *plan of action*. Figure 24.1 illustrates such a plan for a retail operation.

The entrepreneur should draw a T-chart and list the things to do on one side and a deadline date on the other. This will bring the business plan to life. Once the initial steps are taken, things start to happen quickly and will snowball into accumulating steps. The action plan should be flexible as it will change once you start to develop the business. For many, getting started after writing the business plan is difficult; there is confusion as to

New Store Checklist	
To do	Deadline Before
Select store location	16 weeks
Select lawyer and accountant	16 weeks
Sign lease	16 weeks
Prepare floor plan-measure site	16 weeks
Plan dollar stock investment by resources	12 weeks
Purchase floor covering, wall paper, etc.	12 weeks
Plan store hours	12 weeks
Order cash register	12 weeks
Prepare stock control system	10 weeks
Order wrapping supplies, store stationery	10 weeks
Order pricing tickets	10 weeks
Place merchandise orders with resources	10 weeks
Plan bookkeeping system	8 weeks
Select store manager	8 weeks
Plan grand opening promotion	8 weeks
Conduct store management training program	8 weeks
Secure insurance	8 weeks
Notify utilities	4 weeks
Secure licenses	4 weeks
Buy fire extinguishers	4 weeks
Order cleaning equipment	4 weeks
Buy tools and stepladder	4 weeks
Order office equipment	4 weeks
Secure forms, job applications, W-4's, etc.	4 weeks
Make merchandising signs	4 weeks
Hire salespeople	2 weeks
Install telephone	2 weeks
Install shelving in stockroom	2 weeks
Install carpeting, wallpaper, paint	2 weeks
Prepare customer request book	2 weeks
Secure sales tax charts	2 weeks
Buy supplies	2 weeks
Open bank account	2 weeks
Receive and price merchandise	1 week
Set up fixtures and merchandise	1 week
Set up weekly schedule for salespeople	1 week
Place advertising for grand opening	1 week

Figure 24.1. Action plan steps.

where to start. Use the action plan to get started and the natural momentum of a developing business enterprise will take over.

Types of Business Plans

What you have been putting together is a complete business plan to help guide you through the maze of getting started. In its present format, it is for your use only. It is probably too long to take to a bank or potential investor to review. Bankers and investors are interested in the guts of the matter, not necessarily the step-by-step procedures. Your formal business plan will have the same parts as your action plan. They will be presented in a more concise manner. The following is a business plan for a software manufacturer and producer.

Medical Management Systems—A Sample
Business Plan

Business Description

MEDICAL MANAGEMENT SYSTEMS is a small systems development
company that is dedicated to providing Medical physicians with a
comprehensive software system that suits their individual needs.
Computer related industries are among the fastest growing industries in
the United States and MEDICAL MANAGEMENT SYSTEMS hopes to
capitalize on growth and expansion of this industry. MEDICAL
MANAGEMENT SYSTEMS is a partnership operated and owned by
Charles and Mark Fuller. MEDICAL MANAGEMENT SYSTEMS was
founded in February of 1993. The primary product, Medical Office
Management, underwent a development and testing period of
approximately 10 months. Over 600 hours of programming and research
was performed before the product was completed. In order to control
expenses, MEDICAL MANAGEMENT SYSTEMS operates out of Mark
and Charles Fuller's household in Livingston, NJ.

MEDICAL MANAGEMENT SYSTEMS' mission is to provide
Medical physicians with a comprehensive, cost-effective, and
user-friendly software system that fulfills the needs of even the most
demanding doctors. We are dedicated to providing long-term
relationships with our clients by providing them with helpful and
friendly support, training and by being known as a company who will
go out of their way to make sure their client's are happy. Mark Fuller
is a practicing physician and provides MEDICAL MANAGEMENT
SYSTEMS with professional input which allows us to provide our clients
with an extremely functional and comprehensively designed product.
The goal of MEDICAL MANAGEMENT SYSTEMS is to steadily
increase software sales and becoming profitable after nine months.

The software has many unique features and benefits over our
competition. Medical Office Management enables doctors to keep
track of patient records, provides a comprehensive billing and
insurance system, tracks referral sources, manages inventory, and
provides the doctor with detailed management and financial reports.
The two primary advantages of our system when compared to our
competitors are that it is extremely easy to learn and operate, and is
priced $7500 less than our closest competitor. The entire system can
be operated from an easy to use menu system and for which no
previous computer experience is necessary. We also sell complete
turn-key systems. These systems may be a single computer, or can be a
complex 10 station network system. We provide turn-key systems as a
customer service, rather than for profit motives. We recognize that
most of our clients are very computer illiterate and would rather
spend a few hundred dollars to have someone deliver them a
complete system than try to purchase their own hardware. We also

believe that providing our clients with complete turn-key systems will significantly reduce technical hardware support and provide them with the most effective system available for our software. All software and hardware systems are customized to each individual practice. Every piece of software is customized to suit the demands of differing practices needs. We feel that by customizing each system we can cater to the special requirements of each customer.

Through market research we have been able to pinpoint our specific differential advantage. Our primary advantage and selling point of our system is its ease of operation. Our competitor's systems routinely demand many days (three or more) of in-office training in order to become acquainted with the system; this often results in a large amount of lost office hours and is extremely costly. Our competitors typically charge $600 per day for in-office training plus expenses. MEDICAL MANAGEMENT SYSTEMS charges roughly half this amount for one-on-one training. Another competitive edge our product has is its price. Our single user version costs a mere $2495, while our multi-user network versions range from $2995-$4495. Many smaller practices can not afford the expensive $10,000 price tag, not to mention an additional $2500+ for hardware. The fact that a doctor can purchase a complete turn-key system for $4500 dollars places our product easily into the hands of smaller practices, as well large ones.

Our competitor's advantage is the length of time they have been in business and their established reputations. All of our competitors have been in business for at least four years. Our competitors have good training centers and facilities.

Market Analysis

MEDICAL MANAGEMENT SYSTEMS targets small- to medium-sized practices primarily in New York, New Jersey, Connecticut, and Pennsylvania. The characteristics of our market are:

- Age: 40-55
- Practice Size: Two practitioners
- Income:$100,000/practitioner

When attending national trade shows, our target market expands to the entire United States. Using a phone survey as a marketing tool, has indicated that approximately 47 percent of medical practices are not computerized and that the market conditions are expanding. This would mean that 2515 out of 5240 doctors throughout the country are potential clients. The total number of Physicians per state is:

New York: 420

New Jersey: 207

Connecticut: 123

Pennsylvania: 319

Previously, many doctors did not computerize because of the complexity of the hardware and software, and extremely high start-up costs. To computerize an average size office (two physicians) five years ago would cost approximately $25,000 (hardware and software). Many of those software packages did not perform well and were subsequently "shelved." Today, a much more comprehensive system can be purchased for $4500. This lower price, improved programming, and low-priced "fast" PC's stimulated an increase in the number of systems purchased over the last two years. The number of Physicians throughout the United States has remained relatively constant over the last ten years. This indicates that the market should respond well to our product and that sales should remain constant over the next ten years.

Currently, there are three companies that sell medical software. Our three competitors are:

- Micro-Practice Management, NY
- Micro-Medical, FL
- H-PROFESSIONALS, CA

These three competitors currently charge $10,000 for their single-user software product. Micro-Medical offers a stripped-down version of their software for $999. However, this package is not very useful and does not include the many necessary functions that the other products offer. Micro-Practice Management is considered to be the industry standard for functionality. However, MEDICAL MANAGEMENT SYSTEMS offers 85 percent of the features, of the $10,000 product, at one-quarter of the price. We feel that the 15 percent that we left out of our program were the unnecessary "bells and whistles." We left out such things as computer generated graphs and spreadsheet modules. One of the many drawbacks of these three systems is the fact that they are very difficult to learn and operate. The systems can not match the simplicity of our system and often require many days of in-office training at significant cost. Another problem that we have discovered about our competition is the costly phone support. H-PROFESSIONALS and Micro-Practice Management offer a 1-800 phone number, but require you to pay a monthly fee of $50-$100. After speaking with many doctors, we found that most felt that they should not have to pay $600 for support after spending $10,000. Many doctors felt that this was a drawback.

Micro-Medical offers support via a 1-900 phone number, thus doctors would have to pay for each call, rather than a monthly service charge. This is another flaw in Micro-Medical's marketing and management. This 1-900 number seems to relay the message that they want the doctors to call with problems. The more phone calls the more money they can make. MEDICAL MANAGEMENT SYSTEMS incorporated a new approach to software and technical support. First, we are the only company that offers support via computer modem and this is one of our differential advantages. By dialing into a client's computer system, we can instantly analyze software and hardware problems. This saves time and significantly reduces the client's maintenance fees. We also offer complete modem support for our software product. If the client's question can not be easily answered on the phone, then we can access the client's computer from our office and show them how to solve their problem. This is an invaluable tool for support.

Market Share	
Company Name	Number of Clients
H-PROFESSIONALS	1000
Micro-Medical	150
Micro-Practice Management	900
MEDICAL MANAGEMENT SYSTEMS	6

Micro-Practice Management, H-PROFESSIONALS, and Micro-Medical provide services to all surgeons throughout the United States. Micro-Practice Management and H-PROFESSIONALS also offer training centers in major cities. Instead of providing one-on-one training in the doctor's office, the doctor can elect to send his/her employees to these training centers. In many instances, the practice does not run efficiently because a portion of the office staff is missing.

Micro-Practice Management and H-PROFESSIONALS use various methods of promotional strategies. They both use direct mailing techniques to reach their potential clients. Micro-Practice Management sends direct mail monthly to its potential clients. Their literature often includes one-page brochures and catalogs. They also mail a 60-page brochure which outlines the entire software package bi-yearly. They do not offer any financial incentives to purchase their product. H-PROFESSIONALS mails a newsletter (approximately 6 pages) every three months. This newsletter not only has information about their products, but also includes information pertinent to office management, insurance claims, and medical updates. Micro-Medical typically mails a poorly photocopied order and information form. We have yet to see any "quality" advertising coming from them.

Marketing Strategy

MEDICAL MANAGEMENT SYSTEMS has used numerous
promotional strategies throughout the last seven months. We
primarily use direct mail, and it is the company's key marketing tool.
We currently have a database of over 700 Medical physicians. Most
are from the New York, New Jersey, Pennsylvania, and Connecticut
area. We have performed two direct mailings since our establishment.
Our first mailing, which resulted in 31 responses, included a three
fold brochure, a rolodex card, and a personal letter from Dr. Mark
Fuller. The respondents were then mailed a 25-page catalog outlining,
in detail, our entire product and its functions. This packet along with
a price list and thank-you letter is mailed in a crimson colored folder.
After mailing these folder's we received request for four in-office
demonstrations. These in-office demonstrations typically lasted $1\frac{1}{2}$
hours. With a color notebook computer and portable printer, we were
able to demonstrate the entire system on a one-on-one basis and
answer any questions that the doctor had about our product. We feel
that these in-office demonstrations are usually the deciding factor in
whether or not to purchase our product. A typical demonstration
usually involves the following discussion and presentation:

- Reason for product development
- Features, advantages, and benefits
- Ease of use of system
- Relating a case history
- Demonstration of software product
- Determining the individual needs of practice and stressing those
  points during demonstration
- Showing how product can reduce operating costs and increase
  office efficiency
- Listen to doctor or office manager
- Stress how it will benefit practice
- Asking if he/she has any questions or needs to see something
  re-demonstrated
- Make a closing statement

Mark and Charles Fuller currently make up the sales force, but over
the next two years plan to hire salespeople who will take over a
majority of the sales role.

After the initial sale is made, we will be offering practices the
option of purchasing our upgrade package. The upgrade usually
includes new features and changes. After the initial sale is made, we
will be offering practices the option of purchasing our upgrade
package. The upgrades usually include new features and changes. We

will encourage all of our customers to purchase this upgrade by pointing out the benefits and advantages of staying up-to-date with the latest version available. The updates will typically cost between $100-$250, depending on the complexity of the update. Updates will be available at least twice a year. We have also used sales premiums to encourage purchases. In two instances, we have agreed to include special customized applications pertinent to the individual office. For very little work, we can often use these premiums to effectively close the sale. We also tell our clients that if they recommend us to someone we will provide them with a free upgrade.

To keep track of customers we use a contact management software that tracks all transactions, conversations and mailings. With this software we can keep accurate and detailed records of all of our clients and potential clients. This helps to reduce lost sales due to failure to follow-up leads for potential clients.

Our pricing strategy has basically involved penetration pricing. Our initial price was ⅕ of our closest competitor. At the end of nine months we raised our price by $500. One concern that we have about having our price so low is the fact that some clients might feel that the product is inferior because of its price. This was one of the reasons we decided to increase the price. In 1994, we plan to raise the price another $500, bringing the price up to $2995. We have not noticed any change in our competitions price to date, but we presume that some company will release an abbreviated version for approximately the same price as ours. Our software is currently protected under a copyright.

Our product is currently distributed via direct channel. The software is simply mailed to the client, or if in-office training is requested, installed prior to training. If the client purchases a turn-key system the system is set-up and configured in our office and then mailed or delivered to the client.

We also plan on advertising in medical trade publications such as: The Journal of the American Medical Association. Over the next two years we will be increasing our direct mailing data base to include most of the country. We hope that this effort will effectively increase our product awareness and convince doctors that there is an alternative software package available for their individual needs.

Organization Structure and Initial Capitalization

MEDICAL MANAGEMENT SYSTEMS is currently a partnership which is owned and operated by Mark and Charles Fuller. We are currently in the process of becoming a sub chapter S corporation to take advantages of the tax and limited liability benefits.

Pro Forma Statements and Cash Flow Projection

Income Statement

	1993		1994		1995	
Income						
Gross sales	$86,860.13		177,700.00		266,550.00	
Less returns and allowances						
Net sales	86,860.13		177,700.00		266,550.00	
Cost of goods	38,184.17		57,900.00		86850.00	
Gross profit	48,675.96		119,800.00		179,700.00	
Operating expenses						
Sales expense						
Commissions	0.00		4,000.00		6,000.00	
Marketing	3,047.58		5,000.00		7,000.00	
Total sales expenses	3,047.58		9,000.00		13,000.00	
General and administrative expenses						
Payroll	27,706.00	31.90%	66,500.00	37.42%	115,000.00	43.14%
Professional services	1,316.73	1.52%	2,000.00	1.13%	2,500.00	0.94%
Rent	0.00	0.00%	9,600.00	5.40%	9,600.00	3.60%
Insurance	0.00	0.00%	1,500.00	0.84%	1,650.00	0.62%
Depreciation and amortization	0.00	0.00%	1,906.00	1.07%	1,906.00	0.72%
Offce supplies	5,954.90	6.86%	3,000.00	1.69%	3,500.00	1.31%
Interest	616.40	0.71%	0.00	0.00%	0.00	0.00%
Utilities	1,668.57	1.92%	2,000.00	1.13%	2,000.00	0.75%
Postage	536.20	0.62%	900.00	0.51%	1,200.00	0.45%
Travel and entertainment	1,348.80	1.55%	2,500.00	1.41%	2,500.00	0.45%
Taxes	2,216.00	2.55%	5,320.00	2.99%	9,200.00	3.45%
Maintenance	0.00	0.00%	500.00	0.28%	500.00	0.19%
Equipment rental	0.00	0.00%	0.00	0.00%	0.00	0.00%
Furniture and equipment	0.00	0.00%	2,500.00	1.41%	1,500.00	0.56%
Bad debt	0.00	0.00%	0.00	0.00%	0.00	0.00%
Total general and administrative expenses	41,363.60	47.62%	98,226.00	55.28%	151,056.00	56.67%
Total operating expenses	44,411.18		107,226.00		164,056.00	
Net income	4264.78		12,574.00		15,644.00	

Figure 24.2. Pro forma income statement.

A loan of $5000 was made to MEDICAL MANAGEMENT SYSTEMS on February 1, 1993. This was used to purchase capital, office supplies, pay for application and legal fees. Most of our capital purchase (i.e., desktop computer, notebook computer, and laser printer were financed on a low-interest credit card). Over the last nine months, we have steadily paid off the credit card balance and plan to complete the payments in October of 1993.

Management

Currently Charles and Mark Fuller and a secretary are the only employees of MEDICAL MANAGEMENT SYSTEMS. Charles has a background in Accounting, Marketing, and Management. Dr. Mark Fuller is a practicing physician and is very familiar with Hospital Management. Over the next three years, we plan to hire marketing and training managers to handle most of those aspects.

Employee Skills

Marketing Manager—comprehensive knowledge of all aspects of marketing. Responsible for all direct mailing, trade shows, journal advertisements, and publicity.

Secretary—good communication and telephone skills, 35 words per minute, and computer word processing and basic hardware use skills.

Training Manager—good teaching skills, friendly, speaks English clearly, computer literate, proficient in hardware and network use, familiar with dental terminology.

Chapter Summary

Upon completion of the business plan, the entrepreneur should design a separate plan of action. This action plan lists the specific activities to be undertaken in order to get the business open and lists the dates that the action must be completed by.

If the entrepreneur is planning to take the business plan to investors or bankers for financing, he or she should condense the information into a concise report stating the essence of the information.

Cash Flow—1993

	Jan.	Feb.	Mar.	Apr.	May	Jun.	Jul.	Aug.	Sep.	Oct.	Nov.	Dec.	Total
Cash receipts													
Income from sales													
Cash sales	0.00	0.00	0.00	1495.00	3411.92	234.88	0.00	10533.33	7685.00	37850.00	20980.00	4690.00	86860.13
Collections	0.00	0.00	0.00	0.00	0.00	0.00	0.00	738.33	783.33	738.33	0.00	0.00	2214.99
Total cash from sales	0.00	0.00	0.00	1495.00	3411.92	234.88	0.00	11271.66	8468.33	38568.33	20980.00	4690.00	89075.12
Income from financing													
Interest income	0.00	0.00	0.00	0.00	0.00	0.00	0.00	0.00	0.00	0.00	0.00	0.00	0.00
Loan proceeds	0.00	5000.00	0.00	0.00	0.00	0.00	0.00	0.00	0.00	0.00	0.00	0.00	5000.00
Total cash from financing	0.00	5000.00	0.00	0.00	0.00	0.00	0.00	0.00	0.00	0.00	0.00	0.00	5000.00
Other cash receipts	0.00	0.00	0.00	0.00	0.00	0.00	0.00	0.00	0.00	0.00	0.00	0.00	0.00
Total cash receipts	0.00	5000.00	0.00	1495.00	3411.92	234.88	0.00	11271.66	11271.66	8423.33	20980.00	4690.00	94075.12
Cash disbursements													
Expenses													
Purchases	0.00	0.00	0.00	0.00	0.00	0.00	0.00	6944.17	2695.00	15870.00	9980.00	2695.00	38184.17
Gross wages	0.00	0.00	0.00	0.00	0.00	0.00	0.00	0.00	0.00	0.00	0.00	0.00	0.00
Payroll expense	0.00	0.00	0.00	706.00	0.00	0.00	0.00	0.00	0.00	0.00	0.00	0.00	706.00
Outside services	0.00	0.00	0.00	0.00	0.00	0.00	0.00	0.00	0.00	0.00	0.00	0.00	0.00
Supplies (office and operating)	0.00	0.00	761.50	7.41	2293.77	1071.37	75.85	950.00	200.00	250.00	150.00	195.00	5954.90
Repairs and maintenance	0.00	0.00	0.00	0.00	0.00	0.00	0.00	0.00	0.00	0.00	0.00	0.00	0.00
Advertising	0.00	426.38	304.66	24.35	170.00	1533.44	299.95	0.00	350.00	50.00	350.00	75.00	3583.78
Car, delivery, and travel	0.00	94.35	150.00	809.00	0.00	38.45	157.00	0.00	100.00	0.00	0.00	0.00	1348.80
Accounting and legal	0.00	0.00	0.00	0.00	0.00	0.00	0.00	816.73	0.00	0.00	0.00	500.00	1316.73
Rent	0.00	0.00	0.00	0.00	0.00	0.00	0.00	0.00	0.00	0.00	0.00	0.00	0.00
Telephone	0.00	159.46	0.00	295.59	125.68	165.88	165.03	126.95	130.00	200.00	175.00	125.00	1668.57
Utilities	0.00	0.00	0.00	0.00	0.00	0.00	0.00	0.00	0.00	0.00	0.00	0.00	0.00
Insurance	0.00	0.00	0.00	0.00	0.00	0.00	0.00	0.00	0.00	0.00	0.00	0.00	0.00
Taxes	0.00	0.00	0.00	0.00	0.00	355.02	0.00	0.00	1860.90	0.00	0.00	0.00	2215.92
Interest	0.00	0.00	71.66	81.63	82.80	79.67	90.64	95.00	90.00	25.00	0.00	0.00	616.40
Loan principal payment	0.00	1495.00	2210.00	0.00	0.00	0.00	0.00	475.00	275.00	5800.00	0.00	0.00	10255.00
Capital purchases	0.00	0.00	0.00	0.00	0.00	0.00	0.00	0.00	0.00	0.00	0.00	0.00	0.00
Bank charges	0.00	21.38	37.01	22.85	23.27	24.74	43.46	23.27	24.00	26.13	25.00	23.27	294.38
Owner's withdrawal	0.00	0.00	0.00	0.00	0.00	0.00	0.00	0.00	0.00	10000.00	10000.00	7706.00	27706.00
Total cash disbursements	0.00	2196.57	3534.83	1946.83	2695.52	3268.57	831.93	9431.10	5724.90	32221.13	20680.00	11319.27	93850.65
Net cash flow	0.00	2803.43	-3534.83	-451.83	716.40	-3033.69	-831.93	1840.56	2698.43	6347.20	300.00	-6629.27	224.47
Opening cash balance	0.00	0.00	2803.43	-731.40	-1183.23	-466.83	-3500.52	-4332.45	-2491.89	206.54	6553.74	6853.74	3711.13
Cash receipts	0.00	5000.00	0.00	1495.00	3411.92	234.88	0.00	11271.66	5724.90	38568.33	20980.00	4690.00	94075.12
Cash disbursements	0.00	-2196.57	-3534.83	-1946.83	-2695.52	-3268.57	-831.93	-9431.10	-5724.90	-32221.13	-20680.00	-11319.27	-93850.65
Ending cash balance	0.00	2803.43	-731.40	-1183.23	-466.83	-3500.52	-4332.45	-2491.89	206.54	6555.74	6853.74	224.47	-93850.65

Figure 24.4. Cash flow.

Balance Sheet
For Year Ending December 31, 1993

Assets			
Current liabilities			
Cash	$4,264.78		
Accounts receivable	750.00		
Inventory	300.00		
Prepaid expenses	0.00		
Total current assets		$5,314.78	
Fixed Assets			
Land	0.00		
Buildings	0.00		
Equipment	8,360.00		
Furniture	200.00		
Fixtures	0.00		
Less accumulated depreciation	2,186.67		
Total fixed assets		6,373.33	
Other assets		0.00	
Total assets			$11,688.11
Current Liabilities			
Accounts payable	$5,500.00		
Accrued payroll	500.00		
Short-term notes payable	300.00		
Total current liabilities		$6,300.00	
Long-term liabilities			
Long-term notes payable	0.00		
Total long-term liabilities		0.00	
Net worth			
Owner's equity	$5,388.11		
Total net worth		5,388.11	
Total liabilities and net worth			$11,688.11

Figure 24.3. Balance sheet.

The Last Step

Design a plan of action with deadlines and move out. Do the first step, and let the momentum start to build. Prepare a second more concise version of your business plan to present to lenders or investors.

Review Questions

1. *What is an action plan?*
2. *Why is it necessary to label deadlines for completion of activities?*
3. *What is the difference between the complete business plan and the one that can be presented to lenders or investors?*

Part 6 Case Study—Hindsight

"Oh my God," thought Joe, "I have a major problem!" Joe Novak had just received confirmation of his greatest fear—his prime customer, a major national airline company, had officially closed down. He was sitting at his desk looking at the $300,000 of machinery that had been financed and purchased to produce the luggage loading equipment for the airline company. Two years ago this development was the furthest thing from his mind. It was then that he had turned down an offer of over $2,000,000 for the 30-year-old company that he had founded and developed.

The 30 years had brought great satisfaction to Joe and, in some years, significant financial rewards. He had started by distributing and producing aircraft parts to private pilots and small charter airlines. Along the way he had developed a light weight luggage transport cart that had caught the eye of the major airline company. They had approached him with a supply contract that would make him a wealthy entrepreneur in five years.

Word got out of their interest which brought a group of investors to his doorstep with the offer to sell and give them the contract and the rights to the equipment. It was a tough decision.

His wife wanted Joe to sell the business. He was 62-years-old at the time and the offer would ensure them a secure and comfortable retirement. But Joe couldn't let go. If he could produce his product for the airline for five years he could more than double the offer extended to him. Of course, to produce in the quantities requested he would have to invest heavily in machinery, which he did at the cost of collateralizing all that he owned.

It took six months to get the machinery set up and he revamped his business by cutting off ties with former customers in order to have the time and production capacity for the new customer. The next six months were spent building production runs to accommodate the orders. Finally after one year, he was poised to start making the huge profits guaranteed by the contract. About the same time, rumors started to grow that things at the airline were getting a little tight. Joe had no recourse but to move ahead and keep his fingers crossed that the rumors were not well-founded.

The announcement was a stunning blow. All operations would cease, the company was in Chapter 7 final bankruptcy. Not only were there to be no orders, Joe would not receive the $165,000 owed to him for the last delivery.

Joe knew he was facing bankruptcy himself. The orders he had collected to this point were not anywhere near enough to pay the bank on the equipment loan. He could quite possibly lose everything he had worked for, including his home. At this point, he had no retirement account as it had been liquidated when he had put together the financial package for the equipment purchase.

Thirty two years of building a successful business were in danger of being wiped out. Joe was in shock.

Case Questions

1. What were the many mistakes that Joe made in handling this situation?

2. What should Joe have done?

3. Is there anything that Joe can do now to escape his undoing?

Answers to Chapter and Case Study Questions

Chapter 1

1. A successful entrepreneur senses the needs of the market.
2. Self-confidence, creativity, determination, goal-oriented.
3. To discover the environment you have performed best in.
4. You will work closer to your potential in an environment suited to you.
5. Retailing, wholesaling, manufacturing, services.
6. Poor planning.
7. To control your own destiny, be free from supervision, opportunity to earn great profits.
8. When you are not tied into great personal obligations and you have set capital aside.
9. Your family must understand the challenge facing you.
10. Write out personal satisfaction and income needs.

Chapter 2

1. Service businesses.
2. To make sure a business opportunity is compatible to your expectations.
3. Will vary by community, but should include local Chamber of Commerce, colleges, and Small Business Development Centers.
4. A resource center for small business owners that is funded by the SBA and state government.
5. They possess insider information.
6. To serve as a guide to reach goals.

7. Executive summary, business description, market analysis, marketing plan, management plan, legal considerations, financial plan, and supporting documents.

8. Size of market, sales potential, and identification of target market.

9. A description of how money flows in and out of a business.

10. Testimonial letters, contracts, advertising examples and any other evidence that supports declarations in business plan.

Chapter 3

1. To learn about the business and the industry you are considering entering.

2. It has a track record, a customer base, suppliers in place, employees are trained, it is easier, and there may be seller financing.

3. You may be buying someone's problems if the elements in question three are not present.

4. To improve your negotiating position.

5. Accurate tax records, a list of assets, a copy of leasing arrangements and contracts.

6. Poor recordkeeping.

7. The rate of return of the investment.

8. The lowest value of the assets.

9. To determine profit potential under new management.

10. An opportunity that will grow because the new owner can add an element that the former owner was not capable of adding.

11. Possibly lower interest, continued seller assistance in business operations, less risk to buyer.

12. Collect data, verify data, analyze, evaluate, and negotiate for best possible terms.

13. Classified newspaper ads, trade journals and publications, local community sources, industry representatives, ask the business owner directly.

14. Yes—the projected rate of return on investment exceeds 25 percent.

15. Asset value on the balance sheet shows purchase price less depreciation. Current market values of assets may have changed considerably.

Chapter 4

1. A business operation legally obligated to operate under a prescribed manner.
2. Experience is generally not necessary. In some cases, there is less risk.
3. Service businesses are growing the fastest. Business services and fast foods continue to grow.
4. Training is available, the product has proven customer acceptance, possibly less risk, use of trademarks and logos, assistance available in site selection.
5. Procedures and policies restrict the owner's freedom in decision making.
6. Franchise shows and franchise publications are two excellent sources.
7. A document offering all vital information concerning the franchisor.
8. All information pertinent to the purchase, operation, and obligations of the franchisor.
9. The terms of the purchase agreement.
10. Direct questions to current franchise owners regarding the relationship between franchisor and franchisee.

Chapter 5

1. Define question, determine information needed, collect data, analyze data, implement data, evaluate action.
2. Size of the potential market.
3. In order to achieve a level of understanding of significance of information.
4. Population × sales per capita × percentage share of market + sales forecast.
5. Secondary is previously published information, primary information is that which is collected firsthand.
6. Directing marketing efforts at a specific segment of the overall market.
7. A detail description of a business's ideal customer, including demographic and psychographic information.
8. A directory of manufacturers in the United States including size, officers, and location.

9. To develop an effective marketing plan that discovers unsatisfied needs.

10. Needs are perceived wants, perceptions are how we view things from our internal locus, motivations are why we act in a particular manner, attitudes are how we feel about something.

Chapter 6

1. Direct competition is any business which derives its primary source of revenues from selling similar products to the same target market.

2. Indirect competition are those businesses that sell similar products to a similar market but not as a secondary source of revenues.

3. To determine potential market share, to determine profitability of marketplace and to gauge competitive reaction when a new business enters the market.

4. Yellow pages for the consumer market; the *Thomas Register* for an industrial market.

5. Visit all competition to determine size, location appeal, number of employees, inventory levels, customer traffic, management availability, appearance, how long established, customer satisfaction level, suppliers and community reputation.

6. Attend a trade show to determine industry leaders, strongest competitors, weakest competitors, geographical differences, and selling terms and dependability.

7. Where to position your business in the market.

8. The different marketing strategies of the competitors and what they consider their differential advantage.

9. Insider information as to future plans of the competitor in addition to strengths and weaknesses.

10. It allows you to monitor their progress in the marketplace.

Chapter 7

1. To offer the greatest customer convenience.

2. The more convenient something is to buy, the more you buy.

3. Neighborhood shopping centers, community shopping centers, regional shopping centers.

4. Poor parking, poor lighting, limited hours of operation.

5. Businesses that benefit from drive by traffic.

6. An area in a community set aside to attract industrial companies by offering accessible location, good facilities, and reasonable purchase and lease arrangements.

7. A facility designated for use by start-up companies that shares general operating expenses.

8. Improved and more affordable telecommunication technology has allowed home-based businesses to perform the same as professional offices.

9. Common area maintenance charges; heating, ventilation, and air conditioning charges; merchants association fees; pro rata real estate property taxes.

10. To the business owner an opportunity to find another tenant to take over lease obligations in the event he or she wishes to close down or relocate.

11. An agreement that the tenant will pay a guaranteed base rent or a percentage of sales whichever is higher.

12. In order to be relieved of long-term commitments until the business is on stable financial footing.

Chapter 8

1. Product (satisfaction), place (location), price (value), promotion (selling).

2. The cumulative effect of all of the four Ps drive the marketing efforts of business activities.

3. Advertising, packaging, merchandising, brand names.

4. Price determines the value exchange perception of the product.

5. Guarantees and brand names are two strong attitude enforcements.

6. The easier it is to buy a product, the more will be purchased.

7. A message is sent by the sender, encoded as to the most effective way to express the message, a vehicle is chosen to relay the message to the receiver, who decodes the message as to how it is perceived. Noise factors in the channel interfere with effective communication.

8. Repetition will combat noise factors.

9. Bachelor stage; newly married with no children; full nest I; full nest II; empty nest I; empty nest II; solitary survivor; solitary survivor, retired.

10. Introductory stage; growth stage; maturity stage; decline stage.

Chapter 9

1. The price should cover the cost of goods, overhead expenses, pay the owner, pay back the investment, contribute to the long-run stability of the business operation and serve as a marketing tool to attract customers.

2. Determining the fixed and variable cost per unit and adding the needed profit.

3. Determine the number of units that must be sold at what price to cover all fixed and variable costs.

4. As price goes up, demand will go down.

5. Markup is the difference between the cost of the product and the selling price, if a profit margin has been added. Markdown is the difference between the original price requested and the price advertised or sold if lower.

6. As a percent of the retail price.

7. Divide the cost by the markup percentage you wish to achieve.

8. Broken assortments, out-of-date merchandise, damaged goods or to meet competitors' prices are reasons for taking a markdown.

9. Continuous discounting can alter the customer's perception of the value of a product(s).

10. Fees must cover time and overhead expenses of the provider.

11. Initially setting prices intentionally low to secure a desired percentage of market share.

12. Setting prices as high as the market will bear.

13. Setting one price to cover a category or classification of certain type of products.

14. Deliberately setting prices at or below cost on particular products to entice customers to visit a business with the hope that other products priced at a satisfactory profit margin will be purchased.

15. Maintaining a pricing strategy that is comparable to competition.

Chapter 10

1. The promotional mix includes advertising, promotions, personal selling, publicity and word-of-mouth referral.
2. To draw attention to the superiority of a product, service, or business.
3. The advantages are the ability to reach large markets—the disadvantages are their impersonalization and costs.
4. Direct mail allows the advertiser to be one on one with the potential customer.
5. It entertains and creates a positive image.
6. It announces to customers that the business is open and makes a first impression for a positive image.
7. The parts of the sale are identifying qualified prospects, the approach, the presentation, handling objections, making a trial close, asking for the order.
8. Yes, sales training teaches skills and acts as a motivator for sales personnel.
9. Design a program that brings what you sell to the attention of media representatives.
10. Determine opinion leaders and sell to them in a satisfactory manner.

Chapter 11

1. A capital needs statement shows the amount of money needed to start a business, including an operating reserve for working capital.
2. The amount needed for assets and the amount needed for initial operating expenses.
3. A statement showing an individual's assets and liabilities.
4. Only those personal assets that can be easily converted to cash or are considered as good collateral due to a confirmed and consistent market value.
5. The SBA loan procedure starts with a cooperative agreement with a bank.
6. Start up business loans have a high rate of failure.
7. A partner who invests, but has no voice in management and is only liable for the amount of the investment.

8. Create a stock prospectus that shows the profit potential of the business.

9. Normal high technology businesses with the potential to make hugh profits when introduced to the market.

10. Long-term installment loans on purchased equipment.

Chapter 12

1. Personal sources from friends and relatives, partners, investors and government assistance programs are sources for financing.

2. A partner can be taken if there is a specific need for capital or technical assistance that the originator is not able to supply.

3. General partners share a voice in management and have unlimited liability, limited partners do not have a voice in management and are only liable for the amount that they have invested.

4. Create a stock prospectus showing the profit potential of the business.

5. Strictly by whatever the investor is willing to pay.

6. A stock prospectus is a business plan made available to prospective investors.

7. To keep management control of the business.

8. To determine the amount of money that must be made available to meet your personal financial obligations.

9. There are too many things that go wrong to risk your retirement future.

10. Yes, most lenders like to see a 2:1 equity to debt ratio, or at least a 1:1 ratio.

Chapter 13

1. A business plan must show pro forma income statements, balance sheets, and cash flow projections.

2. The income statement shows the net profits generated from the business.

3. The balance sheet shows the financial status of the business.

4. The net worth of a business is the difference between the assets and the liabilities of a business.

5. Current assets are those that can be converted into cash during the next 12 months, the fixed assets are those that the business uses for operations and are normally more difficult to convert into cash. Current liabilities are debts that will be paid in the next 12 months, long-term liabilities are debts with a maturity date of longer than 12 months.

6. A sales forecast must be made to determine expenses and the amount of assets needed.

7. To show the expected growth of the operation.

8. To show how the revenues of the business cycle in and out of the operation.

9. Any change of patterns or expectations of these variables affect the cash flow of the operation.

10. The cash flow analysis will show any initial deficit a new business will incur that must be covered with a cash injection.

Chapter 14

1. The five functions of managing are planning, organizing, directing, controlling, and staffing.

2. The business owner must be able to look past the day-to-day operations of a business into its immediate and long-term future.

3. Planning the arrival of inventory as close as possible to selling it.

4. Determining the beginning and desired ending inventory levels.

5. Beginning inventory plus purchases minus sales minus mark downs equals ending inventory.

6. Daily adjusting inventory levels to account for new arrivals and current sales.

7. If money is not received as planned, accounts can not be paid as planned.

8. Early pay discounts are offered as an enticement to get customers to pay early in order to have the use of the money.

9. Management by objectives requires that objectives to reach be stated in all functional areas of a business operation.

10. Customer satisfaction and continuous improvement should be goals of all business enterprises.

Chapter 15

1. Through honesty and sharing the challenge, participation, and profit potential of a small business.

2. Theory Y managers are very conscious of human relations.

3. Challenge, participation, sharing, and acknowledgement of contribution are motivators.

4. Applicants can be found through classified newspaper advertisements, college and professional placement agencies, window signs, and employee referrals.

5. Vacation time, sick leave, insurance, and pension plans.

6. Simplified employee pension plans are investment programs available for small business owners and employees. The contribution limit is 15 percent of employee earnings, not to exceed $30,000.

7. Offer discounts on products or services the business sells.

8. Performance evaluations should be conducted in an informal environment without rankings or other numerical methods often found in larger businesses.

9. To show opportunities for advancement and explain employee obligations.

10. A small business employee must be better educated as to product knowledge and customer service techniques than large businesses.

Chapter 16

1. Computers can be used to help control cash management through effective bookkeeping systems.

2. Cash receipts, cash disbursements, accounts payables, accounts receivables, capital assets ledger, payroll activities, perpetual inventory systems.

3. By keeping track of all receipts, purchases, accounts payables and receivables, expenses, and inventory levels.

4. A computer can be used to create advertisements, brochures, and direct mail letters.

5. A customer data base allows a business to keep in contact with its customers.

6. A business can keep in touch with its customers through the use of newsletters and direct mail letters and advertisements.

7. Some of the more popular include Quicken™, Quick Books™, and Lotus 1-2-3™.

8. Popular word processing software programs include Word Perfect™, Micro Soft™, Wordstar™, and Multimate™.

9. Lotus 1-2-3™ can create cash flow spreadsheets.

10. All software may not be compatible with all hardware, therefore, decide what you need to have performed and than match the hardware to the software.

Chapter 17

1. Accountants, attorneys, financial planners, and insurance agents.

2. As an advisor and tax consultant and preparer.

3. To plan for future financial goals, particularly retirement.

4. An advisory board should consist of individuals with different career backgrounds to assist the entrepreneur in making key decisions.

5. The Chamber of Commerce supports local businesses and promotes its community to outside business interests.

6. Answers are individually different.

7. Small business development centers, Department of Development, Department of Labor, Department of Transportation, and the Office of the Secretary of State.

8. The SBA will assist small businesses in securing government contracts, provide financing assistance, counseling services, and published information.

9. The Census Bureau provides demographic information, The Office of Small and Disadvantaged Business Utilization assists minority owned and disadvantaged businesses, The Economic Development Administration provides financial support, The Bureau of Economic Analysis provides published information.

10. The International Trade Administration assists businesses engaged in international trade.

Chapter 18

1. A sole proprietorship is easy to start, has a minimum of paperwork, and the owner has total control. Its disadvantages are that its technical

and financial support are dependent on one person and that person has unlimited liability in regards to financial adversity.

2. A sole proprietor registers with the county or city where the business is located and commences business activity.

3. A partnership has two or more people as capital sources and more technical support. Its disadvantage is the potential for internal disagreement, split control, and unlimited liability of partners.

4. An Articles of Partnership is a written document that declares all input, profit sharing, management responsibilities and contingency plans of   all partners.

5. A limited partner has no voice in management, only the rights to profit sharing. He or she is only liable for the investment made in the business.

6. A corporation offers limited liability to its stockholders and employees. It is more expensive to start and has to abide by more reporting regulations.

7. Limited liability means that an individual is not personally liable for the actions of a business entity. He or she cannot be sued individually unless found personally negligent.

8. The Articles of Incorporation are filed with the state where incorporated and declare the purpose of the corporation, where located, its officers, and the amount of stock authorized to sell.

9. To incorporate the business owner must file an Articles of Incorporation with the state, register for a name, pay a fee and have the incorporation published in the newspaper,

10. A subchapter S corporation is for small private corporations that wish to report all profits or losses under the same basis as a proprietorship or partnership.

11. The corporation must have less than 35 stockholders and its stock cannot be sold through public exchange.

12. A sole proprietor reports income taxes on a Schedule C attached to his or her 1040 Form.

13. A partnership reports income taxes on a U.S. Partnership Form and each partner reports his or her profits or losses on their respective 1040 Form.

14. Subchapter S profits are taxed at the personal income tax rate of the shareholder. Regular corporations at taxed at the rate for corporation income taxes.

15. The regular corporation has less expense limitations and does not necessarily have to pay taxes on all earnings for a given year. The biggest disadvantages are the possible higher tax rates and that it must pay taxes on profits before dividends and the receiver of dividends must also pay taxes on the dividends—a form of double taxation.

Chapter 19

1. An eight-part course, conducted by the SBA, that teaches proper tax reporting procedures to small business owners.
2. A form filed by business owners to summarize employee tax withholdings.
3. If the individual has self-employment income that exceeds 20 percent of all income.
4. 15.3 percent
5. There must be an agreement, it must be lawful, there must be consideration, the parties must have the capacity to understand, and there must be a clear form.
6. Invoices, purchase orders, and customer exchange.
7. Land, buildings, and fixtures.
8. A warranty deed states there are no claims against the property. In a quitclaim deed the buyer assumes all liabilities outstanding against the property.
9. The form of ownership.
10. Joint tenancy, tenancy by entirety, tenancy in common.

Chapter 20

1. The local government has the right to know of all commercial activity in its province.
2. If the business sells at retail it must obtain a state sales tax registration reporting number. If the business has employees, it is necessary to obtain an employer's identification number from the IRS.
3. The Federal Trade Commission is a federal agency created to oversee business activities.

4. Product warranty and safety, consumer credit reporting, advertising and business competition.

5. An express warranty is written, an implied warranty is not.

6. The Truth-In-Lending Act, the Fair Credit Reporting Act, the Equal Credit Opportunity Act.

7. Bait and switch advertising and advertising the true price as a sale price.

8. Answers will vary.

9. The Clayton Act, the Sherman Antitrust Act, and the Robinson Pactman Act.

10. Any violations of safety precautions that should be followed in a work place (i.e., no fire extinguishers).

Chapter 21

1. The risk must be calculable, it must occur in large numbers, it must have a commercial value, the policyholder must have an insurable interest in what is insured.

2. Experienced agents are more knowledgeable in ways to reduce insurance premiums.

3. Basic property coverage covers fire, explosion, and acts of nature. There is also business interruption to cover the insured while a business is shut down due to a misfortune; vandalism coverage will cover against looting, etc.; water sprinkler insurance covers against faulty equipment; dishonesty insurance protects against crime, credit insurance covers against a supplier's insolvency; and surety bonds protect the failure of another business to fulfill a contract.

4. General liability and employers, liability insurance.

5. Coinsurance is bought at reduced rates as the insured has a stated limitation of percentage amount of coverage in the event of total loss.

6. Workman's compensation.

7. Seek relief from your insurance company, not the offending parties'.

8. Personnel, customer, and market-related risks.

9. Install effective prevention programs.

10. Create loyalty and comraderie among employees. Follow security procedures if necessary.

11. Do not become solely dependent on one source of revenue or supplier. Write out contingency plans.

12. Diversify and create strategic plans for worst case scenarios.

Chapter 22

1. The business life cycle has four stages: introductory, growth, maturity, and decline.

2. Too many businesses expand to satisfy the owner's ego.

3. Normally soon after entering the maturity stage.

4. Investigate ways to explore expansion without making long-term commitments.

5. The essence of being in business is to produce profits, including those that may come from selling the business.

6. Sell a business when it is considered at its peak value and the future market is strong.

7. Choosing a successor to a family business can result in conflict among family members if not done properly.

8. Who is most qualified and who is most interested. Potential successor should be properly evaluated for abilities.

9. The market for selling a business can change drastically due to competition, economic cycles, and technology development.

10. From the beginning of a business operation.

Chapter 23

1. The changing lifestyles of consumers and the difficulty of securing money for larger investment operations.

2. The government must provide more tax incentives for business start-up investments and there must be more confidence in the economy.

3. Contact assistance agencies, conduct market research on potential foreign markets, plan your strategies, arrange financing, and learn how payments are exchanged.

4. The International Trade Administration assists and promotes businesses involved with doing business with foreign markets.

5. Through fax transmissions, computer modems, and more affordable overseas telephone service small businesses can now compete globally.

6. To assist in the financing of accounts receivables from foreign companies.

7. Recycling and remanufacturing.

8. Answers will vary.

9. The downsizing of large corporations.

10. It may increase demand for temporary workers as opposed to full time employees.

Chapter 24

1. An action plan states precisely what must be done and by when.

2. Deadlines serve as motivators for action.

3. Normally the plan presented to investors or lenders is more concise than the complete business plan.

Case Study Questions and Examples of Suggestions

Part 1—To Create or Franchise?

Barry is in a very familiar situation for an aspiring entrepreneur. There is some research he should do. Most importantly is to visit other franchises and talk to the owners. Even though in this case he might have to travel to a neighboring state or even farther he should not hesitate to get in his car. He can not make a good decision without experiencing first hand the operation of a Gift Managerie. He should visit several and those he cannot he should contact by phone and ask the questions suggested in the chapter.

Questions 1 and 2. The other part of his decision-making process lies in his personal goals. If working under supervision, no matter how limited, is a problem for Barry he needs to address the future implications of inspections and reports. If he truly seeks independence he will struggle with running his business as someone else sees fit. Decisions of what to buy and how to merchandise are the creative part of the job and he may wish to keep these responsibilities as his own.

The profit motive of joining the franchise might be the determining factor. If there is reasonable assurance that profits will soar as a franchisee, it might overcome many of his reservations. Barry must closely look at what he is getting for his fees. Five percent of gross sales will accumulate into a great amount of money over a number of years in business. Is there enough evidence to warrant the expense. Is the name—"The Gift Managerie"—an asset that will attract customers that he would probably not have? Probably doubtful at this point since it ia relatively new franchise, but what about the future? If the anticipated growth does occur, it might be a very timely decision as the resale value of the business should grow appreciatively. He also must factor in the cost of financing the purchase from the franchisor, including the terms. Barry will have to find these answers through questioning, research, and self examination.

Part 2—Delicate Decisions

1. They should run a 5000-unit production run and expand their mail order circulation since it has shown potential and has the greatest potential gross margin. Once they have made the production run they could simultaneously explore selling to retailers on a limited basis.

2. They could seek investors using the market research that they performed as the interest motivator. This would reduce the risk and possibly allow them to investigate other markets.

3. There are other markets to investigate such as the educational toy market. They can attend trade shows of other industries to seek a solid customer base that will not fluctuate and give more stability.

Part 3—The Loan Officer

1. Holmes can recommend that by securing a second mortgage on her home Paula can qualify for an $88,000 loan ($40,000 plus 80 percent of the $60,000 home equity). Since this is still not enough, Paula should see if there is the possibility of negotiating an installment loan with her equipment supplier.

2. If the bank rejects the loan, Paula should inquire as to whether they would be willing to do the loan if it was guaranteed by the SBA. If so, the bank and Paula together will apply to the SBA. She can also shop the loan request to other banks or consider taking a partner or selling stock to investors.

3. Paula is close enough to providing enough collateral that she should really put pressure on Holmes to get loan approval. Presuming her financial projections are solid, she needs to point out to the bank how they will benefit from her intended business deposits and that she is quite willing to discuss her business plan with their closest competitor.

Part 4—A Problem with Control

1. Alan neglected to do a cash flow analysis for this business. If he had he would not have allowed the payment terms that he did.

2. Alan must attack the problem on two fronts. He must bring his receivables into line by not allowing any payments to exceed 30 days and, in most cases, should collect on delivery or within 10 days. He must discuss the situation directly with customers and those that cannot or will not cooperate should be dropped from his account list since they are costing more than they are contributing. At the same time he should firmly request better terms from his suppliers. He has now been in the market for four months and should use that as an argument to be allowed 30 day payment terms. If successful on both fronts, Alan should have a very profitable business. He will have to close if proper arrangements cannot be made.

3. The accounts payable customers must be constantly monitored to detect potential problems. All future customers must be screened by credit checks before agreeing to sell to them. He should design an effective letter for reminding customers of past due payments and seek the advice of an attorney for how to force collections when necessary.

Part 5—Breaking Up Is Hard to Do

1. The partners did not sign an articles of partnership which would have addressed these conditions.

2. A negotiation must prevail. If necessary, a neutral arbitrator should be asked to determine each partners contribution and asset values. The partnership should be terminated as the partners are no longer working towards mutual goals. Joan is not in the position to investigate the new location until after a settlement is reached, which will more than likely absorb any funds earmarked for expansion.

3. The partnership was created for the wrong reasons. Only if technical expertise or significant financial contribution is needed should a partnership be formed. Friendship and shared interests often do not have staying power in a business environment.

Part 6—Hindsight

1. The greatest mistake Joe made was becoming too dependent on one source of income. He should not have dropped his smaller customers. The risk involved with taking on the new contract was too great if it required liquidating his retirement holdings. He also worked without a contingency plan for a worst case scenario.

2. Needless to say, he should have sold. He allowed his emotions and personal involvement to cloud his business thinking. Once he turned down the offer and decided to move ahead, he might have been able to carry insurance to help cover this situation.

3. There is little hope here, unless another major airline can be secured as a customer. This will likely take time, which Joe doesn't have. He also needs to go back to his smaller customers and start again to rebuild his customer base. It is the equivalent of starting over, however, now Joe is 64 years old.

Index

Final Examination

The McGraw-Hill
36-Hour Course in
Entrepreneurship

If you have completed your study of *The McGraw-Hill 36-Hour Course in Entrepreneurship*, you should be prepared to take this final examination. It is a comprehensive test, consisting of 100 questions.

Instructions

1. You may treat this as an "open book" exam by consulting this and any other textbook. Or, you can reassure yourself that you have gained superior knowledge by taking the exam without reference to any other material.

2. Answer each of the test questions on the answer sheet provided at the end of the exam. For each question, write your response on the answer blank that corresponds to the number of the question your are answering.

3. Questions are true/false, multiple choice, and matching columns. Always select the answer that represents in your mind the *best* among the choices.

4. Each correct answer is worth one point. A passing grade of 70 percent (70 correct answers) entitles you to receive a Certificate of Achievement. This handsome certificate, suitable for framing, attests to your proven knowledge of the contents of the course.

5. Carefully fill in your name and address in the spaces provided at the top of the answer sheet, remove the answer sheet from the book, and send it to:

> Allyson Arias
> Certification Examiner
> *36-Hour Course in Entrepreneurship*
> Professional Books Group
> McGraw-Hill, Inc.
> 11 West 19th Street
> New York, NY 10011

True/False

For each of the following true/false questions, write T or F on the answer sheet blank that corresponds to the number of the question you are answering.

1. The majority of small businesses fail or close down within one year after opening?
2. When purchasing a franchise a business plan is NOT necessary?
3. Convenience entices consumers to buy more?
4. Incubators are used for small business start-ups?
5. The difference between a $5 cost and a $10 selling price is markup?
6. Publicity is paid advertising?
7. Knowing the inventory turnover rate helps entrepreneurs project operating expenses?
8. Cash flow analysis is used to determine net profits?
9. It is important to include resumes for active partners in a business plan?
10. Public stocks can be converted to cash in a matter of days?
11. All inventory should arrive at the business location at the same time?
12. Small businesses should be more concerned with preventing theft than catching thieves?
13. The use of credit cards has made credit less of an issue for small businesses?
14. The purchase of real property requires a written contract?
15. The reason a business is for sale is NOT an important consideration to the potential buyer?
16. The goodwill value of a business can be calculated by adding all asset values?
17. The Small Business Administration is a federal agency in charge of licensing small businesses?
18. The business plan is useful only during the design and start-up phases of the business?
19. Entrepreneurs who do not need to borrow money do not need to create a business plan?
20. A demographic study analyzes population statistics?
21. There are three types of competition?
22. Purchases of convenience goods are often planned?
23. Neighborhood shopping centers almost always have large anchor stores?
24. Loss leader pricing strategies are often used by grocery stores?
25. A good salesperson avoids objections?
26. Pro forma financial statements are projections?

27. Sales minus cost of goods minus operating expenses equals net worth?

28. Interest or dividends paid on investments that are held as collateral are paid to the lender?

29. Theory X managers often presume that workers dislike their work?

30. An employer who uses top-down management does not listen often to employees or customers?

31. Open to buy is the money available for making inventory purchases?

32. Computers are too expensive for small businesses?

33. The Small Business Administration helps small business owners secure government contracts?

34. Workers' compensation insurance provides compensation for displaced workers?

35. Advertising is a paid personal public notice?

36. The exact amount of consideration must be included in a sales contract?

37. Once it is attached, a fixture becomes a part of real property?

38. Any person may insure the life of another as long as the premium is paid?

39. Sellers sometimes assist in financing the sale of their businesses?

40. It is illegal for a business owner to show the business lease to a potential buyer?

Multiple Choice

For the following multiple-choice questions, write the letter of the answer that best completes the statement or answers the question on the answer sheet blank that corresponds to the number of the question you are answering.

41. Which of the following occupations would be considered an entrepreneur? (a) a postal worker (b) a professional football player (c) a bank teller (d) an inventor.

42. A person with a technical anchor would be happy (a) managing a chain of fast food restaurants (b) refinishing furniture (c) selling door to door (d) creating a marketing plan for a department store.

43. In addition to making profits, a successful entrepreneur must (a) be well known (b) receive a favorable rate of return on the investment (c) be able to expand the operation within five years (d) be active in community events.

44. A retail store owner would consider a large national chain department store as (a) direct competition (b) auxiliary competition (c) indirect competition (d) communal competition.

45. The starting place for finding competitors in an industrial market is (a) the yellow pages (b) the Chamber of Commerce (c) trade shows (d) the *Thomas Register*.

46. A demographic study is (a) a study of consumer lifestyles (b) a study of industry trends (c) a study of population statistics (d) all of the above.

47. In doing a demographic study, it is important to (a) illustrate the findings in a graphic format (b) compare the data to other markets (c) discuss the findings with the bank (d) keep the purpose of the study to yourself.

48. Aspirin is an example of a (a) specialty good (b) shopping good (c) convenience good (d) drive-in good.

49. A shopping center with less than 20 stores is a (a) neighborhood shopping center (b) a community shopping center (c) a regional shopping center (d) a super shopping center.

50. An incubator is a (a) new business (b) a facility that houses new businesses (c) a new industry (d) an inventor's workshop.

51. A poor business for sale opportunity is often characterized by (a) a seller who is hesitant to provide information in the initial meeting (b) a business with poor records (c) a demand for cash only (d) a business which does not advertise.

52. The liquidation approach to evaluating a business for sale opportunity (a) compares relative value to other similar businesses (b) bases the decision on the book value of assets (c) is concerned with return on investment (d) checks with salvage buyers before making a decision.

53. A franchisor must (a) assist in financing the purchase (b) disclose civil litigation history (c) supply training (d) secure the site location.

54. Which of these is not one of the four Ps (a) process (b) price (c) product (d) place.

55. A customer profile is used to (a) identify the best location (b) determine price (c) design promotional strategies (d) all of the above.

56. The breakdown in the communication channel is usually a result of (a) decoding (b) feedback (c) noise factors (d) encoding.

57. The break-even point is reached when (a) profits are received (b) a gross margin is received (c) all costs are covered (d) a business closes due to poor sales.

58. The price of a product must cover (a) cost of goods (b) overhead expenses (c) profit (d) all of the above.

59. The financial statement that shows the financial worth of a business is the (a) income statement (b) the balance sheet (c) the cash flow statement (d) the bank statement.

60. For initial start up capital, most entrepreneurs rely on (a) banks (b) investors (c) joint venture capitalist (d) personal savings.

61. A cash flow analysis shows (a) the short-term profits (b) the money cycle of a business (c) open to buy reserves (d) capital appreciation.

62. The bank would consider which as good collateral (a) inventory (b) equipment (c) automobiles owned (d) certificates of deposit.

63. An individual's net worth is (a) the amount of assets accumulated (b) home equity plus savings (c) liabilities paid (d) assets minus liabilities.

64. Normally banks will loan on the equity of a house (a) 80 percent (b) 90 percent (c) 70 percent (d) 100 percent.

65. A good equity to debt ratio is (a) 1:2 (b) 2:1 (c) 1:1 (d) 1:3.

66. Theory Y managers are (a) very authoritative (b) human relations oriented (c) marketing oriented (d) customer oriented.

67. Listening is very apparent in (a) down to top management (b) top to down management (c) horizontal management (d) vertical organizations.

68. Performance evaluations in small businesses should use (a) rankings (b) weakness critiquing (c) classifications (d) motivational psychology.

69. How a customer feels about a business or product comes from (a) perceptions (b) motivations (c) attitudes (d) needs.

70. Determining a purchase plan starts with setting (a) sales objectives (b) markdown strategies (c) ending inventory objectives (d) open to buy budget.

71. Just-in-time inventory control requires (a) COD terms (b) supplier dependability (c) immediate collection of accounts receivable (d) fast inventory turnover.

72. Open to buy is (a) money available for nonplanned purchases (b) used to purchase capital assets (c) reported as income on a tax form (d) a discount marketing strategy.

73. Small business advertisers should (a) over reach their market (b) stay away from mass media advertising (c) personalize their messages (d) advertise only during their busiest seasons.

74. The Small Business Administration is a (a) state agency (b) a federal agency (c) a private agency (d) a community agency.

75. The Federal Trade Commission (a) helps businesses to secure contracts (b) acts as a government lending agency (c) oversees business practices (d) collects taxes.

76. For a contract to be legal it must (a) be witnessed (b) be written (c) have consideration (d) be signed.

77. Small businesses have done well in the environmental industry with (a) hazardous waste disposal (b) chemical clean up (c) pollution inspection (d) recycling.

78. Small businesses are doing well in international trade due to (a) lower tariffs (b) the elimination of trade barriers with Eastern Europe (c) government loans (d) improved telecommunications.

79. Due to the balance of trade deficit, the ITA has special emphasis on assisting (a) importers (b) exporters (c) foreign sales agents (d) gold dealers.

80. A business should be held onto until (a) it produces for 20 years (b) it can be passed on to family members (c) it goes into the decline stage (d) the owner can make a handsome profit selling it.

Matching

Match the following terms with their definitions and write the letter of the term that matches the definition on the answer sheet blank that corresponds to the number of the question you are answering.

A. secondary data

B. psychographics

C. self-actualization needs

D. shopping good

E. incubator

F. customer profile

G. target marketing

H. variable cost

I. markup

J. income statement

K. balance sheet

L. fixed asset

M. collateral

N. Theory Y manager

O. controlling

P. directing

Q. corporation

R. limited partnership

S. Small Business Development Center

T. real property

81. A separate legal entity that can sue, be sued, buy, and sell. Its owners have limited liability.

82. The difference between the cost of a product and its retail sales price.

83. Shows the net profit of a business.

84. Buildings, land, and fixtures.

85. A business's ideal customer.

86. A person who owns part of a business but has no say in its management.

87. A product that is compared to other similar products.

88. A desire to feel worthy.

89. Previously published information.

90. Keeping abreast of progress towards goals.

91. A facility for start-up businesses.

92. An asset that can be used for borrowing against.

93. Purchased to be used in the operations of a business.

94. Shows the book value of a business.

95. A learning resource for small business owners.

96. The observation of consumer lifestyles.

97. A well-defined segment of a market.

98. A human relations person.

99. Controlled by sales.

100. Guiding to reach an objective.

Name _____

Address _____

City _____ State_____ Zip _____

Final Examination Answer Sheet: The McGraw-Hill 36-Hour Course in Entrepreneurship

See instructions on page 1 of the Final Examination.

1. _____	21. _____	41. _____	61. _____	81. _____
2. _____	22. _____	42. _____	62. _____	82. _____
3. _____	23. _____	43. _____	63. _____	83. _____
4. _____	24. _____	44. _____	64. _____	84. _____
5. _____	25. _____	45. _____	65. _____	85. _____
6. _____	26. _____	46. _____	66. _____	86. _____
7. _____	27. _____	47. _____	67. _____	87. _____
8. _____	28. _____	48. _____	68. _____	88. _____
9. _____	29. _____	49. _____	69. _____	89. _____
10. _____	30. _____	50. _____	70. _____	90. _____
11. _____	31. _____	51. _____	71. _____	91. _____
12. _____	32. _____	52. _____	72. _____	92. _____
13. _____	33. _____	53. _____	73. _____	93. _____
14. _____	34. _____	54. _____	74. _____	94. _____
15. _____	35. _____	55. _____	75. _____	95. _____
16. _____	36. _____	56. _____	76. _____	96. _____
17. _____	37. _____	57. _____	77. _____	97. _____
18. _____	38. _____	58. _____	78. _____	98. _____
19. _____	39. _____	59. _____	79. _____	99. _____
20. _____	40. _____	60. _____	80. _____	100. _____